Wakefield Press

T0359559

Last Bed on Earth

Teri Louise Kelly (Ratso) lives in Adelaide, South Australia, with her partner Mel (Jo Buck), where together they find yet more ways to defy the laws of nature.

By the same author

Sex, Knives and Bouillabaisse

Last Bed on Earth

Teri Louise Kelly

Wakefield
Press

Wakefield Press
1 The Parade West
Kent Town
South Australia 5067
www.wakefieldpress.com.au

First published 2009

Cover designed by Liz Nicholson, designBITE
Text designed and typeset by Clinton Ellicott, Wakefield Press
Printed and bound by Hyde Park Press, Adelaide

National Library of Australia
Cataloguing-in-publication entry

Author: Kelly, Teri Louise.
Title: Last bed on earth/author, Teri Louise Kelly.
ISBN: 978 1 86254 822 0 (pbk.).
Subjects: Kelly, Teri Louise.
                 Tourism – New Zealand – Employees – Biography.
                 Tourist camps, hostels, etc. – New Zealand.
Dewey Number: 338.4791092

Publication of this book was assisted by the
Commonwealth Government through the
Australia Council, its arts funding and advisory body.

To Hank, thanks for the ride.

Sleep tight.

WANTED!
Couple to manage 100-bed roach motel on South Island for
high season. Live-in accommodation supplied. Fresh young
meat required, please apply in writing to –
The Owners c/-

Contents

1.

Some Sort of Jet-Lagged Introduction . . .

Pennies do not come from heaven.
They have to be earned here on earth.
Maggie Thatcher

Auckland, Year of Your Lord 2002.

There is nothing beautiful about today, not in the least. It is grey and cold and unwelcoming, like Port Au Prince in the old days, when the first things you saw were decapitated heads on stakes. We are a long way from anywhere, marooned by circumstances and brain-shrunk decision-making. There are *signs* of life – but not as I know it. Naturally, there are no hire cars available, at least not in our price range. There are no hotel rooms in our price range . . . this is what they call the budget traveller's dilemma. And I *really* am a budget traveller, a person renowned and admired for thriftiness, as well as for being a light-fingered cheapskate.

Our price range is called 'low end', which is even lower than 'budget'. It is the range between absolutely free and not more than twenty bucks a day, all up. There isn't anything in that range apart from park-benches, skips, railway viaducts and abandoned buildings – oh, and police cells. But all of those are taken; Auckland is a rough-house kind of town.

It's a price range that hasn't worked particularly well on our trip, which is why our credit card no longer functions as it ought to. The card got cancelled in London, or was it Dublin? Whatever, but at least we'd used it to purchase the tickets here. Though I still can't fathom *why* it got cancelled. Okay, so we've been on the road for almost two years, of no permanent abode, and with nothing in the way of stable long-term employment to hold up as material evidence. But these are not good reasons to deny a person – especially a person who is perennially 'between situations' – extended credit.

Without that card we're going to have to do it hard, well harder I guess. No more on-the-slate mid-range hotel rooms, no more en suites, no more continental breakfasts, and definitely no more pillaging of the mini-bar. When it's someone else's money I'm squandering, I'm all for those little luxuries that make extended travel enjoyable, but considering we're unlikely to be able to take a room with crisply laundered sheets ever again, I guess that's not much of an issue right now.

What are of concern are my feet. Somehow my brain has lost contact with my nether regions, in particular my ten digits way down south, and it is becoming somewhat alarmed. Begrudgingly I get up and start shuffling to and fro like a vagrant. To the orderly assembled group of tourists over to my left, I must look a bizarre sight; unkempt, under-dressed, malnourished and shuffling about like Ratso Rizzo in *Midnight Cowboy* while I wait for my own Jo Buck to return with good news. Finally he does, return that is, although he's a she and doesn't have good news – or, I suspect, clean underwear. There was no joy on the free-call phones, no chance of a free ride or a stay-two-get-one-free deal, no deals at all in fact – especially without credit. No one wants to take the risk.

It's entirely my fault, of course, as everything that's gone wrong on this trip to date has been. It was my *idea* in the first place. I am admired for many traits, but astute judgment is not in the top five. So thanks to me, we're out of credit and stranded at this bleak airport on a frigid dull day. I just keep on shuffling; it seems for the best insofar as my toes are concerned.

Around us, laughing people are clambering into heated vehicles. These people with credit can go anywhere they damn well please, that is how the modern world works, even here in New Zealand. They are all wrapped up and warm, whipping out gold cards and platinum cards and heavy-duty corporate Visa cards ... and frankly, I hate the lot of them.

Jo Buck scavenges in her bag for some kind of foreign currency, then goes back into the terminal to convert it into something legal. I sit on our bags – forlorn specimens that have seen more provident days in the ownership of better prepared travellers – and I watch these strangely competent people go about their business.

Once I had business to go about, but it seems too long ago. Right now I have none, and no business watching other people go about theirs, but what else is there to do? Breakfast is a slim hope – for the past 30 hours we've been eating nothing but re-hydrated airline food and chocolate. My brain, having been momentarily distracted by the lack-of-blood-flow emergency, has now turned its undivided attention to the blockage that is stopping my bowels from functioning. I am gripped by cramps, and a desperate urge to unburden myself – only I can't take the bags with me and I can't abandon them ...

The Iron Lady was right, goddamn her. That is the moral of this sordid tale, the eternal need for money. When I cast my addled mind back, I can see that was how it all started.

Greed, that was my demarcation point. Ground zero for me was 1987. That year I finally fled the auld country with a sack full of cash and a stupid picture in a passport, and it was all Maggie's fault. Before the greengrocer's daughter got her hands on the reins of power, England was still an okay place to live, I was still proud to be an Englishman. And then one day the old dart couldn't intoxicate or entrance me any more, I was so over it, sister, and I had cold hard currency in my hand. It was the time of super profit and ME ME ME. So I left, vamoosed, took a jet plane to somewhere far away and I've been running ever since, one way or another. And I have seen worse times than this. The outlook is grim, sure, but not desperate. I have driven hire cars across the United States to depots in the most dilapidated ghettoes of the Union. I have served as the cook on luxury yachts around the Caribbean with skippers whose only credentials to pilot such sleek beasts were multiple bank accounts loaded with freshly laundered drug money. I have eaten the foulest entrails man or beast could stomach when my belly was empty and my taste buds eroded, and I have drunk water that even New Delhi street cows would turn their noses up at.

No matter what the current predicament, there are always positives if you are prepared to look for them. At least these people speak English and, I guess, are civilized. Communication will be straightforward and our seemingly dire straits somehow negotiable. All we really need is a break – and a toilet.

Fortune, to be sure, comes when you least expect it. Our luck-o'-meter was obviously swinging, with the offer of a free ride into town. A man had taken pity on us after he and I struck up a conversation about how unseasonably cold it was, and from that little acorn would grow ... well, I guess you'll see.

2.

Follow the
Yellow Shit Road

Once I thought Jamaica was *the* place, after I'd fled from Bermuda like Ronnie Biggs looking for a bolthole. I had these wild thoughts after an even wilder night at the Notting Hill Carnival one year – the same year Marley was big and reggae da thing to chill to.

Kingston was happening, or so they said, everyone was going out on charter flights ex Luton – it just seemed like the sanest thing to do when insanity was all about. I'd thought about dreadlocks, maybe a few beads for authenticity, but the girl said I didn't have that kind of hair. Out there life was sweet, ganja was the substance, Red Stripe the beer, calypso the rhythm of life, the beach a throbbing party – all those clichés that wandering freaks assume as gimmees. It wasn't anything like that, of course. Ganja was a damned expensive, not to mention, soul-destroying habit, and the beer was served too warm; when you popped the ring it always exploded. The only steel drums you heard were when the tourists hit the beach, and rooms with walls were hard to find. Sand fleas were easier to get acquainted with than the locals. The expatriate colony had drawn up a code of conduct and entry requirements that defied reasonable logic. There was no work, not work I'd consider anyhow, and my Caribbean dream simply evaporated like a cheap joint or a hashish bong passed around the wigwam once too often.

But this time, here in New Zealand, it won't be like that. The lessons I learned in Jamaica and Mexico City will stand me in good stead – easy communication is the key; the basic ability to converse on many levels about topics common to the white man. This driver of ours is pretty loquacious. By the time we're in the city itself he's already lined me up for a few days cash-in-hand work helping his brother with some kind of house extension, which is fine, so long as the cash reward meets my expectations. Despite my girlish appearance and feminine wiles, I am the grandson of a master builder and I've done my time with the hod, ladies. Anyhow, just because I'm new in town doesn't give someone the god-given right to treat me like a patsy.

Five in the morning though, seems like a ridiculous time to start work the day after you've flown almost two thirds of the way around the globe and your pipe work still isn't tickety boo. But it *is* money, and money is the manna on which we must gorge if this particular adventure is going to be successful. I have many pressing concerns weighing on my mind, not least of which is the cost of this hotel room. A quick mental calcula-tion tells me that I'll work three days just to pay this wretched bill and we will still not come out in front.

This room ain't even finished, says Jo. Cheapskates. This is her first utterance in the Land of the Long Grey Cloud other than a few grunted 'bollocks'.

Which is why we've got it at a discount price, baby, I remind her.

This window doesn't shut properly and it's bloody freezing and there's no hot water! Jo groans.

I look around the room. The built-in furniture isn't quite built-in and the legless bed is propped up on phone books – a bummer if you need to call Alcoholics Anonymous at the twitching hour. The television works, but only when one of us stands directly in front of it – which kind of defeats the overall objective. By modern standards the room isn't inexpensive, or modern for that matter, and somehow I can't shake the belief that I've been screwed . . .

You've been screwed, Jo accosts me. Look at this bloody dump. I should never have trusted you. Jesus, you're on more pills than a lab monkey!

I'm too exhausted to traipse downstairs and make a scene or have it out with the fiesty blonde sprawled on the sagging bed. At least it's a goddamned room, I tell her wearily.

It's a kennel. That's what it is. Suits you actually, a kennel for a dog.

What?

Puppy eyes. Wagging tongue. Pricked-up ears. Don't think I haven't seen you making eyes with every woman who's smiled at you between Heathrow and here. She turns away from me.

No one forced you to come, baby.

Bollocks. You did. You and your crazy ideas. She shoots me one of her contemptuous looks, the same look she once gave punters she'd just flogged to within an inch of their miserable lives, I guess.

There'll be a silver lining, I tell her . . . and miraculously there *is* – in the shape of a toilet, although it's only after my bowels explode back into action like a hyperactive geyser that I realise there's no loo paper and that a tanker-like turd takes an eon to commence its journey out into the Bay of Plenty or wherever anti-clockwise gravitational interference takes it.

That goddamned stinks! young Jo moans.

Can you go get me some toilet paper, babe, huh? I plead.

Screw you. Use your hand.

We sleep like thieves, without any conscience or conscious interludes. At four in the morning, I am awakened by reception with my wake-up call – I thank the lady sincerely for her diligence and then slip back into a coma. It is past midday when we finally awake.

Well, there goes the labouring. I am already behind the eight ball. It is a bad start to a new life, a blown chance, a real bummer. At least breakfast didn't cost anything as we've missed it. I go downstairs and call my new buddy on his mobile. He is stuck in heavy traffic someplace I can't pronounce, but will let his brother know, see if we can set things up for tomorrow.

The next night is cold, and the thermal qualities of the thread-bare blanketry quite inadequate for the climate. As the temperature plummets even further, I can feel my feet turning blue, then black and finally no colour at all. At four thirty in the morning I'm rude to the wake-up lady, for which I apologize downstairs and impatiently wait for my ride. My employer arrives and we set off. I don't even know my chauffeur – for all I know, this might be my last ever trip on earth. My last glimpse might be of the inside of a black zip-up bag as my final breaths condensate and wispy skits of green dewy grass and English afternoon tea skip across my fading consciousness like old Pathe news footage.

I let the guy talk while we weave through already congested streetscapes until we pull into a big old place with no roof or possibilities. The guy is building some type of conservatory on the rear, though from what I see he's unqualified for such a technical task. I have seen many renovations on my travels, folks are always keen to show off their handiwork or aspirations, but I've never seen anything quite as shoddy as this effort. The whole job is a botch; there are crudely bent nails sticking out of roughly hacked wood and enough bad joints to make a professional carpenter break down and weep.

I'm loath, however, to advise my paying host that not even Noah would use him to build an ark if by some fluke all of the ark builders had been washed away in an un-forecast flood. So I tell him it's a dandy job all right and this seems to set us up for the day. The first task is coffee, and that's about the only job that has a resonance of reality about it – everything else is like a skit out of some unreality show. The guy has all the tools but none of the knowledge, so instead he uses the hammer and nails, the hallmarks of every backyard home renovator. All day we pound in nails and curse bits of stubborn timber while we claw them all out again, and by dusk we're no further forward than when we had started.

Maybe the guy can smell a rat. Perhaps he suspects I'm playing at being what I'm not anymore. He keeps asking me questions all day like:

Aren't you hot?

You sure you can work with gloves on?

Say, you're working up a sweat there, buddy, and it ain't even summer!

Well sure, I do sweat, it's a side effect of the hormonal invasion. My oestrogen-ravaged body can no longer heat or cool itself – but hell if I'm going down to a muscle shirt, no sir, that'd most likely involve a long walk home through some abrasive neighbourhoods. So I just keep telling him I'm okay, that I came in from the Sudan and that it was hotter than a charcoal pit at high noon over there, I'm still acclimatizing.

Three days looks an optimistic time frame to work within,

three years might have been a surer estimate. But I tell the guy, on the trip back, that three days is the most I can spare because after that I'm off. He takes the news well, which is more than Jo Buck does. Tomorrow she wants to get yet another tattoo, though I'm not sure there's enough skin available. But she's been a trooper on this journey into the unknown, so I tell her she can get the tattoo and somehow we'll work it all out. Septicaemia isn't so bad when you get used to it.

My day of hammering in nails has left me as deadbeat as a flogged dog. My silky soft hands are sore, unaccustomed as they are these days to physical activity, and as I lie traumatized from my sudden switcheroo vis-à-vis genders while mourning five broken fingernails, Jo Buck goes and gets us a curry. We sit in bed and watch the ghosts in the television as we eat, and I can't help but think that love is a fine sweet thing, it is good company to have on the road and a hot-water bottle in a cold bed. Maybe this place will turn out okay you know, just maybe it's our kind of place . . .

3.

Bob's Got
Way-Sweet Deals

Overnight the weather has deteriorated even further. I am deliriously happy. My senile old god has provided for me yet again. There are no extra blankets delivered, but on site there are plenty of nails. Hundreds of the buggers, scattered everywhere like artillery shrapnel. This guy is crazy – he has one building motto: 'Bang that mother home, bro!'

Thirty bucks a day is not easy money, it is hard money, and money for which my fingers have bled and my thumbs swollen. I have lost my left thumbnail completely; it has withered and died after one too many wayward clouts. I have seen nothing of this city other than gridlock and plywood walls. Our room has no view – the view is also under construction. Everything is being built. There are cranes, scaffolding, cement trucks and surly tradespeople everywhere, scavenging about like bull ants on a hot day. Traffic doesn't move – I can peer at the highway at five in the afternoon through our thinly glassed window, and if I look an hour later, it's the same cars in formation. No one goes anywhere fast, which is fine in a country where no one has any aspirations to get someplace smartish. It's deadly enough out on the sidewalks, where everyone is a jaywalker with suicidal tendencies. When one goes they all go, like wildebeest; never mind the bumper-to-bumper vehicles just waiting to bag a stray.

Life here is perilous, I have garnered that much information in a few days. Almost everyone is rabid with fear: of job losses, of wage cuts, of being undercut or cut from the socio-economic loop. The big stick is everywhere, wielded freely it would appear. This is a hard-work town with a snub-nosed ethic and while I freely give my admiration to types who live that kind of cutthroat lifestyle, it is not my cup of Darjeeling. Life, I'm told, by those in-the-know, is considerably easier down south. I heard the barman in the pool hall tell some down-and-out backpacker that the other day, just before he threw him out on the street with the disdain of a city slicker tired of low-life bums spending all day sipping one beer.

So what? That's what Jo said, laying there picking at her freshly weeping sore. The tattooist, she tells me, was a large shaggy specimen with the bedside manner of a paedophile. I tell her to stop making the damned thing bleed because it's making me woozy, then lay the hard word on her. She doesn't want to head south because we're south enough, and the souther you get the colder the weather. She's not a damned seal and she doesn't have the necessary blubber reserves.

The day after being pawed by the junkie tatt man, her mood is more upbeat. She's going back to the honest profession that'll turn us enough hard cash to set ourselves up somewhere swanky – like Ponsonby. Hell no, I answer, you can't run that game here, not in a city as gridlocked as this one – have you tried to cross a road lately? How'd you think customers would get to you? Look at the public transport system, the animosity, the mile upon mile of stranded vehicles with bug-eyed drivers. I'm not saying it *won't* work, don't get me wrong, it's just location location location, understand?

Now she's in the bathroom trying to see her latest acquisition in the badly cracked mirror. I'm going nowhere fast –

which is the norm. It's not that I have qualms about this whipping gig, Christ I know too many guys who crave that kind of action. What's bothering me is this fast-growing city. I need something slower, a little more sedated – a place where traffic flows and pedestrians stick to the sidewalks.

I think that this latest tattoo is going to have to be surgically removed, maybe the whole arm. What price a one-armed dominatrix?

It's my last day working on the ark and today I can see that the conservatory looks more like a Viking ship. I don't want to be standing about holding a nail gun when the owner turns up and gets into a frenzied state – nor if the authorities unexpectedly arrive and start delving into my status and competency to wield a hammer. This is not stuff I'm keen to be involved in, litigation and suchlike. At least the guy pays cash and he rounds it up to the hundred because he's enjoyed my company.

I give the readies to the reception lady, who appears surprised, and tell her we're checking out routes south tomorrow. She tells me to go see Bob at the rental place just up the street – Bob's got way sweet deals.

He has, too – you can drive an eight-seat wagon down to Christchurch for the cost of gas and ferry. What's the catch? I ask him, and Bob just laughs until he almost suffocates himself. The catch, of course, is that you have to do it in three days, four max, after that you're on the daily rate. Only it'll take at least four days to crawl out of this damned place! I tell Bob I'm not interested, daily rates haunt me everywhere I go.

So it's the plane, I figure, no way do I want to be on a bus for a week. The only people who travel by bus are the very same types who frequent pool halls. No thanks. Christ, I wish I'd had the good sense to just fly there in the first place when our credit was still good; those banks wouldn't have missed the extra 50 quid each. The travel agent tells me that there are tickets, for tomorrow, all I need now is the money to buy them with.

I know Jo has a *stash* because she's *always* got one some-place – it's the German in her.

What about all that scallop money, huh? Don't play the dumb broad, you know as well as I do that we got paid in cold cash for those five days; do you know how many scallops I shelled? What effect it had on my central nervous system? It's no wonder I'm paranoid about sex, must we go through this elaborate charade every time we need to come to a decision? Didn't you just get a tattoo? Hellfire and damnation, I have to go south – it's in my blood, like poisoning is in yours, do we have money or not?

A day later, despite what Earl the tattooist had warned vis-à-vis pressurization, we're on a jet. Outside it's a beautiful day; we are skimming snow-capped mountain ranges, kicking up a whiff of powder here and there. Thor can see us and he is smiling, until he sees those bloody tattoos, and then he hits us with some turbulence. It's only a touch of turbulence, babe, okay? Like we had that time over Acapulco during the lightning season. Don't sweat it – God loves us all, that's what the Rastas say.

Fuck the Rastas.

Now, this is more like it. Christchurch airport is a manage-able size, not too big, not too small, and there are rows of empty shuttles, like shiny pins on a bowling alley. The air outside is so fresh that after all of that gridlock and smog it makes me sneeze. Bless you! a passing lay preacher says, and if that isn't a sign then I don't know what is. Come on, grab those bags, I tell my Jo Buck, and stop bitching about that arm – a bit of fresh air will do it the world of good. Smell that, huh? Smells like shit, you think? That's God's country, babe, everyone stinks of shit down here. Get used to it. Where there's muck, huh?

I ain't livin' on no farm, she tells me bitterly as she rummages for another jacket and a pair of shoes.

Why haven't you got shoes on, don't you know it's winter?

It was hot in Bombay.

So?

I took my shoes off there; I think some goddamned beggar stole 'em.

Jesus H. Christ.

We are in a shuttle with fifteen Indians, not red ones. They are all looking at my tattooed partner in crime, and staring at her feet. In some parts of the Hindu world it is an insult to show your feet, and so what? We are a long way from Rajasthan. In fact, we are on the Plains as they say down here – we are Canterbrians. Are there such beings?

This motel is adequate for our purposes, which are meagre. It has a kitchenette, a hot shower, a TV with cable, and is within spitting distance of a supermarket. It is about time we ate our own food; I was a celebrity chef for twenty years and understand food in any language. So off we go to shop, following the directions the one-eyed cripple gave us. Finally, an hour later, we come to the supermarket and spend up small on a few necessities. The air is good and the exercise invigorating; already I feel like a new woman.

Me too, Jo says sarcastically.

We eat in bed. Jo slugs greedily from a quart bottle of something local, Tui maybe. Anyhow, she's enjoying the ride and skipping channels with the remote. I'm taking my umpteenth shit of the day, rectum inflamed and bowels like torpedo tubes on a U-boat. Just as I'm deep into it, the whole movement thing, Jo shrieks crazily, and I'm off the throne as quick as an English-born king. She's jumping around the room like a freak-head and I have to wrestle her to the ground. Well, I'm used to it.

What the hell's the matter this time? I hiss as she squirms beneath me like a death adder.

Something goddamned bit me, that's what!

She's right, there's a huge red welt on her calf – no, two actually, sorry, make that three.

There's something in that fucking bed, a rat maybe.

A rat? Good grief, woman, get a grip, we aren't in the Bronx now.

Well whatever it is, it fucking bites, get rid of it, huh?

Sure, I tell her in a manly kind of leave-it-to-me-honey way, and then start savagely ripping the sheets from the bed looking for the culprit. No fucker, man nor beast, bites my woman in a bed I've paid for. But there's nothing live visible among the old piss stains on the mattress. Christ Almighty, what a deadbeat fucking life: cold weather, nasty bugs, bad tattoos and a financial problem, maybe we oughtta just cut our losses and head home, it ain't too far, just across the Ditch.

We can't go home, she tells me stonily.

Can't? There's no such word!

There is after you haven't paid the phone bill, the electricity bill, and the rent – let alone all of those goddamned credit card bills. They'll arrest us both for sure as soon as we set foot back in Australia – those kind of people never forget.

Hmm, she's got a point. Maybe we will have to stake our claim right here, fucking bugs 'n' all. It is a bad and restless night – painful too. By morning we both look like drug-test patients.

4.

The Reciprocal Welfare Agreement

Gone, all the money was gone. We were down to eleven buckeroonies, give or take. Jo and me are sitting in Works & Income looking for a hardship benefit. And why not? We were in dire straits: homeless, penniless and morose. Even the free whisky had gone, and the mini-bar gins. What else were a couple of girls down on their luck supposed to do?

The staff weren't too pleased to see us – not at all amused that a couple of expatriate Aussies were in their backyard looking for a government-funded sub. I thought it was a two-way street? I told them. Look at how many of your mob have fleeced the Aussie taxpayer over the past half a century, and you haven't even paid the goddamned bill!

The only thing you can do, they told us unsympathetically, is call your embassy in Wellington, see if they'll fly you back to that roach-infested place on the next charter – if they won't, you'll have to get the reason why in writing.

Jesus, that was how we came to be talking to the Aussie government about repatriation – and like you know already, they just thought we were a couple of roos short in the top paddock. The government did send us their letter, eventually. No can do, they said, you wasted your own money, you're Caucasian and you can work – get a fucking job, okay! Armed with that we returned, cap in hand, to Works & Income and under the Trans-Tasman Reciprocal Welfare Agreement they dutifully signed us up to the teat. It is always comforting when you know where your next meal is coming from.

We'd rented a house not far from the city, within walking distance, and that was good because we had no money spare for bus rides. When they say hardship, they really fucking mean it. If you have ever wondered how the other half lives, then let me tell you that they don't, they simply exist, like algae in a stagnant pond; that is the way of hardship. There is the daily struggle to appease the stomach and titillate the brain before too many cells self-implode through tedium and the degeneration becomes irreversible. You cannot afford to be ill, warm or contented. Each day is a new nail in your coffin – and if you slide too far into the abyss, your head will become as fucked-up as an adventure bus driver's. The one good thing about poverty is that the only way is up. You are right at the bottom of society's slop barrel, in the residue, and if you don't start paddling fast the shit soup will consume you like acid in the giant gut of life. At a time like this you need good love and a keen sense of right – and failing that, the ability to lie your way into the first available opportunity that slides your way.

5.

Positions Vacant

I loathe morning afters. Even after the sanest decisions, you wake up feeling like you've made the wrong choice and, after that, the day is a write off. So, here I am lamenting my rashness. I have hauled us a long way south to where the air is chillier and this is the terminus. It's an unsettling feeling, appreciating that you've come as far as you can on luck, girlish charm and cute lips, and now you've nothing left to give other than lame excuses. That is about as low as it gets, unless you are stuck in a lift with a pillhead, or maybe Jack Nicholson.

The first thing to do is get down to the tax department for a number – a number gives you legal status, it entitles you. New Zealand is a liberal country, there is no mandatory physical examination or the pre-requisite of surgical papers from Bangkok to establish what genitalia you're hauling around – and anyway, I have several letters from eminent doctors testifying to the fact that, to all intent and purposes, I'm a woman. Ergo, obtaining the number isn't hard. The New Zealand public servant au fait with all manner of weird and perverse gender issues, bats not an eyelid when he slides my documentation over the counter, giving me a tax file number that states my chosen name and gender – gender as in 'F', you understand. Which is all very nice, only I might have a problem (according to this new piece of documentation I've acquired), if I have to pretend I'm the person I used to be and not the person I am now, simply to put stale bread on the table. Not that we own a table yet . . .

After this, we stroll up to Cathedral Square. This is where it all happens, where the hot pot of multiculturalism-in-practice bubbles along nicely. In summer, I hear, they have some guy called the Wizard who stands on a box and lectures the gathered throng on any topic that springs into his mind, which sounds okay to me. I like Christchurch immediately; it is nothing like the Christian-English-loving-mission I had been led to believe it was. It is vibrant, even now in the off-season. People seem reasonably happy and no one is rushing around manically like they do in Auckland. Down here they even obey the road rules – cars actually stop at red lights. Everything looks new and fresh to tired eyes. I have a feeling that we'll do okay here once this rough settling-in patch clears and we find our feet again, and Jo a decent pair of shoes.

And then Jo gets hit with some wild bug that's sweeping the place, some new strain of flu fresh off the plane from Taipei. This entails a trip to the doctor, and one for me too, as despite my change of gender I still have to find someone to implant me with the female hormone; without it there's every possibility that I could detonate. It's then that it hits us – there is no medical paradise down here, drugs are expensive. This is ugly karma as we are both reliant upon pharmaceutical cocktails to survive the trials and tribulations of life; prescribed drugs are our bag, as they used to say in the Haight. This puts a downer on our mood because even though we're attached to the System, the stark nerve-jangling reality of it is you can't survive on welfare.

Life, however, has taught me to be patient, and generally I

am a happy-go-unlucky minstrel. Once my eyes have re-gained their focus and my brain funk has cleared I can see the bells, and amazingly, I can hear them too. Say, don't those bells sound pretty?

Pretty? Bells don't sound fucken pretty, Jo responds sweetly.

These sure do, listen.

What are you? A born-again choir boy?

I never made the choir . . .

In a city like this, where jobs go to the lowest bidder, anyone can work. I was titillated by all the new and challenging positions vacant. I could make cosmetics – which sounded right up my street; I am good with recipes and even better with make-up. I could load bread, and so could Jo, who rather fancied the cap and the steel boots if not the ungodly hours. There were a myriad of openings across the tourism and hospitality sector: New Zealand encapsulates the word 'adventure'. The place has everything a speed freak or gravity-defying numbnut could desire, and lots more besides. You can shoot rapids with your balls on fire or climb mountains and parasail off the summit, if you're inclined to such recklessness. You can go fast, and even faster, until your tits are wrapped around your ears – whatever. All tastes, no matter how bizarre, have been catered for. No one leaves New Zealand muttering about how fucking little there is to do – except the three million or so who fled to Australia and then sit around drinking beer all day while they claim the dole. But no sooner had those wasters gone to the big island penitentiary across the swamp, than the whole adventure tourism gig was totally re-vamped. And now New Zealand has rightful claims to reaching the epiphany.

Gone are the days when Kiwis farmed and buggered sheep, threw rotten eggs at the Queen, and called each other silly names. New Zealand has embraced cultural diversity and mind-warping, adrenaline-rushing thrills and spills. Everyone is in on it, even the goddamned whales and dolphins. If you have ever sat at home on a miserable fucking good-for-nothing night in Stoke-on-Trent or Winnipeg or Gaza, pondering where you should invest your hard-earned to gain that once-in-a-lifetime, brain-damaging mother-of-all fucking rides – well, ponder no more shithead, here's your destination.

Ye gods, if I were that way inclined, if I placed no more value on my life than I did on a bank full of stocks and bonds, then brother I'd be up there too, waiting to bungee jump, shivering my balls off while some heavy-handed monster strapped me into the elastic electric chair for my last ride on earth. And why the fuck not, if you're going to permanently damage yourself either mentally or physically – and sometimes both, simultaneously – then why not do it with a fucking view?

That's what I told the Tourist Board woman when I went for the interview. Fucking oath, I told her, in a place like this I could sell the Irish fucking potatoes or the Saudis gas, hell yes.

I didn't get the job.

But so what? I was happy, oblivious to purgatory and poverty. I had a mattress on the floor, and a good, amply curved and silicone-free woman on that mattress. There's not much else you need when the thermometer hits eight below and your nipples drip icicles. When you get up and your shit plops straight on the frozen toilet bowl water next to a couple of fur seal pups. That's about the point you can rest assured that it *is* cold! And in the cold people go crazy, I mean look at the Finns and the Icelanders.

On the corner of our wee street one frosty morning, when Jo and me set out on our daily riverside stroll to search for dropped cash, there were two bikini-clad women holding up placards at a busy intersection. They were doing a stunt for a radio station; the temperature was two below. Where else can you see stuff like that, huh? Those fucking crazy Kiwis. Maybe Jo and me could get a gig like that?

I tried all sorts of weird approaches across a plethora of shiny new opportunities; at the English school I told the head lecturer that I'd only recently been teaching English to the French in Scotland – which was perfectly true in a roundabout sort of way. I blew the interview for the secretary job at the Antarctic Benevolent Society, or some such, by claiming I had just arrived from Dresden where I had been selling used Travant parts. At the chicken-boning interview – a gig for which, I might add, I was qualified – I squandered my shot by claiming to have been a poultry industry health inspector in Latvia. The guy didn't even know where it was ... but I think it was the word 'health' that put him off. I even got sucked into some insane notion that I could work in the bureau de change – and why not? I am good handling money, especially other people's, but they didn't much take to my 'close friend of Ronnie Biggs' story. You can say what you like really when you arrive in a fresh new country. It's fun to concoct tales that flatter your own bent perspective of you as the great adventurer. As ever, life decrees that sooner or later you will have to fall back flat on your rump and trust in the skill you know and understand.

Jo had skills, and an attitude to go along with them. While I was deep into sophisticated fabrication, Jo was sticking to the truth, but sometimes the truth makes it even harder to find a suitable opening than the little white lies.

Suffice to say that Jo's CV read like a page out of a Marquis de Sade manuscript, and people find themselves sweating when they read stuff like that. There were some takers though, as there always are; the massage parlour rather fancied the idea of a PVC-clad receptionist-cum-hostess who could handle a crop if the need arose, maybe a pair of nipple clamps too – but to be honest, I didn't fancy the idea at all. If you ask me it's not easy money – in fact, it's probably hard money. And even at a time like this, when the cash was gone and we were investigating the pros and cons of armed robbery, I still couldn't bring myself around to the idea. I am flexible, sure, but I am also possessive of my woman.

The art shop sounded better, standing around all day fully clothed hawking pastels and gouache to would-be Picassos, that's a fine and honourable job and insofar as I know, it doesn't involve any prerequisite to understand the aerodynamics of a cat-o'-nine tails. She didn't get the job, something about her Attitude. But haven't all of the great artists had Attitude? What about Bacon, huh? I bet he never got kicked out of an art shop . . .

6.

Infiltrate and Destroy

*They banged the door and went off up the stairs, their keys
jangling in the distance. I looked around me. Bare concrete walls
and floors. The door was a massive piece of timber and steel.
The window was high up in the wall, below ground level and
looking on to another wall. A bare electric bulb, over the door,
shone through wire grating.*
Brendan Behan – *Borstal Boy*

That is institutionalization, and the scenery rarely changes.
Not just in Borstal – but in the mixing bowl of life. There is no
such thing as a room with a view. I know, as I have been institutionalized one way or another since the day I was born. I am
accustomed to it, and for the most part it has served its intended
purpose, which is not, as they claim, to break you, but rather to
adapt you. All that lock-up serves to do in the end is to make
you freer of mind than when you entered. There is nothing like
being confined in a five-by-five or a stinking rotten staffroom in
a skanky hotel to set the mind flying off to better, more open
pampas.

Maybe that's why I'm here in New Zealand. Not only
because it's the last stop on earth, but also because it's still free.
Maybe, maybe not: nowhere is truly free, and no person either.

So, here I am again, scanning the voluminous Saturday jobs pages, circling all the positions that have a ring of institutionalism about them – but not fucking chefs' jobs, no thanks, buddy, I've done my time on the line. I'd rather eat shit and die than don those stupid whites and funny hat again. What I need is a job the human canvas and me can do together, one of those couples' jobs – and by couples, I mean in the heterosexual sense, where you share the load and get paid peanuts. And, for the love of Christ, wouldn't yer know that there's a whole page of them! But how do two women get a job where they can still claim the free shared accommodation on offer without raising a few eyebrows? Easy. One of 'em pretends to be a boy, and if that person just happened to have been born a boy, so much better for the deception. Live-in is the way to go when you're down but not quite out, and if you have to yank the wool over a few pairs of eyes, who really cares? This is New Zealand, for god's sake, the country is covered in sheep.

I have to broach the matter of live-in occupations delicately, however, given that Jo lost it completely up in haggis heaven and almost ruined the bartender's chances of becoming a father. She can be vicious when roused, and carnal when aroused – she is a woman of extremes, with an attention span for the mundane akin to that of the gnat. There will be no point in me charging at this subject like a castrated bull – which, technically, I am. What I need are my skills in subterfuge and manipulation. Common logic, I'll tell her, dictates that we will be vastly better off without such burdens as rent and utility bills. Why work just to keep a roof over your head when someone else will provide it?

And that was how, a fortnight later, we came to be sitting in the tawdry lounge of a large and dilapidated building being interviewed by the 60-year-old owner, Zsa Zsa, and her toy boy lover. It was so cold that what remained of my testicular sack shrivelled up to nothing, and I couldn't stop my teeth chattering. Probably those people thought I was a junkie on some big cold-turkey jive, but somehow it all seemed to be going our way. We were young and hip, even me (by some medical miracle I am actually getting younger instead of older). What with our bleached hair and the multiple piercings it seemed we were just the types that these odd people had been searching for: a young, groovy couple able to take up the reins and run with them, dragging everything else behind – even if it was kicking and screaming.

The best bet, when you are down and dirty and relying upon a mythical CV and your good looks, is never to ask about money – as soon as you do that you are fucked. That's why you're there in the first place, of course, but the rules of engagement stipulate that he or she who appears disinterested in such trifling matters as rates of pay, will always come out on top.

While I was au fait with these techniques, Jo was not renowned for her tactfulness in such delicate situations. I was certain that at any moment she would interrupt our prospective employers' oral lava flow with a choice Jo-ism along the lines of the place looking like a roach den or smelling like a crypt. Which it did on both accounts – but precisely because of that, I knew we were in with the shot.

Instead of letting off her numerous verbal cannons, Jo began to steal my own weak thunder and work our prospective employers like a couple of rubes at the town carnie. Next came the grand tour, and once you get that, you can be pretty sure you have one foot over the threshold. The only thing that could go wrong would be a conscientious employer trying to contact your fake referees in Kabul. My gut told me, however, and my gut is rarely wrong on such matters, that these people wouldn't go to such bother. They were tight-arses, and cash hungry, and people like that never fax Afghanistan.

The place was much bigger than I'd envisioned, three floors and about a hundred beds, maybe more. The staff flat was on the second floor, furnished after a fashion with a TV and VCR – having been without visual stimuli as entertainment for two months, the modernity was enticing. That little hideaway swung it for us, it was easy street, but on easy street nothing is as it seems.

After the big tour Zsa Zsa and the toy boy said their good-byes. They would be 'in touch' as soon as they had interviewed the 'numerous' other 'interested parties'. That is the professional spiel that mercenary bosses give to potential inductees; sufficient to instil hope, but not enough to bring on an out-break of bravado or alcoholic celebration. We walked back to our mattress on the floor and our clock radio, back to instant mashed potato, home-brand tinned peas and yesterday's sausages, and spent the night conducting a rigorous post mortem of our performances while analyzing our chances of getting to roost in that adequate little nest. We had put on a good show, there was no doubt about that, though while the woman had seemed keen on us, the guy had been reserved. Jo dubbed him the Doc because he looked as smooth and authentic as a 40-year-old soap star medic. Sure, he knew how to keep his cards tight, but he wasn't The Boss, he was just the Boy – so maybe we had impressed the right one. And, if not, well we'd just have to do it all over again; we had other sticks in the fire as they say in Ho Chi Minh City.

After a fortnight with no word, we assumed the worst, although we couldn't fathom why we'd failed. I mean who could be better suited than us to manhandle foreign types on budget holidays?

To boost our flagging morale we went for another interview in the same field, only this place was much smaller – a 'boutique backpackers' they were calling it, at the vanguard of the movement toward low budget cost, but high expectation, hotel-like services and accessories. This trend was starting to flourish about town, and was proving quite divisive insofar as I could ascertain.

This couple were odd to the point of ludicrousness. She was on the verge of giving birth to identical septuplets after eight years of IVF treatment in Dallas. He was a religious freak who dressed in a cassock and Jesus sandals. There were seventeen cats scratching a brand-new sofa to pieces in the Spanish-tiled foyer. The receptionist, apparently a product of incest, was putting designer sunglasses into one of those rotunda-like display units you can twirl around. Sure, I thought, these people are new to this game and all of those sunnies will be half-inched during the opening week. Security was slack; a fat dachshund is no guard dog and a chubby boy with bitch tits even less so. I got the distinct impression that this was one of those tax dodge, employ-your-own-slack-jawed-relatives kind of gig. The woman kept arching her back and letting out small moans of pain. She was indeed heavily loaded, and after she gave birth they would have enough kin to start some kind of up-market hostel chain – maybe called 'Puppy Love'.

Still, they had done good work. The old homestead had been completely revamped, all fresh paint, indoor hanging baskets and double-glazing. A real home away from home. They had thought of everything, even chocolates on pillows. Pillows? Now that really was style, especially after that other place with just bare slats. I was impressed by the attention to detail, but not at all by this pair's Manson-esque style of living. The guy was obviously some kind of crazed sex fiend who fired blanks and felt he had open slather on humping anything that writhed. I looked at the dachshund and the chubby boy with wobbly bitch tits. Then at the cross-eyed receptionist with the missing ear lobe – I was in the house of goddamned wax. If the boss guy had overseen the renovations you could be damned sure that all those mirrors everywhere were two-way.

Grandma was there, too. I hadn't noticed her at first because a giant vase filled with Venus flytraps was obscuring her diminutive frame. She was in a rocker, like Ma Baker, crocheting up tablemats for the all-vegetarian communal restaurant. Out in the courtyard were three Krishnas, attired in their day-glo orange robes, stacking stone near an ornamental pond. The whole place gave me the heebies. I am not into religious conversion, nor lentils, nor fucking crocheting for that matter – and besides, Granny looked like she'd just paddled herself down the old Miss on her bed base. They were piping in Gregorian chanting music – an obvious ploy to appeal to all denominations. A few joss sticks burned in the atrium; the place had a come-hither ambience tainted with institutional neurosis.

We didn't make the Tour. The woman began clutching at her huge writhing belly and moaning in unison with the Krishnas while Granny's knitting needles sped up and the dachshund started licking its evil lips. She was going to drop them there and then, on the Persian rug, one after the other; plop plop plop plop plop plop plop . . . urgh!

The man, too busy telling us about the Joshua tree he was going to plant by the hot tub, paid no heed to the forthcoming event. The chubby boy with the tits was digging the hole and we stood there a while watching him, fascinated. In some parts of the world a boy like that would be considered a delicacy. As he dug, his excess flesh wobbled, giving him an undulating aura of sensuality. The man ogled him eagerly, swallowed hard, then turned on his heels so fast his sandals left a burn mark on the patio. We followed him back into the foyer where the woman was now prostrate on the couch covered in purring cats.

This scene was too bizarre even for me; it was a whole new Babylon and it stank of dirty pink skin and lust. A few beads of sweat began the long trip down my spine as I stood there somehow fused to the spot. No one spoke. I had been kidnapped by aliens and they were now communicating tele-pathically over my fate; would I be slow braised or spit roasted?

Fortunately, Jo took hold of my moist hand and led me toward the door. She had seen all she needed to see. The whole gang of them followed us with their watery eyes, but still they did not speak. A little bell jangled above the door and we walked slowly to the gate along a path lined with whitewashed stones that looked like runes.

Back in the sanctuary of our barely furnished abode I lay on the mattress staring at the flaking ceiling. I knew exactly how Alice felt, although she, at least, was in Wonderland. There weren't any talking rabbits up the road, not that I'd seen, but there were Mad Hatters and herbal tea parties. Ye gods, this is a strange and surreal place, everything is a mirage and it vanishes the moment you reach out to touch it. Or was I just dreaming, the result of too many prescription drugs and not enough food?

Without television or alcohol to fall back on, I endured a listless night full of hallucinogenic skits that featured the chubby boy digging holes, and woke with my head on fire and my body frozen. And then the mobile rang. I sat up groggily and listened to Jo's side of the conversation. She seemed happy.

What news, pray, fair lady, maketh you smile like a beautiful morning? I asked her once she'd finished.

That was the other place – they want us to go up there and try out.

Try out? What kind of a gig is that?

It's a free labour gig, that's what. I said we would anyhow.

Why the hell not, I shrugged. We'd come this far. Say, I asked Jo while she ate one of yesterday's cold roast potatoes for breakfast, can you hear monodic liturgic chanting?

You and those fucking bells.

7.

If I Should Die Here, Bury Me in Powder Blue Satin

We will now discuss in a little more detail the struggle for existence, said Charles Darwin in one of his saner moments. And that is the very same thing the doctor once told me in respect of the sperm I was about to sacrifice for the cause of female uniformity. He thought that maybe, given the struggle for existence, I should freeze a few million just in case.

Just in case of what? I asked him point blank.

Well, just in case you, uhm, change your mind one day or meet a good woman and you want to ...

Want to what?

You know, procreate artificially.

Well sure, Darwin was goddamned right – and those gals from Salt 'n' Peppa who once wanted to rap about sex. Why in the name of Bethlehem would the world want more of me?

More voracious spores blowing along on the trade winds, aren't the killer bees enough? No thanks, I told him, the thought of a million me's snap frozen in some deep freeze along with a hundred years supply of Icelandic cod fillets just leaves me cold. And that's what Darwin said about the Japanese once, after he'd seen them slicing sushi steaks off a still wriggling sperm whale up by the Pole. But not Cooky, old James knew all about cannibals and Pacific islanders, about weird voodoo ceremonies by twilight – that was how he managed to keep his head on his shoulders and his tackle swinging free.

I am hacked from the same chunk of salt-jerked beef. I travel well, like James and Charles, and although I understand some men's needs to feast on the different-coloured flesh of other men, and know that once they have tasted that kind of char-grilled rib with earth-baked kumara they will never again be able to sate that craving, I am, myself, a person of simple needs and tastes (apart from when it comes to bedmates or prescription drugs). But I just wanted to tell you about Cook because his great grandchild is Thomas, he of the foreign exchange monopoly, 100% vinyl attaché cases, radioactive umbrella tips and worldwide travel bureaus. The Cooks have done well for themselves, but not the Darwins, they have been pecked at by insanity, and all they got was a desert shanty-town made of old corrugated iron named after them, in Australia's Top End. And even that got blown away by a mean-tempered motherfucker of a storm on Christ's birthday one year. God moves in mysterious ways.

We English are all stark raving mad and we cannot blame the sun for that. We are not really men at all (by the true definition of the word) and I will go further: we English are the most underhand, conniving, and sexually deviant men on this good earth, other than the Swedish. I know a bit about the Swedes and their hard-drinking Baltic nights when the glug flows, and the smuggled chewing tobacco causes the Viking sap to resurface as they slide out on the ice to gaff critters to death and roll around in the still-steaming blood. The Swedes are animals and they couldn't even con me with Abba or IKEA, I know what goes on behind the scenes. Oh, hang on, do I mean the Norwegians?

So what? you're thinking, up there at high altitude with your intelligence molecules frozen and your mouth as arid as the Gobi desert on an August long weekend. Well, what, my dears, is what you're going to encounter as soon as your bloated feet touch good Kiwi terra firma, and the sharks circle around you like a school of jackals patiently tracking a wounded wildebeest. They are patient people in the Land of the Long White Cloud, they have had to be. The only new face they saw for half a century was Harvey Keitel, and then they had to haul that bloody piano up a sheer cliff face. That is a very long time to have been insulated from the great throbbing world beyond, and all of the marvellous technical inventions thereof.

New Zealand is a wild, untamed country, a reckless theme park run by stoned hippies and ex-marine types, and that is as dangerous a mix as badly stored TNT. Tour bus drivers are recruited on the Poppy Trail, from high up in the Tibetan mountains right down to the teeming desperate streets of Kabul. Those people do not understand the meaning of the words 'suicidal risk', and before you board any bus painted in happy-coloured livery for the 'ride of your life', my advice is that you should sign off on an iron-clad insurance contract – one that specifically covers acts of God and pillhead bus drivers – before you climb up those steps. Perhaps a letter to your mother wouldn't go astray either. Adventure bus driving is a murky business full of weird handshakes, knowing facial expressions and heavy drinking – oh, and cheap sex, of course, and there's no sex cheaper than that engaged in when the temperature is hovering around zero and your thermals are scrunched about your ankles.

I took that ride once, and only once mind you – twice would have led me to the confines of well-manicured gardens behind very high hedges while a nurse with an undulating cleavage wheeled me about in a bath chair. I have a strong disposition for many things: ex-communist-bloc airlines flown by ex-Soviet paratroopers still fucked-up from the Afghan adventure; runaway trains en route to Tierra del Fuego and probably beyond; midnight on the dark continent when the beasts roar hungrily and the tribesmen dance around in zebra-skin loin cloths with big ivory smiles like cluster bombs going off in Al Hillah; happy hour at Papa's Bar in downtown Port au Prince while the scarlet hats beat the living bejesus out of a mouthy American tourist. I can take all of that, and more besides, without reverting to prayer but, mother, putting my life in the hands of some grasshead who has not once, but twice, wiped the side-vision mirrors off a bus rattling across a perilously rickety bridge at 90 k an hour over a gaping chasm while he sings 'Don't Worry Be Happy' is enough to fry even *my* nerve ends and pan sauté what's left of my balls.

By the time we hit the kayaking school, I mean *hit* it, as in clipping the verandah, only to find that its 'former' owner was already en route to Nairobi after having just drowned 30 Albanians in what the authorities were calling an 'unfortunate accident', I was already suited up in a full immersion vest and equipped with my own portable floatation system, K-packs and a GPS. No way was I going to find myself unequipped for a day at sea, halfway to the Falklands, on the fickle whims of some ex-banker with Panamanian credit problems. These are the risks you run once you've deposited your valuables in the hostel safe and bought multiple tickets to ride; that's why they insist you fill out an overseas registered packet to your next of kin. It looks macabre, I know, and it makes some travelling types feel pithy in the pit of their guts, but this, friends, is what we in the trade calling dotting the i's and crossing all of the t's. In our line of work you cannot afford to take unnecessary chances, or hold a bed for some fool who is obviously already plankton some-where deep off the shelf. Well okay, it's all there in the 'small print' as they say at every Mitsubishi dealership, you pays your moolah and yous takes your chances.

This is the meaning of existence, especially in the context of modern travelling. Cook and Darwin never had to undergo such thorough scrutiny. If they wanted to seize indigenous artefacts, boiled skulls, potatoes, tobacco or nubile Polynesian virgins to utilize as creature comforts on the long sail back to civilization, well, no one was there to countermand them. Like I've told you already, when you find yourself this far south you would be a dumb fuck if you still thought that polar bears were cuddly. These are dangerous waters, even more so for the mob of white-trash thrillseekers who pile through New Zealand immigration every high season looking for cheap highs and the whole lexicon of uncomplicated sexual encounters.

Where there is prey, there will always be predators, crouched belly-low in the long grass breathing heavily ... a passport, a book of traveller's cheques and a letter of recom-mendation from your filthy old lecturer means nothing way down here on the mud flats. Just remember that, the very next time you're tempted to hitch a ride to save twenty bucks. Given the rates of exchange Thomas offers, you're putting a very low marker on your own existence ... remember Charles Sobhraj.

8.

Jeez, We're a Couple of Lookers

The Maori have the blessing of second sight. Trouble is, the Maori, and especially Maori women, with their 3D vision and honed intuition, saw straight through my identity scam as if I were nothing but a pane of flexi glass. I hadn't allowed for that; I hadn't calculated it into my perambulatory thesis on being able to fool all of the fishheads all of the time.

That trial period was a knuckle-chewing ride, made even wilder by the fact that it coincided with the hostel being full to the white-ant riddled rafters with a Maori school group, in town for some gospel-singing eisteddfod. The only way you can survive this kind of heavy reverse karma is if your virgin boss is so engrossed in the methodical counting and re-counting of legal tender not to notice that his guests are referring to his about-to-be-hired management couple as 'gals' and 'ladies' and 'lookers', as in, Jeez, you're a couple of lookers, huh?

Money talks in the hostelling world and, thankfully, it talks louder than second-sighted indigenous women and their broods. It must have been the noise of all of that coinage clinking in canvas moneybags that drowned out the Truth. Either that, or our about-to-be boss didn't give two sloppy slurps for the fact that his newly acquired mercenary managers were both blonde and somewhat buxom – so long as the cash rolled in.

And, man, that Doc guy knew how to count cash, like a squirrel counting up his nuts for winter, whipping those coins into clear plastic bags like there wasn't gonna be any brand-new dawn. I watched fascinated while his agile fingers did croupier-like acrobatics and his banker's eyes stayed dilated and greedy. Yup, I recall thinking to myself, we're fucked.

The next I knew he was loaded up like a drug trafficker's mule high in the poppy fields, weighed down with hard currency, grunting under the mother lode. That guy won't make it five yards once he hits the Outside, that's what I thought – but the guy wasn't as zonked-out as he looked. The armoured four-wheel drive had already been brought around to the No Standing zone by Dick, the trusty steward of many a past campaign. Dick knew the ropes, and most likely all of the knots too. Dick looked, on first impressions you understand, like the kind of guy who'd be head of the queue for the public hangman's position, should it ever become vacant. He was thin and in his sixties and I swear he tucked his flannel shirt into his undies.

They made a good team, like Burke and Hare, I guess, a couple of gruesome grave robbers who hauled cash instead of stiff white corpses. They both had money on the brain and the boneyard in sight; one shovelled and the other grabbed, and they had the moves down pat – engine running, passenger door slightly ajar, and then SCREEEECH! the sound of squealing tyres and the nasty smell of burned rubber as they made haste to the express deposit line.

I stared at Jo chin-deep in vagrants, the off-season fodder on which the vast hostel feeds while it awaits the return of warm days and cashed-up plankton. The Maori kids were emptying the out-of-date candy faster than I could find dust-covered confectionary to re-stock the shelf. Down in the restaurant-cum-communal-gathering-place, the choir was striking up something Polynesian, and the whole place had a swinging vibe, just like on coronation day. Shit yeah, even the bums Jo was turning away with a hard-bitch stare and a get-the-fuck-outta-here disposition seemed to be taking it all in good humour, a few even swaying rhythmically over by the long-since plundered vending machine. Right about then I wouldn't have wanted to be anywhere else in the world. This was a good place, despite its overbearing feel of desperation. The place oozed neglect the way that house in Amityville oozed blood. Maybe the Good Doctor was right when he'd alluded to the fact that come high season, the whole joint would be as alive and jumping as a pile of bedbugs chowing on a stoned hippy.

But what of this 'trial' business? That's what my family solicitor once said while he attempted a plea bargain to save my sorry arse from forced invasion. I mean, one minute the Good Doctor is showing us the intricate technicalities of the ex-Nazi IBM punch-card register, the next he's vamoosed with his trusty sidekick-cum-acolyte-bodyguard, and I'm left trying to jemmy open the till with a crowbar like a common criminal – not that there's any shortage of experienced advice on how to get a mother like that open. Like, do we work through until the night porter shows up, or do we just drag down the wire-mesh shutters and say fuck this?

I'm of the mind to ask Jo, but she's deep in a pointed argument with some wino about sleeping arrangements and the need to pay for them first.

An hour later, Jo is sat in the office, simultaneously eating house beef jerky that is a year out of date, flipping through the Doc's private files on his laptop and closely monitoring the CCTV screen. The last time she saw moving pictures on a tube was on the Air New Zealand flight and now she's absolutely fascinated with the scurvy-riddled goings-on of the in-house miscreants. She's on split-screen, watching all three access points and the main stairs, engrossed in the silent movie antics of a leery-looking mother trying one door knob after the other up on landing two near the fire-escape.

Where's the mace? she asks me in-between studying pornographic images on the Doc's PC.

Should you be eating that, and for that matter, looking at that? I ask her.

She shrugs nonchalantly. Seeing as how we ain't getting paid, or fed, I can pretty much do as I please, I guess. Now, the mace?

There ain't no mace, only these knuckledusters in the lost property drawer, you seen all the cool shit that's in here?

I already stashed the truncheon, she said. Never know when a tool like that'll come in handy, especially in a fleapit like this. Bung 'em here.

She's studying the CCTV while slapping the brass knuckleduster hard into the palm of her other hand. It makes a soft, malicious thud as it strikes pink skin and I'm guessing the sound is somehow soothing to her, given her penchant for the infliction of pain. Fearing the juice might be cut off at any moment, I've found myself a pair of Ray Bans and two of those headlights that cyclists or miners wear.

It's only after a further twenty minutes of watching the same evil-looking dude seemingly trying the same door handles, that the laundry token drops: this is just some continual loop re-wind gig set-up to appease the relevant authorities vis-à-vis in-house security provisions. I eject the tape from the machine and study the date: July 1999. Ye fucking gods – these fools are so busy counting cash they haven't had the wherewithal to insert a new tape since the year of the big party.

I find a blank tape, of which there are hundreds, slide it into the malnourished machine and switch the panel to RECORD. Suddenly we can see everything clearly. Shit, Jo moans, I really fancied pounding that fucker's head to mush.

Well, some you win and some you lose, there'll be plenty of time to use those knuckledusters, babe, that is, if we ever find out whether we've got the FUCKING JOB or NOT!

All of the soon-to-be-crim faces on the candy-hungry kids stare balefully at me across the counter, silently pleading for more high-energy glucose intake. I spread my hands to signal that we're all out of everything that's bad for the nervous system – at which the little shitheads go hypo and start throwing rent-a-car brochures all over the fucking show.

Give me those fucking knuckledusters, I tell my Jo Buck.

It's then that the chilling reality strikes so hard that my fillings rattle. Good Jesus Christ, I was born to do dirty work like this.

9.

Number-Crunching Safe-Cracking Jaw-Dropping Hijinks

We'd been on our feet for twelve hours answering deadbeat questions and roughing up lippy Maori kids.

Time can really fucking drag in a cavernous hostel, especially the last two hours of a shift you ain't being paid for. Silence falls hard, like a magistrate's gavel, and suddenly there's just you, the quiet purring of the CCTV, a few bums eating the dead skin off their toes, and a huge kea perched atop the vending machine croaking NEVERMORE! There's still no sign of the Good Doctor, that suave prince of the fiefdom, or fucking Dick, the King Rat. Maybe they never made it to the bank, with all that jangling cash, and they're lying comatose in a litter-blown back alley like a couple of just-tossed out-of-towners. Never mind, the clock is plodding its way wearily around to the handover time, and then the rudder of the good ship *Rip Van Winkle* can be handed over to some safe cracker of a night watchman. Are we supposed to come back tomorrow, or maybe just vanish into the fog?

I'm about to ask Jo this, but before I can she tells me she thinks the Good Doctor is more like the Reverend Jim Jones, that she's sure he's got a cult stashed away someplace and all afternoon him and Uncle Fester have been hard at it, banging nymphets for the cause.

Frankly, I don't think so – like, there are cults and there are cults and while I can feasibly see the Good Doctor embroiled in something as sordid as that I don't think King Rat would be the type of lay any nymphet would acquiesce to, no matter how funked up she was on spiritual messages or codeine. Most likely they're up at the Big House, up at the mansion the Good Doctor and Zsa Zsa are building on the back of high season windfalls. I can see everything now as it nears the witching hour. I see exactly why the cash is being shipped out of here faster than diamond dealers cut zirconium and pass it off as the real deal. That money might be going to a 'bank', but it isn't any bank that deals with this joint. This hostel's official bank account is probably as empty as an Egyptian tomb, and the bottom line was most likely passed so long ago that now you'd need to dive deep in a mini-submarine to see it again.

Yeah, this is what they call a tax dodge in some parts of the world – and a money-laundering scam in other places. This joint has more holes than Ned Kelly's tin helmet and your Dutch girls would need meaty digits to plug them. No wonder the accounting system looks like something archaeologists would salivate over – the last time I saw anything with so much white out and double-entry fraud it was my school report. We are deep in the red, the whole place is haemorrhaging cash and even with a Doctor at its head, it can't be saved. Well, okay, so be it, none of this is my concern – so long as Jo and me get paid.

Just as I'm mulling the possibilities such a slipshod place would offer a person with few scruples, who should reappear in our midst like a just-paged locum but our presumed-MIA boss hog.

The Good Doctor, full of apologies, haversack slung over his shoulder, a brace of squash racquets in hand, wears a fine film of sweat on his brow – just enough to convey the image of physical exertion. As the Doc scans the register eagerly, King Rat emerges out of nowhere like a murderer from the swirling fog of Victorian London, and immediately bellows furious rhetoric about some fuckhead having screwed up his CCTV apparatus. Like, now he can actually *see* just what the fuck is going on.

I ignore Dick; there will be plenty of opportunities for him and me to learn the steps of the Russian tea dance. The Doc, on the other hand, seems happy with our efforts; he has a smile on his dial like a brand-new coffin plaque. We have done a real swell job, especially given that we've been thrown in the deep end like a couple of wild ducks. He announces somewhat grandly that our trial has thus ended – we should immediately take up lodgings on the second floor, sign the disclaimers and take a well-earned 24 hours of R&R before we start up again for real. This Doc is a man of sudden shifts and swings, one minute placing a metaphorical laurel around your neck, and then encouraging you to drink a small shot of Gatorade laced with cyanide for the greater good.

Marlon, the storm-ravaged night porter, arrives – albeit very slowly, like a milk train. Time on his shift has no real meaning. He lives by the moon and sun, and navigates by the stars. Marlon plops a half sheep on the counter and meticulously, but laboriously, studies the day's events, all block printed for him in fluorescent magic marker. I watch him awhile, absorbed in his caveman-like aptitude for the modern hostelling world. He is a brave man, I know that because King Rat has told me.

Don't fuck with Marlon, he'd grinned while deftly replenishing his stock of roll-ups and cuffing small Maori kids accidentally on purpose around the lugs. Does the little fuckers good now and again, he'd said, teaches 'em some manners.

Sure, I'd thought, that's what the missionaries always say. He told me that Marlon had just been awarded the Hostelling

Star of Honour for finding six big ones in a plastic Pak 'n' Save bag left sitting in the TV lounge after lockdown. Six grand, I'd whistled enthusiastically, sweet Jesus, we must have some real dopeheads bunking down here.

Fucking A, Dick had said, the big dumb bastard just picked it up and put it in the lost property drawer – think what a fucken riot it'd have caused if he'd just thrown it in the skip or maybe onto the 'abandoned groceries' shelf, huh?

Indeed. I could just see some stone-broke Korean student thinking he was getting weevil-infected free brown rice and turning up hard cash instead. Dick was always ready to lavish praise on his co-workers, and even quicker to measure them up for execution. He was gonna tell me more but he broke down with some kind of coughing fit sending phlegm all over the show.

Don't worry Dick, I'd told him, it ain't the coughing that carries you away, it's the coffin they carry you away in.

Finally, it is time to go – and the Doc must be feeling a twang of guilt for his prolonged abstinence from duty, for he rings the shuttle company and asks them to give Jo and me a ride home on the company tab. It's not safe around these parts at night, he tells us, and I am thinking that the seeds of disaster can germinate real fast given optimum conditions. The shuttle arrives and Ranjid is a happy smiling dude – any fare is a good fare, and he fair rattles through the empty streets, navigating the confusing one-way system New Zealand traffic management are obviously besotted with.

Before we know it, we are back in a still, silent and absolutely bloody freezing real world. Tomorrow we will be decamping to the mausoleum, taking up the reins and taming that brute – but that is tomorrow and cold or not, we waste no time finding sleep.

10.

To Serve and Protect

It looks like a hostel, it smells like a hostel, ergo common logic dictates that it must be a hostel. Okay, so it's kinda sleazy – what with the tattered canopy billowing about in the winds that blow down off the hills, and that flickering pink neon sign at night that gives it a Dutch brothel ambience – but this is a mean street in the more squalid part of town. It ain't quite the Hood, but it's where the gangs from the Hood decamp on frigid nights, when the only other folks still awake past a certain hour are club managers counting the night's takings. Once you get inside, the décor reinforces the message that you're going budget. In a grungy way it's homely, come hither and seductive almost, but with an edge that glints. Reception looks like any other budget accommodation reception anywhere else in the world – one big steel cage with a hole cut in it.

There are all the usual boards: car sale boards, fair exchange is no robbery boards, work for peanuts boards, useful shit boards, sex wanted boards, you know the drill. There is a drinks machine, a plastic plant left over from the America's Cup winning party, a fish tank with no fish because the Doc got fed up re-stocking it after every Japanese tour group had left, a rumpus room with smooth surfaces and minimalist furnishings, two phone booths, a test your own IQ machine that never gets used seeing as no one's yet been bright enough to figure out how to use it, a book exchange full of German language adult tales, rack after rack of out-of-date brochures designed to ensnare the gullible into handing over their cash – like the 'how to sell your own blood' leaflet. There's an organ donation booth, and big signs that say in a hundred languages you shouldn't under any circumstances leave your cash, documents, valuables, virginity, soiled underwear, scruples or FUCKING ROOM KEY unattended!

But no one bothers to read any of 'em, because budget travellers quit reading shit like that at the post office back home. Budget types don't want to read anything other than kindergarten ABC instructions on how to find hot sex, or even warm to the touch sex – that's all they're interested in, which is why the 'Friend Wanted To Ride/Travel/Fuck ...' is by far the most popular and constantly updated board in da house.

A hostel is nothing more than a giant barrel of gimps in heat. This is what budget travellers do: drink, fuck, take dope, steal other people's food, drink, fuck and ride a bus to someplace where they can drink, fuck and steal food again. Once you have a handle on the make-up of your average traveller, you have a one-size-fits-all photofit that can go out on the wires like the hostelling equivalent of an APB.

Under the register there is a fucking rogues' gallery of ugly leering driver licence and passport snap shots all marked like permanent records: under NO circumstances let this guy stay!! Wanted for theft, rape and buggery!!! Police ALERT – car thief!! LOOK BEFORE YOU BOOK SHITHEAD! CAUTION! FLASHER! This Creep Steals PANTIES! Would you let your mother/sister/wife/lover sleep in a communal dorm with THIS!!! BEWARE! Uses the aliases Lord Lucan, Sir Edmond Giles, Right Honourable, etc ...

DON'T BE FOOLED! THIS GUY IS A PIG! Arrest Warrant Outstanding! RING CIB!

Sweet fucking Jesus, the Doc was right when he'd alluded to the fact that eyes in the back of your head weren't good enough in hostelling – you needed them in the goddamned *front*, too! One slip-up through tiredness, apathy, sheer desperation or clinical depression and you could shoot what was left of the hostel's tattered reputation straight to buggery. If in doubt call Dick – Dick has the evil eye and a mind for faces; Dick has photographic recall and the gift of premonition, which is why Dicky rolls down the cage during his night shift, switches off the CCTV and skims still-life porn on the net, when he should be vigilant. Dick has two bronze stars, a purple heart, three letters of commendation from the hostelling association of the Pan Pacific region, and a nose like a bloodhound. Dick sees trouble the same way some folks see blurry flashes of the future. And that is why Dick stalks the halls and corridors during the daylight hours rousting up soon-to-be infringers with his half metre of bike chain and mail-order handcuffs. Dick is the sheriff around this part of Dodge City, and he wears his badge on a puffed-out chest. You can be minding your own during a lull in business – of which there are many before the madness of high season rocks up dressed to thrill – and periodically see Dick whooping some raggy fucker's arse straight outta the doors and onto the cold mean streets without so much as a chance to get their stow from left luggage.

You want me to sign that geek out and refund his key deposit? I might ask Dick. And Dick'll just glare at me like a kill-hungry serial killer on a deserted highway squinting hard into the midday sun for a rube.

That shithead don't need a refund, he'll say curtly, fucker lost his key anyhow – and then he'll slam the poor fool's key on the counter and give you that louche cockeyed smile that passes for a gesture of comradeship in Dick's world. Dick always has the Doc's vested interests at the very forefront of his booze and gambling addled mind. And that, friends, is why he sits content and fluffy on the second highest perch in the henhouse.

Once your name is on the roster it is your sworn duty to serve as a deputy and as such you must always take the side of the Law. Well, okay, we are still learning the ropes and sometimes we get them all tangled underfoot and need a wily old coyote to come along and cut the deadbeats out of our ever-growing flock; and sometimes, even before those deadbeats have the opportunity to put the key you've just given them into the corresponding door, Who the fuck's this wanker? Dick'll ask me, his senses all riled up and buzzing like happy bees in springtime.

Uh? I'll reply, somewhat dumbfounded.

I know that face . . . let me think a mo, yeah . . . that bastard tried to grope some Swedish sweetmeat last summer . . . where's his fucken ID?

It's not easy work, simple, yes, but not fucken easy, and I don't know how these people cope with so much crap on an hourly basis. It'll take me a full week to realize that they don't. And just when I think that things have calmed down, that the Doc is gonna give us some real hands-on tuition in the art of hostel management, he's in the office wearing a white Adidas tracksuit and carrying a sports bag. I get the weird impression the Doc never sleeps, and that, and the fact I can never see his reflection in the two-way when I'm peering over his shoulder learning the intricacies of false accounting, gives me the kind of creeping bejesuses that innkeepers in Transylvania get when there's a hard rap on the saloon door in the wee hours. But so what, huh? Just look at this way-sweet deal; old Bob up at the car rental place in Auckland could learn a lot about incentives from a contract like this.

Shit, yeah, we only have to work four-and-a-half days a week! Can you fucken believe that? That's a way sweet fucken deal in any language, even Icelandic. But hang on, this don't look right because four-and-a-half days somehow equates to 80 goddamned hours? That can't be right, can it?

Course it is, the Doc says all knowingly while he rests contentedly on the latest copy of New Zealand's draconian labour laws guide – in fact, the Doc can do what he damned well pleases with any flesh he hires as help. That's called 'job-sharing', the Doc smiles beguilingly – like you both *share* the workload and so long as one of you is always manning the portcullis then the other is free, see?

Free? Did he say free? Free to do what exactly?

You're never fecken off in this caper, Dick had said only yesterday while he re-stocked the fridges full of no-label 200% sweeter-than-Coke substitute. Even when you're fecken off you're still on and there's always some meathead hammering at your door at any fecken hour wantin' you to help put out a fire or find a day 'n' night quack for some broad who's OD'd. You just get used to it, see, learn to sleep with one eye open and with your pants on coz you never know when a joint like this might go up in flames – tinder fucken dry it is, tinder, I say.

Yeah well, okay, there's another thing to ponder over in-between everything else.

You seen this? the Inkster says to me angrily. Jo's at the roster wondering why the fuck we're working from eight Saturday morning until two thirty Sunday afternoon. She's quick with mental arithmetic and in no time at all she advises me that's 35 fucking hours – STRAIGHT!

Before I can allude to the fact that it'll be a way-easy gig given that we're double-teamed, just like in the WWF, the Doc has smelt mutiny brewing and has whisked up his kitbag and all of his troubles therein and is giving us a pep talk about safe money handling. Next he's handing me the combination to the safe while simultaneously telling me he is booked on the next plane to Pango Pango for the inter-dominion pan-Pac hostel owners 96th annual squash jamboree. The winner gets a beach hut plus a year's supply of mango body rub – he'll be back a week Friday and if we need anything else just ask Dick, okay?

The Doc is disappearing fast, like a partial eclipse, and there are a hundred facts I need to know … but all I hear is him telling me something about nuns. Did he say fucking nuns, or buns? I ask my other half – but she is still in a zombie-like state of suspended animation, still staring at the roster, both hands balling up tight and then releasing slowly. I think about ratifying that situation but before I'm able there's some crazy old lady banging on the counter, just as mad as if she'd just been denied a 'HOUSE!' in the bingo hall. She is spouting senile gibberish and is obviously as crazed as a rabid fox on a stinking hot afternoon. Who the hell is this crazy old bat anyhow and why is she in OUR hostel? Why don't we have immediate access to security of some kind? These are sensible questions but they are not worth a pile of dung right now – she wants me to accompany her to the dining hall, and from her use of olde-English I can tell immediately that this certifiable woman has been institutionalized most of her life one way or another. I drag Jo away from the roster and manipulate her still gaping jaw with my hand to get the blood flowing again – instinctively she tries to land a right uppercut on my chin but as it's still early in the day, my co-ordination is at its peak – and, Man the desk, I tell her abruptly, I have to go attend some kind of domestic in the dining hall.

She stares at me in wonderment – not at my firm hand in times of crises, but wonderment that I have obviously decided that a 35-hour-straight work shift is nothing out of the ordinary any more. The dining hall? she utters robotically as the trance breaks and colour floods back into her cheeks like morning rays de-crisping a still-white valley. You're going to the fucking dining hall?

It's too late now to stand toe-to-toe and bitch slap it out. The old granny has a hold of my arm and we are full steam ahead to calamity. It is then that Dick appears, just appears you understand – you have no inkling that he is within the proximity, as they say aboard aircraft carriers, he is just suddenly There. Ping. He stops us both, the wild grey-haired grandma and me. Where the hell are you going? he enquires menacingly. Don't you know you can never leave reception unattended?

Don't worry, I tell him, I left a blow-up doll there.

It ain't Lulu, is it? he asks me ... but before I can explain that I'm only speaking figuratively he is racing down the hallway pushing aside Krishnas and other vagrant flotsam, and screaming, Don't worry, Lulu, daddy's coming!

What the fuck?

Bear in mind this is not high season and there are, at a quick guesstimate, about 40 vacant tables in the 'dining hall'. I am frog-marched to a corner nook near the blazing heater where a very young pyjama-clad Confucius has squatted on a tabletop in the lotus position. He is deep into some kind of heavy funk Zen. The old bitch points at him angrily, her lips tight and body quivering at the injustice of it all.

What? I ask her.

She just points again. Confucius doesn't so much as flutter an eyelash.

I don't get it, not at all, so finally the woman spits it out; he is on her table, and not just on it, but on it! I gaze around at all of the empty tables but before I can articulate what I'm thinking there is another ghoul beside us. I take two steps sideways, this 'sudden materialization out of thin air' shit is really gnawing at my raw ends. This guy is some unwashed Jesus freak and he is nursing a bowl of something putrid smelling like it was the son of Mary itself. That's her table, friend, he tells me softly, and right about now I really don't give a dry hump whose table it is. This ain't the fucken Four Seasons and we don't take reservations. This place is a god-damned nuthouse, all we really need is a happy bus and we can start up our own version of the adventure tour thing. No need for fucken seatbelts either as all of these loons'll be in straightjackets.

Still Confucius hasn't twitched. He is far out on the astral waves riding a big one and only his physical person remains – cross-legged on a tabletop in a filthy backpackers' communal chow-down hall. A crowd assembles in mumbling discontent, perhaps summoning up the strength to start hurling stale bread or set up a lynching post, who knows, but my time for deliberation and peaceful resolution is fast vanishing.

I am saved by Dick. He pushes through the throng like a Roman Centurion and grabs Confucius by the pyjama top like he was a fucken black belt ready to rumble. Okay, Ho Chi Minh, he says, tabletops are for rissoles not arseholes so take it somewhere else, all right? Dick ain't got no time for Zen, not now, and certainly not Zen.

Shit Dick, I start, but he waves my protestations away like a bug from a half-eaten pizza. You won't get no fucken time for negotiations once high season comes, just show 'em who's boss and use a firm hand, this ain't a fucken chapel we're running.

Maybe he's right – I'm new at this caper and sometimes when you're the new kid on the block you need guidance. But no fucking way am I gonna get some heavy dose of weird karma thrown at me by a disgruntled Zen practitioner. Let Dick have that bag to haul about – limp or no fucking limp.

Back in the cage Jo Buck is still transfixed by the horror of having to face 35 hours straight at the coalface once a week. Look, I tell her, as soon as Sunday lunchtime rolls we'll be free for two-and-a-half days, huh?

She doesn't buy it, not one fucking bit of it – this is a cheap-skate rort being perpetrated by money-hungry ogres with no damned intention of investing one cent in the 'upkeep and re-development' of a dive like this, there ought to be a set of pawnbroker's balls outside. I know she's right – but that doesn't mean we should harness our wagon to another circle, maybe it's better this way, better to camp out on the fringes of good business practices and see what kind of injuns finally end up encircling us?

Stop fucking talking in metaphors, she tells me angrily – we've been had good and proper and it's all your stupid fault, just accept the fact and start thinking of a way to get us out of here. Pronto!

Shit, but I like it here. I like the smell of damp that perme-ates the place, the creaky floorboards, the fact that modern technological advances have given the joint a very wide berth. I like the conceptual sparseness of the place – the fact that they don't give a rat's arse whether other joints are providing free morning-after pills or not. This is my kind of place; I come from streets just like these and I've always understood these kinds of people. To me they're crystalline and I can read their every move. These people can't get a jump on me.

Even Dick doesn't faze me, not Dick with his 1950s cowlick and heavy dollop of Brilliantine, his teenage rebel stance and his tales of bygone years when he burglarized the corner dairies and terrorized the high school prom. Nah, there's always been a Dick in my life, and if that ain't a skewed metaphor then I don't know what is.

As for the Good Doctor, well … him and me already have a kind of telepathic understanding. He understands that there's something not quite right about me, and I understand that there's something terribly wrong with him. And that is a match made in heaven.

11.

Shit Pots and U-Bends

There are many sights you wouldn't wish to see in life but sometimes events conspire to maroon you. In the budget accommodation world you will witness unsavoury and disturbing things, that is just the shit that goes with the Job and hostel management is certainly not for people who cannot stand the sight of blood or overflowing lavatories.

No one wants to shit in their own nest and in communal environments, where the hay is cheap and the facilities about as glamorous as a truck stop shithouse, you'd be surprised how many sickly faced delinquents grope their way down two flights of stairs each morning in the hope of finding a shitter that doesn't already have some Israeli slumped over it talking on a private line to Tel Aviv. This is called the 'Morning Dance'. Only a few hours earlier, the large red hands of a psychotic night porter were halfway down the U-bend of the downstairs dunny fishing out hair balls and big black turds, just to keep the plumbing system ticking along.

The Doc has left us several manila folders full to bursting with operational notes and while you can ignore a lot of them, you certainly can't ignore the ones double underlined and then highlighted in alien-green fluorescent swipes. One such item by way of example is 'Check downstairs toilets every HOUR!!';

the Doc knows only too well what kind of foul business is conducted in the downstairs shitters and that is why there is set of pipe rods right under his desk. He is not the kind of man willing to spend 80 smackeroos an hour plus call-out fee to have some ape with a hairy back unblock his in-house inconveniences. No indeed, especially when he has below-minimum wage hired help at his beck and call. The location of the unblocking rods is clearly marked on a diagram adjacent to the stern warning about overflowing shit pots and there is a set of detailed directions on how to use the rods and how to clean them properly post usage. It is all very technical, and I fail to see how Marlon, for example, could decipher such explicit instructions. But maybe that explains why most mornings before the crows commence ripping the mound of garbage bags to bits out in the yard, Marlon is on all fours in the shit-house howling at the new dawn like a jungle beast.

The last thing we need is a severely blocked pipe or two – that is not pleasant when you are still belly-deep in the infantile scrawl of bookings, messages and complaints that Marlon has left everywhere but in the correct place. We cannot rely on Dick at this time of the morning either as he is a renowned late sleeper, and woe betide any idiot stupid enough to rap on his door before eleven bells have sounded. Then, of course, it is our daily duty not only to prepare the float and the banking from the previous day's shady business, but to delegate recently vacated rooms ready for spraying to the very slack housekeeping staff. In between all this, maybe we can answer a query or two about where some stonehead could catch a bus, train, plane, dose of clap, or bronchial disease. I am a problem juggler and that is one of the reasons the Doc has hired me – for in a place such as this, problems have a way of multiplying faster than weevils can infiltrate a Krishna's rice sack.

Today's log will illuminate exactly what I am referring to. First it is the barring from using the laundry before checkout. I do not make the RULES you understand, they were carved in stone tablets long before I arrived on the scene – but there is little point in debating this with a gang of filthy backpackers still wearing the same undergarments they left home in five days ago. It may seem pretty fucking stupid to you that the laundry facilities cannot be utilized for their intended purpose until midday, but it's because they also serve as the in-house linen laundry. And after all, after 60 hours on an aircraft and several more hours being de-loused at immigration, what could be more welcome than freshly laundered sheets? Some knobheads see my rationale, and they drift away from reception like cuttlefish swimming hard against the current. But to some, no explanation, no matter how clear, concise or rational, ever suffices.

You will get used to spotting this type of person in even the largest and most unruly mobs. They are always the ones who are quiet at first and then, just as you have gained a tentative foothold in abating the mob's initial fury, surge to the front like angry chimps and begin beating their chests. All who serve on the front line have found their own manner of dealing with these regular occurrences. The Doc, for instance, leads by example and will always exude an air of calm even in the midst of the most shit-ugly of melees. His is the divine path and he walks it humbly. Then there is Candice, the Doc's idiot savant, who attends to duty during our days off. She is a woman who can find a meagre kernel of good in every ominous situation. Even when she can't, she will quickly fall back upon the Doc's bible of across-counter conflict resolution. But not Dick, that King Rat has his own method and he has never been in a mood to alter it. At the very first sign of heating tempers Dick will roll the cage down and start letting go with the capsicum spray – it is a foolproof method and it has never failed to quell even the most ardent of agitators. You can learn a lot from Dick but, alas, we have been told expressly on the QT that Dick's way is the old way, and there is no scope for violent conduct in an industry based on the policy of the NYPD, which is 'To Serve'.

Marlon must have done a grand job, for there is no bunged-up shitter this morning and I am able to focus my attention to ironing out the bugbears plugging up da System. They are manifold, like scabs on a drifter, but this is why the Job is so interesting. Jo, The Inkster, is still in bed; like Dick she is not a morning person, although she will have to learn how to be when the madness of high season falls upon us all like napalm in the Nang. For now, though, she can rest easy, safe in the knowledge that I have the helm and we are charting a steady course toward rudimentary procedures.

Like, making sure our two room cleaners spend more time actually cleaning rooms and less time looting them. I am not dumb and I have the CCTV fully operational, which means that periodically I can drift into the back office like a stalker and scrutinize the shady goings-on on the back stairway; shenanigans such as creeping room cleaners loaded up with more booty than an Iraqi soldier in the first days of the Kuwait annexation. They have a cunning ruse afoot, one that entails the rear fire door – the one clearly marked 'Do Not Open Unless In Case Of Emergency!' – being wedged open on the flimsy pretext of 'airing out' the dark damp recesses of the Block. Now, in the normal course of events, our good amigo Dick would lather himself up into a fury of spitting rage if he so much as sensed fresh Canterbury air blowing in. But not between eight and eleven, seven days a week, for between those 'cleaning' hours Dick has become accustomed to waking to find a wee gift or two in his locker – every morning is Christmas morning for Dick. This is why he turns a blind eye to the daily blatant contradiction of fire access procedures. Insofar as I know, even the fresh Prince of Fetid Air himself is prepared to turn his golden-child eyes away from such rampant thievery in the name of keeping the Machine lubricated. What's good for the goose, etcetera.

For now, I will let it slide, especially as we are perilously short of gold coinage and I am the only fool on the boat with the safe combination; only I can't fucking remember it because after the Doc wrote it down for me while we rehearsed like tandem safecrackers practising for the Italian Job, he made me eat the slip of paper while he stood there and examined my oesophagus with a pen torch.

I have a number for him, but out in the wilds of the South Pacific there is no such thing as immediate contact, and sometimes there is no contact ever again. I know half the combination, but that is like having half a winning line on a lottery ticket. So while I stand there concentrating hard, which is a particularly fraught task when you are being interrupted every two minutes by numbnuts who can't get their toast out of the toaster and room cleaners who will do seemingly everything apart from the very task they are being paid to do, I have the not-so-bright idea of grabbing up the Brother. Yes indeed, he is an idle log, and his sole purpose it appears is to haul soiled linen to the laundry room each morning before he collapses on a sofa to spend the rest of the day ogling flesh.

The Brother is just called that, no one has told us why. Perhaps it's because he's a big lump in leather sandals like Friar Tuck. In the late afternoon sunshine he takes roost on the reception sofa with Dick, his King Gee pants riding low and his butt crack showing. They look like Dick Dastardly and

Muttley. It is nowhere near past the yardarm and, bone idle or not, he is within my immediate field of vision. Oi, I beckon him, and he sidles over with an armful of filthy sheets like a stoolie in the joint. I give him a hundred big ones, money I might possibly never see again. Take this over the road to the supermarket and change it to one and two buck coins, I tell him, and it takes his mind several minutes on defrost to thaw out my request. His eyes move with the speed of cold gravy congealing and, by Christ, I wish he had a perspex head so that I could watch all the little people inside yanking on levers and tugging on flywheels. But finally the thing inside his head goes PING! and he is back in the same universe as the rest of us, albeit temporarily.

Shop. Money. Change. He repeats each of my instructions to himself in the same way as just-raised-from-the-dead zombies utter their new master's name. Yes, I tell him, nodding all the while to visually reinforce the command. You go now, to shop, bring back change, okay?

CH-AN-GE, he murmurs again, each syllable in his language a struggle to understand.

Sweet Jesus, I could have gone myself and been back already if it weren't for the severe penalties meted out to receptionists who fleetingly abandon their posts no matter how great the cause. But suddenly the Brother is off at great haste, like some kind of freak in the dining hall who has just heard the lunch bell. But ... oh good Christ ... the big fool still has the bundle of filthy linen clutched to his wobbling belly and before I can say no ... he is across the street and on his way, dropping soiled sheets here and there in his rather large wake.

So what? A few sheets blowing up this street won't raise too many eyebrows. The residents along here have seen much worse sights I'd guess, and so long as the big jelly bean gathers them all up on his way back then no one will be any the wiser.

Fate is a fickle bitch of a mistress, however, and you won't be surprised to learn that just when I thought I'd get away as clean as one of Marlon's U-bends, who should grope his way into the office still wearing his night mask other than our trusty steward Dick? It is a ghastly sight and even I am taken aback at the horror of it all.

Dick paws over the register the way a jewel thief paws over a display cabinet on a recce, then stretches and immediately grabs his lower back, then his knee, and mutters disconsolately about lumbago and rheumatism and he is off for a soak in Deep Heat bubble bath to kick start his day – until he sees the sheet wrapped around the ornamental shrub just outside of the main door, flapping there like an abandoned spinnaker. What the fuck is that? he says.

I lean over the counter, then suddenly pull back. Dick might well have goddamned lumbago but I have issues to struggle with as well – issues of anatomy prone to obeying Newton's law of gravitational interference.

I don't think Dick should be meandering out to the street wearing his night mask and crusty PJs, it is not a good look. But then again Dick always has his first roll-up of the day while squatting among the pot plants like an angry gnome. Well, this is his backyard and he can squat where he fucken likes. I can still see him, or at least his shadow, spread out across the pavement like the Phantom, running all the permutations as to Why. But then he darts off quickly – Dick is still pretty spry for a white guy.

There will be all hell to pay for this but I am not overly concerned as yet. What I desperately need is more coinage, a decent shit and to hand the baton of power to Jo Buck, due on the bridge at any moment.

Time beats me. Just as Jo arrives looking all sleepy and hungry, both Dick and the Brother burst through the big front doors like Ratboy and Dobbin, loaded up with sheets and good Kiwi shrapnel. Dick is goddamned irate, first about the sheets, our fucken sheets, all up the road right to the supermarket entrance, and that I've trusted the Brother with a task (like most) he isn't qualified to do. Jo Buck pirouettes in reception and skips away – on the CCTV I catch her amply curved arse doing the fandango up the stairway to heaven. Dick dumps the now even dirtier laundry on the floor and shoves aside some deadbeat who looks like Travis Bickle and is just about to sign on the dotted line for a whale-watching excursion – that is a good sale lost, but obviously there are more important concerns in the day-to-day running of a hostel than flogging trips to gangbangers.

You see this? Count Dick demands, holding up what was once a bargain-bin sheet. Fucken taxi drove right over it in the parking lot up the road. He is awaiting my riposte but I don't have one on hand – there are some circumstances where you know damned well that mitigation won't wash. Dick is like a just-washed sheet himself, I think, one minute billowing in the breeze full of puff, and the next about as limp as a pussy-whipped penis.

I permit Dick the civility of me listening to his rave until he's all out of steam, then I start emptying the change into the ever-hungry till. Dick comes around my side of the counter to paw the register again but is distracted by some pervert by the car-hire brochures rack. Who's that fucken shoe gazer? he says.

Must be one of Marlon's night kills, I reply.

Keep your eye on him, okay? He looks way fucken dodgy to me.

Jo re-enters the reception area, shoots one sharp look of disgust at Dick and vanishes into the nether regions of the back room to slurp her cereal. I have a set of keys that would do any head nurse in a fun-house proud and soon I will be free of my obligations for an hour or two to jangle them around the corridors of power.

You figured out the safe yet? Jo yawns. I tell her I haven't, that I'm putting yesterday's take under our bed for now.

Don't you think that this bunch of backstabbing halfwits might easily misconstrue an act like that? she asks, and it is sound logic. Ergo I shove the cash bag in the Doc's drawer and head out into the great wilderness like Dr Livingston himself. My first port of call is the hostel kitchen where my day goes to shit as they say in emergency plumbing circles.

Now, whether you are aware or not, I spent twenty-odd years in professional kitchens and I would consider myself well-versed in such matters as food preparation hygiene, safe-storage techniques, and utensil and implement cleaning. That is how chefs make their wonga, by understanding that bacteria are a mean and unforgiving nemesis. You will concur if you have ever enjoyed the visual terror of laying eyes on a communal kitchen in a backpackers' hostel.

You might well expect a scene like this in some kolkhoz kitchen in deepest Siberia, but in the First World?

We are not even in full swing, yet 30 travellers have managed to completely destroy an industrial-sized kitchen, and turn a communal dining room into the LZ for *Apocalypse* fucking *Now*. I have seen chimps at a tea party with better table manners and a more rudimentary understanding of rule #1: if you use it, arsewipe, you fucking clean it. This place is ravaged, the barbarians have laid siege to it en masse then scuttled off to sack another joint. I am deep in agreement with Dick's philosophy that we should take a water cannon to the whole filthy lot of them. There is half-eaten food everywhere, dying slowly on grubby plates. There are food scraps all over the floor as if those who thought about scraping their leftovers into the pig bins provided were overcome by some terrible urge to fling tidbits at each other instead. There are condiments scattered over tabletops, in varying sized dollops and misjudged squirts. And it gets worse the nearer I draw to the kitchen.

I have seen some heinous things done to kitchens in my journeyman career as a mercenary-chef – but for the love of Valhalla I have never seen anything like this. As I step warily over broken eggs, pools of spilt milk, and baked beans hopping their way to a bacteria hill, I catch sight of what might have once been a stove.

What remains of a frying pan, one that is terminally past its non-stick glory days, is heat fused to an electric hob, like some kind of weird wreckage in *Mad Max*. The bench tops are even worse. Imagine if the Salvation Army laid out an all-you-can-eat buffet for derelicts by upending all the pig bins on to the benches, and before the derelicts arrived clutching free-meal tickets, Attila the Hun and his fanny-starved hordes have gate-crashed the whole shindig. My head is spinning as my eyes struggle to keep pace with the ruination. I feel like ripping Marlon a new one tonight, surely he has not done his rightful duty down here?

BANG! Dick is right next to me like a headfreak strapped into the jump seat of a souped-up junker. What the fuck ... I start, but Dick has seen everything, and this, he tells me soberly, ain't nowhere near as bad as it gets. I accuse Marlon, but he tells me Marlon would have had this joint shining like a new penny not three hours ago. It only takes shitheads like these about fifteen minutes, give or take, to wreak total havoc on a kitchen. He starts rousting out the stragglers with his piece of chain-link and doesn't accept any kind of whinging, bitching or moaning about stored foodstuffs. Then he bolts the doors shut – restaurant closed for delousing – and takes me over to the grocery shelf, a whole row of large pigeonholes where travel-weary types hoard their dry goods.

Look at this fucken mess, he tells me, and to be sure, 'sound storage' and 'prompt rotation' aren't two of the key phrases travellers employ in their ritual migrations. There are tied-up bags in every hole, all crudely labelled or marked: I know who you are! Buy your own bran! Don't TOUCH! I'll be back! Back from where, I ponder, the emergency ward? Some are dated, as if dating will preclude bowel-sensitive types from wolfing it down and then vamoosing.

It's the fucken boss man, Dick tells me, he's a fucken hoarder. Say, you really wanna see a sight? I didn't, but I was deep in Dick territory and as such honour bound to take the stinking rotten tour. Better pinch your nose, huh, Dick advised as he yanked open the creaky old cool-room door. Even before it gave, the repugnant odour that escaped, like a giant last-gasp for air, immediately put me in mind of embalming fluid, and I don't have time here to tell you how I recognize that particular scent, a dirty, lingering, obnoxious stench, the same fetid pong that used to seep from all those piled-up bin bags during the garbage strikes.

Last time I stepped in here, said Dick, I had to have a fortnight on an iron lung. His eyes filled with fluid and he started groping for air like a just-hooked groper. I wasn't far behind him, nowhere near far enough. The light inside the deep dank recess was gone and no one had wanted to venture that far into the abyss to change it. There were creatures glowing in there, iridescent worms multiplying, viruses that were the still-burning filaments of every microbiologist's wet dreams. Sweet tubular bells on a long wet Sunday, not one of these juvenile delinquents had ever had to sit and watch the *Life Cycle of Bacteria* before lunch in a big cookery school because if they had, then bejesus, they'd never take food out of this cave, not even if they were as malnourished as an Ethiopian farmhand during an El Nino drought. Not one of them has ever been sent to a vast cool room in an industrial kitchen with a scrubbing brush and knee pads while a large butterball of a chef stands by soaping his arm to the shoulder joint in case a more practical hands-on demonstration is required.

No sir, I have seen many cool rooms, cool rooms are my thing; I have been locked in them, almost butt fucked in them, and I have scrubbed them until my hands were raw and my knees as rough as a Dominican priest. But never, not in all my travels, have I ever stood in front of a mosh pit for bacteria such as this one. A biohazard suit and full breathing apparatus wouldn't be sufficient protection to convince even the most dim-witted of apprentice chefs to take one small step for the travelling man.

And what the hell is that? I ask no one, because Dick is already slumped over the farthest table in the restaurant hacking up phlegm the way a miner coughs up black dust. I am on my own, as they say on the space station. I grab hold of something for support but immediately let go, as it feels far too furry for my tastes. I reach up for the bulb cage and by rote – thanks to years of experience – allow the assembly to drop. Standing up to your ankles in brine while playing with an electrical fitting is not recommended. As soon as I can work this mother free – that is, if it doesn't shatter in my hand or I don't feel the warm lovin' of Mr 240 volts surge through me like electric-chair music first – the sooner I can throw light on this whole gig.

Reluctantly it gives and on my return to the kitchen I see the bulb is brown and stamped 'Property Of …' something illegible – most likely a funny farm. I shout to Dick for a new bulb, but he is gone for all money, so instead I step into the cleaning cupboard and find about 8000 of the beggars. After several minutes grappling crazily with the exposed fixture like a cowboy electrician I manage to bring light again to this long-dark storage house for perishables – most of which have long since perished. As soon as I can see the thermostat I understand why – this poor bastard has been working overtime for about three high seasons, it's as balmy in here as Marrakech on a June afternoon. The drip-tray has been overflowing since the planet warmed after the Ice Age.

There are the sounds of hissing gas escaping from god knows what, and the telltale rumbles of a badly malfunctioning cooler unit. No fucking bucket of warm water with a few squirts of pishy home-brand detergent is gonna cure this problem. What this needs is a small nuclear device, the kind you can buy on any street corner in Tehran right after prayer. Just as I'm thinking this, I hear the sound of never-quite-chilled-enough teeth snapping lethargically, like your granddad's dentures used to do after he dropped them in a glass of Alka Seltzer. That's when I step backward and slam the door. I leave Dick there, in the restaurant, and march down to reception, tell my partner to ring a refrigeration mechanic – a real one, one versed in the art of industrial-sized machinery – and, even though it is almost time for our handover, I tell Jo I will be running an hour late, maybe more, as I need to pop out and buy rubber gloves like the ones asbestos removers use, two chain-link butchers' gloves, oh, and a pair of steel-toed

Wellington boots with ultra-grip soles, and some triple X bleach – that stuff that kills all known germs, and a whole lot more that aren't known of yet. I feel like Louis Pasteur.

But what about these . . .? I vaguely recall Jo saying, after I'd grabbed another wad of notes from petty cash and was almost out onto the pavement, where I paid but fleeting notice to the sleek black Mercedes eight-seater with tinted windows and the professionally stencilled gold crucifix on the side . . . or the persons disembarking. In fact, if I had to swear to it in court, I'd claim she said, What about these buns?

Why was everyone so hung up on buns? What fucking buns? No one, no matter their constitution, could think of food if they'd seen what I'd just seen.

12.

The Sisters of Show No Mercy

Jo's intuition that this place had an ecclesiastic bent proved right, taking into account the covenant we have signed with our own blood. She looked at me hard when I finally arrived back at reception resembling a chimney sweep on Christmas Eve. You'll love this, she said, and when she says something like that, with that licentious smirk on her lips, you can bet your last cent of hardship benefit that you won't.

What? I said wearily, licking out putrid food remnants from under my long fingernails.

She showed me the booking sheet and it took me a few moments to climb aboard her boxcar-like train of thought.

Where'd you think he advertises? she smirked. *The Tablet.*

I wouldn't put anything past the Doc – and especially not the bill the heavily perspiring dude has just handed me for a complete cool-room makeover. That bitch is purring like a contented madam, he says, as he wipes frost from his eyebrows. And ain't it weird how men always refer to a piece of machinery as a female?

Did the seals too, boss, just like you requested, he adds greedily.

As I study this statement of account, I am aware of two

things: the first is this guy was obviously the guy for the job, he is 'old school' as his bill is in pounds shillings and pence. The second thing, and the one that reinforces my opinion of myself as the Boss, is the final conversion to decimal that I run on the hostel's abacus. Good Christ Almighty ... I start to say, and then Jo kicks me hard on the shin with her steel-capped Doc Marten motorcycle boots.

Oi, what the shi –

I look up into golden light and, after my eyes adjust to the brilliance, I see six cherubic, well-scrubbed nuns' faces peering back at me. Never take the Lord's name in vain one of the angels says, or maybe they all said it together in perfect nunnery unison?

The fridge man whips off his filthy beanie and bows to the gang of God botherers; even he recognises the significance of such a blessing. Now then young lady, one of the voices says, and the fridge man and Jo stare at me as if I were Mary herself come back to find a crib and breakfast in the poorest lodgings in town. I do not even have time to get the word from Jo because she is already out of the lock-up with an armful of jerky, en route to an afternoon of hot bathing and stimulating literature. I am on my own, surrounded by the sisters of the revolution, still clutching an itemized bill for service and repair that will bring even a nearer-my-god-to-thee man like the Doc to the very steps of blasphemy. But maybe not if these nuns are nearby. This might all fall nicely into place, thanks to the Doc's insistence that the calibre of guest be raised in conjunction with the lowering of services and standards. Even that loveable rogue Dick will have to watch his ps and qs, not to mention his tendency toward flying without a licence, now that the God Squad is in residence.

I don't know why I keep thinking about Three Nuns, I'm not even certain what this strange brand name refers to, although I'm hazarding a guess that it's either some brand of shag tobacco or an alcoholic beverage. Whatever, I've twice the potency of nuns in the House, and not the slightest idea of why they're here. No wonder the Doc fled to Mango Mango or wherever the hell he's gone ... and little wonder that Dick's gone about as timid as a church mouse. In fact, the whole joint has suddenly taken on a reverent ambience since the good sisters from County Kildare arrived, one which I'm not adverse to ... yet.

Like I've told you, there are six of them: Sister Colleen, Sister Mary Magdalene, Sister Katherine, Sister Bernadette, Sister Catherine The Great, and Sister Sarah, and the last one don't have three mules in tow either. They are here, insofar as I can gather, to study religious sites and practices at various locations around the island – sort of like a Catholic sabbatical to the heathen land. Though strangely, right now Sister Katherine is asking me about the perils of bungee jumping.

I raise my plucked eyebrows. Bungee jumping?

Ah, tis just something I've read about, she smiles beguilingly.

Read about where? I ponder. In the travel liftout of the *Catholic Times*? That's a kinda exhilarating habit to get into, I think, especially for a gaggle of godsters let loose in paradise. Once they've tasted that thrill, who knows where it might end? (If, that is, it ever does.)

Now, what about dolphins? another nun says to me, as they crowd into the hatch like practising Catholics hell-bent on being the first to confess.

Dolphins? What kind of a craic is this? Nuns swimming with dolphins in some kind of briny communion of higher intelligence? Someone on high is pressing my doorbell but, as I'm on my best behaviour insofar as foul language goes, I go find all the relevant adventure information from the racks, while the six sisters follow me down the hallway in single file as if I were Mother Superior.

I am the font of knowledge – even though I've only been hands on for 72 hours. Dick makes a brief appearance, morphing out of the gloom that always emanates from the Block. No sooner does he see my flock than he ducks for cover quicker than Dracula at dawn.

One of the sisters crosses herself hastily to ward off such evil, then they are all giggling mischievously over a mound of out-of-date adventure brochures. God knows what they'll end up doing, maybe we can lay the foundation stone for some kind of high-adrenaline chariot rides up to the pearly gates and back. The Doc is far more insightful than I've afforded him credit for: Papal Tours R Us. Sooner or later, my shrink had said wisely, there will be a price to pay for the heathen deeds I've perpetrated on others and myself. Right about now I'm in the mood to agree, especially given that I'm knee-deep in rosary beads and silk purses. These sisters would swear on any bible that I'm a member of their fair sex; just like the Maoris we had last week, these convent-cruisers have the gift of second sight.

To be sure I must be blessed, in fact I just have been, six times. All of a sudden I feel invincible, as if nothing, not this shabby vagrant-plagued doss house, not King Rat, not even the Doc with his pen-is-mightier-than-the-sword pathos, could impinge upon my eventual salvation. I have no understanding of the hows and whys, the scriptures have never been required reading for me – though maybe they ought to be from now on?

When the day comes that some freak leaves a New Testament in a straight swap for *The Seafaring Adventures Of Olga* I might give it a go, but right now I have to practise cracking the safe again, so I leave the sisters debating the merits of jet boating versus paragliding, and amble back down to my steel-caged refuge – where I find the Brother all crumpled up on the foyer sofa like a giant ball of brown wool. It's hard to restrain my rapacious laughter; he really does look like Friar Tuck with the bare feet and tufty clumps of fuzzy white hair sticking out like cotton wool caught on a wire fence. Friar Tuck and the six sisters – how much more monastic can it all get? And why do they call him the Brother anyhow?

Strange days indeed, and known in the trade as the leeward days, all becalmed and neither quite here nor there. It is still several weeks until high season explodes like Guy Fawkes' gunpowder barrels and there is time enough to learn the ropes, manhandle the rigging if you will, of this great big wooden craft. In Britain in the olden days, they would have called this a Spike, a night stop for the homeless, jobless and criminally insane. The Doc must have boned up on such stuff; maybe he's studied Orwell's *Down and Out in Paris and London* as he sure knows how to turn a buck on the taxpayer tab. In that way, me and him have similarities, I guess.

The Doc has fine-tuned the System to the extent that during the off season (i.e. not long after the Jean Claude Killy wannabes of this world have decamped to watch alpine skiing on TV, and before the real gristle of the backpacking world turns up ready to screw anything that moves), he is happy to let Works & Income meet his day-to-day expenses. This is why I have about 16 beds occupied on a weekly basis by various malicious-looking ex-crims suffering all manner of mental problems. These are the people who have slipped through the chasm-like crevices of the modern world and been washed up stony broke at some hostel or another where the rooms are cheap and the linen even cheaper. Backpacking is a viciously competitive game and during the quiet months the continual arm-wrestle for business is at its most viperous. A hostel like ours, an old hotel that was once grand but is now in a state of terminal disrepair, and with far too many beds to be filled in down time – except maybe on the weekends when the Crusaders are at home – must sink or swim on the meagre opportunities for income that still exist.

There is that ever-reliable source of financial manna, the English language student, and one-off parties of guests in town for a night, a weekend or a week. This is how the Doc charts a course safely back to solvency. The bums I can handle for the most part, and even if I can't, Dick can. I have yet to witness my first rugby fan scrum in reception so I cannot as yet comment on that, but the lifers I am growing used to.

The most difficult demographic to handle right now is our complement of Korean students who occupy about seven dorms on landing one. It is Little Seoul up there and despite repeated warnings about cooking in rooms, hanging up laundry in corridors and smoking in bed, there is (as you might expect in such circumstances) a language, and thus, communication problem. Another problem is that the Koreans in residence have long ago worked out that the stupid white dopes on reception cannot distinguish between them. This might explain why a four-bunk dormitory is currently hosting twelve students and why there appear to be only ten actual paying students among the 50 or so who always appear to be staying here. In financial circles they refer to this as 'discrepancies in bookkeeping procedures'. Dick is on to me about it constantly, sweating over the register, studying Korean names, then attempting to put those names to faces during the Friday night pay-up pantomime.

Picture this. There are three stooges reposing on the sofa: the Brother, Jacob the long-distance truck driver, and Tim, the resident Volkswagen Kombi van expert. Each has a cup-a-soup and a bread roll ready for the night's pre-entertainment entertainment, the hors d'oeuvres, if you will.

Jacob has a fetish for Korean girls and Tim has a fetish for engine parts. He has been re-building the wreck out back for the past eight weeks, but every Friday even he abandons his beloved piece of German engineering to come see the Show. Dick arrives with a sharpened pencil stuck behind his ear and a serious look on his dial; he has had a gutful of Korean karaoke and this time everyone is gonna squeal. I know that this is an error of judgment on my part, that by permitting Dick access to the register I am already in contravention of the Doc's one-person-one-highlighter rule. The Doc believes that too many bean-counters spoil the ledger. He may be right, as Dick is already dragging the register away from me and studying the numerous Lees in residence. He is not at all happy about the fraud being perpetrated by our Korean friends and tonight he intends to evict every one of the buggers who is trying – in fact, succeeding – in getting a free ride on the foreign student express. How many Lees do you think there are in Korea? he asks me.

Probably the same as there are Smiths in England, I answer, or Patels in India.

Well, they can't all be called Lee, can they?

The three stooges dunk their bread rolls in unison, waiting impatiently for the Friday theatre to commence, and all the while Dick is sharpening his pencil to the sharpest tip. I am telling him he's not to lose his cool and turn this into some kind of ASEAN rutting contest. I am sure that it's all just a matter of mistaken identity, that if we remain rational we will steer a steady course toward unification. He looks at me kinda odd and starts sharpening another pencil, eager to get into the fracas in the foyer.

The Koreans arrive mob-handed, most wearing boiler or flying suits and some even goggles. This group of kamikaze pilots, all wanting to cram in a final bowl of noodles before the off, swarms over us in numbers and any chance of rational discourse is lost the moment Dick breaks the tip on his first pencil. I know we are doomed when Dick begins barking, rather loudly:

Right! What's your name?

No, not you – YOU!

Look, I didn't ask you yet, wait your turn, okay?

Don't fucken push in – oi, you, yeah, you, have you paid?

What's your name? Oh, Lee, is it?

What room are you in?

Number? No, not that number, your room number?

Where's your ID? Let's see some ID, okay?

What's your name, and don't say Lee!

Oi, come back here you!

And this is what the Koreans are saying:

You no in charge!

Name? What name? Me, Lee. Yes!

His name my name – family name, Lee!

You no push, okay?

Two, only TWO in room, okay?

Me pay two week yesterday, YES!

This my name, here, see! Kim Lee!

What room where?

You no shout!

**Me stay here six year already! Always pay okay!
Him Lee, she Lee, me Lee!**

It is like watching a white-faced explorer trying to fend off cannibals until The Inkster barges into reception and yanks Dick away from the register. She holds up both hands like Noah asking for calm during the last crazy hours of the ark loading, and starts speaking in tongues. The mob go quiet as they sense their funny name-game has been rumbled and, just like the constant gardener, she weeds our beds, one by one. There are eleven Koreans suddenly bedless and rather embarrassed, hands together in the prayer position and bowing very slightly, now full of the humblest apologies for their oversight. Money is plucked from bulging wallets and thrust through the hole. It is over, but Dick shows no joy. He is not used to being manhandled, especially not in front of a baying mob. I figure he will go to find the Bat phone and hot-wire the Doc between sets and passionfruit cocktails, but to my surprise he scuttles away to skim porn on the in-house computers, glaring up in our direction every so often like a just-scolded child.

Well, that went okay, I finally say.

You think so? Jo replies, while erasing names from the register. You two couldn't organize a wake. Jesus, you have to be firm with Dick, remember what the Doc said?

She's right, of course. I'd permitted myself the luxury of falling under some kind of spell and bowing to the older man's approach. Neither Dick nor I will inherit the earth, that much is for sure. Dick because he is never quite *compos mentis*, and me because I'm far too lackadaisical these days when it comes to treading on toes. I've done enough of that in my short life and I'm tired of it.

Say, what language was that you were talking? I ask her.

Jo looks up from her business on the register and ponders the question before calmly replying: Haitian.

Saturday dawns fair but blustery. Marlon has again piped the U-bends with his giant butchers' hooks and he is off to Port Lyttelton to see if there is a spare bunk on a merchant ship to Oz. He has friends in the cane belt of Far North Queensland. Plenty of work there for those who don't mind ball-busting yakka, he tells me. I consider his statement. That must be why they call FNQ the Kiwi Coast. It is a coincidence that Marlon and I should be discussing the Big Island over the water because at the desk are an expatriate Aussie and a Danish girl who looks as if it has been a long time since she posed in pigtails by the Little Mermaid. When I see an Aussie and hear that nasal twang, my heart does weird stuff. It is not quite homesickness, more a sense of faux identity, although right now I would rather be here than there. I give them my *welcome friends* smile and this seems to appease the Danish girl. I know she is Danish because she has the flushed cheeks of a just-smacked bottom. The Aussie is just like any other Aussie; a bedraggled specimen with tousled hair, windswept features and a cocky glint in his eye. He is on the make for sure, one of those Aussies who has been brought up to believe that Kiwis only come in two styles: dumb and dumber. He is in for a shock, however, as I've taken an instant dislike to him, more so as he is indulging in braggadocio with his travelling companion, vis-à-vis this place being a dive.

Technically, of course, he is perfectly correct, but this is *my* dump and *I* decide which rubbish I will add to my ever-growing tip. And he has no money, which is a particularly Australian trait; if they can freeload they will – look at me and the Jo'ster, huh? The mermaid is doing the booking in and paying, two bunks in a mixed bunkhouse for one night. Before I give her the key I ask for the Aussie's ID.

Why? he demands.

Because it's a requirement, I tell him.

You didn't ask for hers, he counters.

She looks honest, my friend. You, I'm not so sure about.

Fucking oath, can't you people get over the trans-Tasman thing? he whinges.

I am not, as you so eloquently put it, one of *those* people, but if I were, I'd most likely have already had you forcibly removed for your impertinence. Now, ID?

C'mon Marta, he says sternly, let's blow this dump?

Marta is not for relocation, however, and she begins in her Scandinavian way to cajole her on-the-road-love into handing over ID.

He sighs dramatically and rummages around in his many cargo pockets until he finds a card, slapping it down on the counter. It is a long-expired student card from some institution in Melbourne. I study it. What the hell's this? I finally ask him.

ID, he moans.

I slide the student card back to him. That's no good, you got a passport or driver's licence?

Not here! he shouts.

Do you intend to work?

What are you, bloody immigration?

Any place will ask you for ID and that, I figure, is why you chose our humble lodgings, because we looked like the kind of joint that would askee no question, eh?

Jesus, mate, have a heart, okay? I've got ID in my bags but they got lost somewhere . . .

So how'd you clear immigration then?

They got lost after I'd done that!

I'll vouch for him, the Dane says, exasperated.

I tap the counter a while, thinking it over. If this guy gets up to mischief, and, by Christ, he looks the type, and there's no ID recorded, it'll be my butt in the slingshot. He is still standing his ground, hands sunk deep into empty pockets.

One night, I finally say, but if you want to re-book tomorrow he'll need ID. I say this to the Danish girl and she nods. I put my hand out for his student card and Xerox it just to cover my arse, no matter how thinly. Then I give her the key to heaven and the two of them scamper upstairs like Bonnie and Clyde desperate for the sanctuary of a hidey-hole. I still don't like him, so I add his mug shot to the rogue's gallery and scribble a few choice comments underneath. If nothing else it'll rouse Dick's interests because Dick's got a beef with the antipodean cousins across the Ditch, something to do with his son doing a stretch for welfare fraud.

Tonight will be our first night shift and we will be on duty until two thirty tomorrow afternoon. Right now that seems like a hell of a long way off. I am waiting for the first of numerous handovers between myself and Jo Buck. This is a tag-team effort, made a little more comfortable after I breezed into reception this morning and busted the safe in one crack. Now we really are in full control, we have the powers of Grey Skull bestowed upon us. As I watch the clock tick slowly, trying to shake from my already sleep-deprived mind the thought that this is our home for the next 30-plus hours, the six sisters sweep by like a pure ray of hope and bundle out through the doors into the waiting limo; they are on a mission from God and today that mission is taking them to Kaikoura to watch the whales. I'm not sure whether they have their sea legs yet but perhaps it won't matter . . . the great one will see to it that it's a beautifully tranquil day out on the bay, and that the great mammals bellow out a hymn or two. All is good in Eden, for now.

13.

The Keys to Babylon

I like Big Kev. He is a rotund, jovial guy, with a booming laugh big enough to hide behind should the need arise, which it would more often than not in BK's line of work. BK is opening the bar that adjoins our place – in fact, by facsimile I have been advised by our boss that it not only adjoins our hostel but is an integral part of it.

Well, I'll be damned, you learn something new every day. And what I've learned today is that come high season, when the place is heaving, I will be able to partake of even more late-night shenanigans, courtesy of a house bar that will be open all hours.

Fucken hell, Dick tells me blithely, the last time that bar was open it was pure bedlam in here on a Saturday night. Raving drunks and skittish women all over the fucken show – rather you than me, eh?

He has been all buddy-buddy with me since yesterday's Lee incident – as it's become known, and now there is a malicious twinkle in the silvery old fox's eyes. He knows all about Saturday nights in high season and just what hell lies in wait for us down the tracks.

I don't think I'll tell Jo all this, no indeed. I'll just tell her that BK's measuring up the place next door for 'future refurbishment'. Anyway, when she arrives for the next handover I barely recognize her: she has spent her break dying her hair a deep shade of red, when I was just getting used to green. Gazing up at my beloved I can't help but think of the saying: it takes a red-headed woman to get a dirty job done.

So I compliment her on her latest look and set off to walk around the perimeter, get myself acquainted with yardage, as the new quarterback says, as well as exits, car-parking spaces and the plethora of useless information your average back-packer hostel manager should know. Like fire-escapes: ever since Dick imparted that pearl of wisdom about tinderboxes into my head, I've had a palpable fear of fire engulfing us all. This is a big place, three floors, and, like everything else in this country, is built almost solely of wood. Perhaps not the wisest choice Kiwi builders ever made, especially given the plague-like infestations of white ants that prevail in such a climate, not to mention the landslides, floods and other wet acts of God this nation is prone to.

All of that I can cope with, but the fact that I grew up with a pyromaniacal sibling is something I will never shift from my subconscious. I spent my childhood years with one eye ajar for signs of smoke and the bedroom window wedged open, even on the wintriest of nights. If, like me, you've ever gone upstairs in your family home one lazy Sunday afternoon, clutching a cup of cocoa and some marmite on toast, only to see your juvenile delinquent firestarter of a brother desper-ately beating back flames with his smouldering dressing gown, you would be fire sensitive too.

So here I am, wandering about the big building with the flaking paint, the building that was once, I'm assured, a swanky up-market hotel. This end of town used to be where top-hatted and tailed diners straight from the riverbank opera disembarked gaily from horse-drawn carriages, and strolled into the grand foyer to be met by the Penguin and his evil minions. What gay days they must have been, huh? And nights too, I suppose. Today our building is as close to council condemnation as a lodging-house can be, without actually being razed. Who knows when these fire-escapes were added? I mean, look at 'em, snaking all over the place like the giant exoskeleton of some mutating alien life form. Very New York.

These drop-down ladders seem a long way up to me. How in the hell do you get them to come down? Maybe you do it from up there but, sweet Jesus, if my arse was already singed, leaning out a third-storey window trying to untangle a drop-down ladder from its rust-encrusted mountings wouldn't fill me with optimism. They're up, as I understand from that demented halfwit the Brother, because if they were down it would be too easy for people to climb them at every hour of the goddamned day or night. But I can't see the logic in having them permanently up and, apparently, seized. Maybe I'll go get Dick and he can explain this conundrum to me – but then again, Dick lives downstairs and he's only ten metres from the rear fire door; maybe that tells me everything I need to know?

I come around the side still peering upward until on one of the few staging platforms, I spy a half-naked Danish girl and a scabby Australian lying there as bold as you fucking like, rolling a reefer. That makes up my mind for me. I'm back inside and up two flights of stairs faster than a trainee fireman. The fire door, the one clearly marked 'Do Not Open Unless In Case Of Emergency' is propped open by a pair of filthy hiking boots. Just as I'm about to go out on the escape and rip that drug-addled Aussie a new one, I am overcome by the urge to shut the door and leave the fucker out there for a few hours. Just until the sun dips over the plains and the air temperature gets down to safe storage levels. Yeah, that'd be a more prudent way of solving this particular in-house dilemma. So, with a devilish smile playing on my pouty lips, I quickly kick free the boots and let the door latch itself. Then I go off whistling to myself, looking for any other rube who might want to test the limits of my intolerance.

And I find one – or, at least, I find his sneakers. They are clanging around in the tumble-dryer like a pair of clogs in a tin trunk, the very same tumble-dryer that prominently displays the notice 'Any Shoes Found In This Dryer Will Be Thrown Away!' Well, fair enough, I think. So I yank open the dryer door and juggle the hot Adidas sneakers for a minute until they're cool. Then, satisfied with my lot, I track back to the rear staircase and at the bottom dump the cooling sneakers into the rubbish bin. Another good job done. I am really racking up the Brownie points now, and the thing is, I'm ENJOYING it.

It must be this huge bunch of keys I have jangling from my hip. They say that power corrupts once you become the jailer rather than the jailed, and it's easy to see why. I veer off into the kitchen to check my cool room, maybe roust up a few gooks for sloppy wok-handling procedures. Surprisingly, it's all fairly clean. It's then I notice the fire-extinguisher. I've come full circle, right back to where I started, thinking of fire. I look at the metal dog tag that the extinguisher is wearing and am shocked to see, beneath the grime, that the last compliance check was performed in 1994. Ye fucking gods. Say this kitchen went up after a wok full of palm oil went BOOM! And some poor fool trying to do the Right Thing wrestled this beast from its wall mounting – that is, if he or she could even get a perfunctory hold on it given the amount of grease it's slathered in. They cocked the trigger, aimed, and pulled the ring … only to find that what they'd hoped would be a geyser-like burst of clean white powder actually turned out to have about as much oomph as a two-pack-a-day smoker?

I add it to my list: check and re-gas all extinguishers. On my night shift I'll check every last one of these mothers too. Unsettled by the laissez-faire stance that my boss has taken toward in-house fire-safety precautions, I detour up to the first-floor TV lounge to check out what's happening. The place looks like a betting shop, with seven or eight world-weary types huddled around an old TV set watching the remains of their day being flogged into last place by a cross-dressing jockey. The oomph has gone from them too, as they begin to shred their betting slips and thereby all hopes of a better Saturday night. Use the bin, I tell them as I wander around wishing I had a hostel-issued truncheon, or the one from lost property that is hanging by our bed in the staff flat – maybe I'll use it tonight.

A red-headed lad with a thousand too many freckles for my liking has his bare, gnarly feet up on an old cup-ringed coffee table. He looks at me sheepishly and I look at his feet, which he immediately removes from hostel property. He doesn't seem familiar. I study him a while longer and as I do he starts to blush. Red-headed people can't help it, I know, I used to be one. What's your name? I ask him.

T-T-T-T-Tommy, he replies.

What room are you in?

Th-Th-Th-Th-Thir-t-t-t-y-one.

Really? I say, interested, because I know full well that the 30s block isn't in use tonight – it's low season and we keep our inmates to one corridor so the room cleaners don't have to traipse all over when they de-louse. Tommy is as red as a plump tomato now and is hurriedly putting on holey socks and grubby trainers. I motion him to follow and, wearily, he does . . . he is a bona fide aficionado of the Game, a player, and his skills of

deception have afforded him the relative comfort of an afternoon in hospitable company far from the maddening breeze
outside. If his horse had come in it would have been a different
matter, but Tommy is having no luck today when it comes to
picking a winner or a dopey hostel manager. I hold the front
door open for him as a courtesy, just like the concierge used to
do for well-heeled patrons in bygone years after a long night on
the sauce. Tommy doesn't tip me, just gives a sly wink, and I
must admit that I'm not indifferent to his plight. There but for
the grace of God, etcetera. And, just as I'm thinking this, that
big black Mercedes pulls up outside and begins to disgorge its
quotient of nuns for the day. Both Tommy and I stand there a
moment and watch the scene from *Sister Act* unfold.

S-S-See ya, boss, Tommy says, as he hoiks up his collar
against the cold, and I can tell that he is going to be my
nemesis, the Riddler to my Batman if you will.

I'll look forward to it, I tell him truthfully.

I am still holding the door open as I greet each sister in turn.
Well now, one says to another as they pass through my portal,
'tis the lovely young lady who runs this fine hotel, to be sure
it is.

I go out onto the darkening street and watch Tommy vanish
into the night. Good Christ Almighty we've at least 60 unused
beds here and ... ah shite, you can't bring that motherlode
down upon yourself, you can't pick and choose, you know?
Maybe keeping those fire-escape ladders up is a wise move
after all.

Dick is supposed to be coming at eleven, the time the night
porter starts – only we're the night porters tonight, even though
we've been the day porters all day. He is going to show us the
ropes, as they say in seaports around the world, as we've only

glimpsed night duties from the night porter's log and from that two hours scrubbing we did during our unpaid pre-trial trial. We get the gist of it; the list of night jobs is pinned up in the office and it looks like a staggering incline of work to surmount before dawn breaks. I don't know how they do it, those who labour while the rest of us sleep with one eye open. The reality, of course, is that they don't. Marlon and that defector Helga, who works two nights a week, don't actually do anything. Okay, Marlon unblocks our pipework, but Helga? No, Helga sells cars and she has quite a line of them, warranted and ready to roll – about as far as the on-ramp for Highway 1.

Sure, look here in the Book, there are innumerable phone messages for Helga and most, if not all, are from disgruntled rubes ringing from emergency phones on the arterial highway. They are standing there holding a blocked fuel pump, maybe a set of gooed-up points, even a split radiator hose or two – and before they even think about professional roadside assistance they are thinking about teaching Helga a life lesson, just for the cathartic hell of it. Helga is like ice, as cold and as steadily moving as the Franz Josef Glacier. In her choice of vocation you would need to be.

Sweet Jesus, doesn't the Doc ever read this goddamned message book? Just as I am beginning to find myself becoming engrossed in Helga & The Car People, Dick saunters into lock up in his PJs and dressing gown. He is no little Lord Fauntleroy that's for sure, though he is carrying a bottle of linctus, some syrupy concoction left behind by a past guest in their haste to flee. It's for this fucken graveyard cough, he tells me, all that fucken dust that blows off the plains, never had a permanent bronchial infection down in Dunedin, no fucken sir. I follow Dick around, convinced he should be holding a candle to give us the period effect. We go through the jobs list, on which the most important chore involves getting the stragglers out of the kitchen-cum-restaurant and the TV lounge.

It's a balancing act, Dick tells me as we lock down the restaurant and kitchen with a chain and industrial-sized padlock. Once you've got it locked you can clean it at your leisure. The longer you leave the fuckers in there the harder it'll be to clean. And get those front doors locked at eleven sharp. If you don't, any piece of passing trash'll saunter in like they own the fucken joint. Guests gain after-hours entry by using the keypad. Although half the time, Dick tells me knowingly, you're gonna have to buzz them in because they'll be smashed or just too stupid to work it out for themselves. If you don't recognize the face or if you don't like it, let the bastard sleep on the pavement. Carry the phone everywhere – see this? I put that sticker on there, not that I need it now, by Christ no. I've rung the fuzz so often the number's engrained on me brain – right here.

I get his point. We meander upstairs to check the lounge, toss out a few insomniacs and pillheads, then check all the shitters and showers. Never know what half-breed's trying to stow away for a free night's shuteye in the shithouse.

That's when we hear whimpering, up by the second-floor fire door. Dick has the phone on speed dial just in case. When he whips off the leather cord from around his midriff, it's like watching the Hulk go green and angry, but nowhere near as fascinating. He listens hard at the door then turns to me and whispers, There's some fucker out there, by Christ.

Oops, yeah … I start to say, and then I clam up tighter than butt cheeks in a communal shower hall.

Who's there? Dick finally says in authoritarian mode. We listen for the response and even though I know who the fuck is out there I go along with the charade.

Who? Dick says again and turns to me. You got some dopey couple in room fifteen?

I nod. One of 'em's an Aussie too, I add, maliciously.

That'd be fucken right, Dick says as he yanks the door open. A partly frozen Aussie and a well-weathered Danish girl fall back through the hole like time travellers who realise their number is well and truly up.

What the fucken hell you doing out there? Dick demands, and before the Aussie can summon up some huff and puff he is on them the way a shepherd is on a just-found sheep.

You fucken idiots, he bleats, don't ya know ya ain't allowed out on the escapes?

The door shut! the Aussie whinges.

Of course it did, those doors are big mothers and they're supposed to shut ... by Christ you'd want 'em fucken shut if this place was snap, cracklin' and poppin'!

But ... the Aussie tries.

But fucken nothing, Dick replies sternly.

Must have been the wind, I tell him, as we corral the two recaptured fugitives back to their cell for the night. The Aussie turns around and asks, Any chance of using the kitchen, mate?

Ha ha ha ... as fucking if.

Do I feel a twang of remorse? Well, a little, I guess. I'd meant to let them back in with a lecture after an hour but time has a uncanny knack of slipping away from you in the Joint. Me and Dick go back downstairs to be met by some clown hammering on the front doors, perhaps an absconder too stupid to realize he's already on the outside. Check out this ape, Dick says to me as he whips the piece of leather cord hard against his bad leg. What sort of cretin would have checked in a monster like that, huh?

Probably the Jo'ster, I think to myself. She's got a funny habit of sheltering the deranged from the long arms of justice.

Go on, fuck off! Dick says through the smeary glass but the big mother with his paws pressed flat against the safety glass just goes on slobbering.

Fucken oath, Dick moans, then tries to get the slobbering bogan to show him a room key ... which miraculously he produces. I just shrug, and Dick, much against his better judgment, lets the brute in. His name is Otto and he is here on business, seedy maudlin' business that is most usually conducted in rooms you can book by the hour ... but not in our joint – we don't go in for that kind of palaver. He is Norwegian, I think. I surmise this because he is wearing an Aran turtle-neck sweater and reeks of booze and herring. He thanks us most humbly for our troubles by producing a hip flask, which we both decline, then stumbles up the staircase like a North Sea fisherman sozzled on the poop deck.

That kind of caper will go on all night, Dick yawns, but if there's any real trouble just come and get me, okay?

Sure, I tell him. He leaves, and I settle down for six straight hours of purgatory until my other half comes to relieve me at six bells. This is what we've decided, that during the night I'll do the wee hours and she'll take over at dawn ... no way I am gonna let some leery old seadog with man milk still to spill get his rubbers – or is it lubbers? – around my woman. So I bunker down and take the night train, another six hours that I'll never have again.

The cleaning ain't too hard and all the while I'm dreaming about that foldin' stuff that Marlon found ... like, six big kahunas. Sweet Jesus, would I hand that in? Hell no, probably not, I think to myself, anyone stupid enough to leave that much stash on a hostel couch deserves everything they get. It's the thought of booty – and the power – that gets me through night shift. That and the fact I rather like it. I am free to rummage through stored property at my leisure, allowed to tramp around in total control with a huge bunch of keys. I am a control freak, I realize at four in the morning as I sit watching the early morning serenade of drunks out on the main drag. Look at those fools out there, staggering along loaded up on booze and pills, too pissed even to know where the fuck they are – women too, not just guys. I've seen at least a half dozen under-dressed women crawl by in the past hour. What the hell goes on in their minds?

Tim the car freak, obviously an early riser, comes down around five and we watch the BBC World Service together. He wants to make toast before the 'rush' starts as he is off today to hunt down a second-hand clutch cable. Try Helga, I tell him with a yawn. I feel kinda good, that I've sailed this ship and all her crew and passengers through a long rather uneventful night. Six bells strike and I watch the CCTV for the first signs of Jo Buck; my appointed watch is over and soon enough I will be free.

As it drags on to half past my stomach feels as empty as a backpacker's head ... and then I see her, groping groggily down the back stairway with a bowl of cereal in one hand, and I know that just as sure as the first customer of the day will ask a dumb-ass question, my other half will be as grumpy as all hell. She is not a morning person. Our very own Mrs Slocombe? Not at all.

When I regain consciousness around eleven I feel as though I have been beaten all over with a wooden mallet by a meaty-handed Mongolian grill chef. It's a real fucking struggle to get downstairs and, when I do, I'm immediately accosted by the Jo'ster who tells me bitterly that she's spent the past three hours arguing with some Arab who's lost his sneakers.

I don't know anything about it, I tell her. Where'd he last see them?

In the laundry, she tells me.

We are handing over at two thirty to Peggy Sue. She is the Sunday girl – well, maybe she was in 1933. She reminds me of that quirky old woman who used to do the dog training show on TV in England, what was her name? Woodhouse? Wodehouse? Whitehouse? Ah shit, my brain's too fogged up to get a clear sight of it. She arrives late. All she has to do is get here by two thirty, you know? After we've done 35, and now, one half hour and still fucking counting. She has a boot load of boxes full of cheap chipped crockery for the hotel kitchen and a couple of purloined antique jugs under each arm just in case the *Antiques Roadshow* comes to town. She is parked about a mile away. Why, I ask myself . . . it is fucking Sunday and you could park on the pavement right by the front doors and still not get nabbed. Good Christ, anything to be spent of this obligation . . . so I hike up the street a ways and haul the boxes back, and then we have to go through the Q&A handover procedure and to be sure Miss Walkies ain't the brightest button on the seamstress's shelf.

Parched, dry as kindling, I can smell Guinness being poured in a nearby bar; the bar boy is putting my initials in the froth with a dab hand while the fire crackles nearby. But as we make our dash for freedom I'm pinioned to the hot drinks machine by the six sisters of Show-No-Mercy.

No, I tell them firmly, we're off duty now. See that crazy old bitch over there? She'll sort it all out now, to be sure.

The first two pints of the black stuff don't even dampen the tonsils. The world is still turning, even though it's anticlockwise down here. No more work till Wednesday!

14.

Work for Bed, Apply Within

Captain's Log – Star date . . .

God is in his heaven. The Doc is back, long live the Doc! It is the Hour of Power first thing on Wednesday morning. The mice have all squealed and there is big trouble in little paradise. Apparently, I am the cause of it all.

Screw the fact the ledgers square, or that no paying guest has a bone to chew. These don't matter when you're surrounded by work colleagues with about as much backbone as a beached octopus. The Doc is full of wisdom on his first day back on the bridge, surrounded again by sycophantic doomsayers and long-term residents with not a clue as to how the world outside functions. And he is irked, and while that might be the result of a dodgy semi-final loss in the squash tournament, it might also be because Dick has been nibbling his ear since sun-up.

Dick is a rakish adversary, and right now he is drinking his morning cup of hemlock and looking like Lazarus. The old bastard looks away from me as the Doc begins his morning sermon to the gathered retinue. The Doc doesn't mind the cut of my jib; he may look a fool, but looks can be deceptive.

As things stand – i.e. precarious – I can see the Doc is oscillating between believing the limping one's litany of lies about

Jo and me, or, albeit begrudgingly, congratulating us on a job well done under trying circumstances. As per usual, he falls on his rump in no man's land with a soft downy thump attempting to placate all parties, as is his way.

There are the Bills. As the Doc reads them to me, he whistles through his teeth like a surgeon with damp x-rays. Either at the magnitude of them, or my balls for authorizing them. I explain to him the basic health and hygiene regulations vis-à-vis cool rooms, then venture on to mitigate my decision to have every hostel fire extinguisher replaced. Look, I tell him flatly, for there is no point tippy toeing around the Doc's maypole, either we get new working extinguishers or stop taking IDs and start taking dental x-rays. I think the Doc gets the crux – I am working in our best interests and sometimes you must spend a little to avoid spending the whole pot later. But then I have to sit there and listen to Dick gripe on like a wind-choked bub about un-flattened cardboard boxes and other dreary shit.

You only have to fucking tell me, I finally spit in Dick's face. As he can see that my hackles are rising, he lopes off to crush cardboard. The Doc reprimands me, but only lightly you understand; he is on to a cushy little number here, having found a managerial pair who can actually manage. This is a barrel of worms he has no interest in upsetting. Thus, lecture over, he carries on checking my bookwork for discrepancies like an old lady guarding her best-in-class sponge cake at the Royal Show.

Later that day, back on shift, after the Doc has vamoosed temporarily to his safe deposit box, I am accosted by five of the six sisters of hellfire and damnation about a WWOOF-ing experience. Now, if you are a seasoned penny-pinching kind of traveller, one who thinks that digging up someone else's spring vegetables in exchange for a bowl of watery soup and a flea bath is a swell type of meet-the-locals gig, then you will know about WWOOF-ing. If, however, you are not au fait with the principle then please permit me to explain: WWOOF-ing is a come-as-you-are assignment for the day, week or month, depending upon your level of sanity. It is put on for those interested in helping local farmers, small holders, hobby farmers and other assorted organic numbnuts plough a few furrows, dig a few ditches or maybe even neuter a few ewes, and all for free food and board if required. Some people, I believe, actually enjoy this kind of on-the-land adventure. They are the desperate kind.

Anyhow, the problem is there are only five sisters; Mary has become separated from her companions either by an act of God or something far more heinous. These events are regarded as natural phenomena in the hostelling industry. As I try to determine where Mary was last sighted, the Aussie turns up. He has no money – this is not new, he had no money yesterday. That, however, is not my problem. My problem is there are no free bunks in this bunkhouse and just as I'm about to delight in iterating this simple business practice to the Aussie, who should return carrying one of those big novelty money boxes other than our esteemed leader?

Problem? he asks me, as he breezes into reception wearing his soap-opera smile.

Nope, I tell him ... but just then the Little Mermaid joins the pregnant throng at the cage window looking for my assistance in severing the umbilical cord between her and her off-again bit of Aussie maleness. Before I can assure her that I've no intention of allowing Crocodile Dundee jnr to re-book, the Aussie is leaning to read the large notice the Doc has just pinned up next to the cage.

WORK AVAILABLE!
Construction/labouring – 15 minutes from town.
Free transport, meals and bed.
One day's work = one voucher. Enquire within!

Things are going from bad to worse, and despite my best efforts I am unable to stop the Aussie and the Doc entering immediate negotiations. This is unexpected; I might never be shot of this lice-ridden antipodean with no hard cash and even less in the way of dignity.

On the up side, Sister Mary has re-joined her flock – and proceeds to tell me that the little girl's room has some kind of plumbing problem. I flash the Doc a quick glance but he is knee-deep in offal, the walking-talking, ready-willing-and-able-to-work kind, so I thank the sister for the information and dig out the WWOOF book, where I see, much to my amazement, that Peggy Sue, the Sunday girl, has some kind of alpaca farm and is a registered WWOOF host. Good Christ, they've all got a scam on the go, sometimes even more than one . . . And what about this giant novelty money box that is sat aside the register?

I offload the Little Mermaid into another dorm, then receive a shuttle of deadbeat types straight from cavity searches at the airport. Among them is a tired Spaniard and, good lord, you rarely if ever see Spaniards this far south. His name is Pedro and he is as bent as a North Island carpenter's nail collection. He is roving far from his usual habitats in the quest for inter-racial-bum-banditry. I check him in immediately, ahead of the waiting two Chinese – even though two Chinese is good luck, and especially two with a little dumpling of an offspring.

I don't know what kind of travel agents they have in Shanghai, but one thing is for sure; whoever they are, they are utilizing outdated reference books. The last time this place had stars to its name James Cagney was Hollywood's leading man. These two Chinese look as if they are moribund with fear in the face of obvious booking errors. They have some pre-paid docket from Sally Lim's Exotic Travel Bureau, all in yuans, and where for the love of Buddha am I gonna find today's conversion rates? Obviously Sally Lim has run some Fan-Tan ruse on these poor souls, maybe even a bent game of Mahjong, who knows? Yeah, maybe the Doc, this is right up his kind of laptop. So I beckon him over, away from his bug-eaten work-force who resemble a gang of wetbacks hoping the watermelon picking truck'll stop by, and back to a more Ying and Yang kinda set-up.

The Doc speaks any currency, no matter how inscrutable, and of course he'll even bow as low as Sally Lim stoops in the name of earning a dollar or two. But I can't see how he's going to extricate himself from the mess Ms Sally of Shanghai has plopped him into. These people think they're getting cable, a mini-bar and an adjoining rumpus room for their own Little Emperor to squat in while he gorges on fortune cookies by the jar load – and all for only eight million yuan a night. That is bad kismet in any language, but now it is in the drawer marked 'Doc's Problems'.

The Aussie is climbing aboard the 'To The Manor Born' bus along with a few other worthless pairs of hands that are only just attached to even more worthless torsos. He will be back tonight with his free bed voucher and I will save him a berth in the dropouts' dorm. They are macho boys in there and quite a few of them, from what I've seen, aren't at all picky when it comes to orifices.

The sisters have gone off to buy gumboots and heavy-duty gardening gloves. They are intending, I suppose, to get as close to aunty nature as is possible in theologian circles without being later accused of some kind of code of conduct infringement direct from St Peter himself. And good on 'em too, I am all for seeing the beautiful, fair hands of God's maidens toiling on the land – maybe they will bring me back a sweet potato or two?

I hand over – we are becoming adept at a quick turnaround, the Jo'ster and I, having already learned, just like the old King Rat had said, that we are never truly off duty. Danger, questions, or even a homesick gay Spaniard lurk in every alcove just waiting to pounce. And so it proves, there, on the first-floor landing, perched disconsolately on a sofa that has seen many such perchings, is my new amigo Don Pedro from Alicante.

Fortunately for young Pedro, I know Alicante rather well; my paternal grandparents retired there to take up a life of whist, gin-slings and expatriate gossip-mongering. The English can be like that; once the crumbling white cliffs vanish from sight and they are ensconced in some foreign land, they set about turning it into *Eastenders*. The whole Med coast of Spain has long since gone this way. Now it's a hotchpotch of old Londoners who survived both the Blitz and Thatcher, only to have to now survive the Spanish health system. They are a motley ensemble of shopkeepers, petty crooks, B-grade gangsters and otherwise upstanding British citizenry fleeing beefs with Customs and Excise or the Man. Actually, I kinda like it – and that's what I tell Pedro, not of course that he and I can actually engage in conversation, but we can do enough with charades and pidgin brogue to get by. We are both a very long way from La Tomatina.

As I understand it, he is down at heel over the rashness that has led him to venture further south than he has ever journeyed before. He is disoriented and fatigued. He has one of those ubiquitous free city maps that you can collect at every airport the world over, and, as with every other mixed-up long-distance traveller, he is turning it this way and that in a vain Spanish attempt to grapple with his current bearings. The large red arrow that signifies 'You Are Here!' means about as much to him right now as a last call tannoy announcement does to a guide dog.

Where iz 'ere? he asks me, his large brown eyes like a couple of cane toads about to hump.

I am a philanthropist, I suppose, of the ilk of Getty, only I am collecting a ragtag assortment of desperados from the Village, and the Village People as well. I've seen the rainbow, in fact, I've even been over it once or twice, and while our gin palace isn't ready to embrace the multi-coloured logo of the bent traveller, the Doc doesn't have any qualms about the colour of the dollars he collects. So I draw a line along the map directing Pedro to a more suitable information centre and then explain it with semaphore. That is a universal language.

Ah! Mochas gracias! he tells me.

Hasta la vista, baby, I reply. Man, I've always wanted to say that.

It seems ridiculous that I am back in the Hole already, but I cannot argue with the practices of quantum physics as obviously I AM. My person is here at least – although mentally I am still surfing an updraft somewhere rather more Leary-esque. Jo takes pleasure in advising me that she, and therefore we, have been instructed to prepare ourselves for an imminent avalanche of coinage. It happens every high season, as regularly as outbreaks of bed bugs, when all those weary souls cross the ditch with their pockets full to brimming with Aussie coinage, the same coinage that invariably ends up in Kiwi hostel owners' money boxes.

But why? I ask her dumbly. You can't convert shrapnel at Thomas Cook.

Of course you can't, don't be ridiculous, she tells me. The Doc and Zsa Zsa holiday at Surfers after every high season finishes, get it?

You mean we've gotta go through the banking and weed out Aussie gold, and then plonk it in a novelty money tin so the Doc can haul it back to Oz as hand luggage?

Exactamundo, my pale-skinned compadre! she smiles. Everyone has a Mediterranean air today. I shrug hopelessly.

But wait! there's more! she announces.

The Doc and Zsa Zsa have invited us to a Go-Go apparently, some kinda welcome wagon tour around the Big House, a night free of in-house obligations, dinner included, oh, and a session in the spa. That's the bit that tweaks my nipples. The spa? I reply, and then I see that big voracious smile of hers. We are on the same wavelength, tuned to the same frequency, and we've no need at all to seek fucking Kenneth's advice. I find myself suffering from a fit of REMs, the first signs of an imminent bout of paranoia. How in the name of Mohammed are we gonna pull off communal spa bathing?

She shrugs. Better get yourself an all-in-one, honey, she whispers, sarcastically.

It never ends, this madness. I mean, aside from the fact that I don't think the Doc and Zsa Zsa would see the funny side of me and the Inkster in our teeny, weenie bikinis, there's the matter of whether even a couple of normal types would want to sit in a spa, barely attired, with their employers. I mean, c'mon, that ain't quite the getting-to-know-you deal I'm interested in. Dinner is one thing, but ripping off your togs and splashing around in bubbling hot water is quite another altogether.

I'm hopeful that we have good reasons to avoid the unavoidable. First, because the Doc will have to pay some poor fool to cover our absence, and ergo he will be paying twice, and second, because we don't have transportation, or indeed any idea as to the wheres and hows of reaching the Big House. Those are good solid reasons, or at least they would have been had not that limping grave robber Dick become involved.

15.

The Addams Family

Dick's got a car. He strips its parts to stop it being filched and, like Henry Ford, he keeps those parts under his bed. Handing over the rotor arm and a coil, he tells me all I gotta do is re-assemble and drive away. Oh, and my first stop ought to be a servo coz there's no juice in it; Dick ain't letting no fucker siphon his tank under the cover of dark.

Yes, the grumpy old man has lent me his vehicle, such as it is, to take the drive up to the Manor. He has given me a crudely drawn map too, sketched on the back of an old betting slip. Regrettably it all looks pretty straightforward, but then again that was what Columbus and Bligh once said in their foolish haste. Helga is coming to cover us, she needs the overtime as used-vehicle sales have been somewhat slack since the recent clash over consumer rights with three resident Slovaks. I saw a picture of them – they all looked like Kojak, only far meaner; who loves ya, baby!

That is *her* dilemma. I have enough sloppy gruel in my own bowl, thanks, like driving up to the Big House and trying to explain my way out of a family friendly night in the hot tub. I think I can do it, I've talked my way in and out of far worse predicaments and feel that my eloquence, and indeed my ability to lie straight-faced, will stand me in good stead again. So we hand over to Helga, who reluctantly takes the reins and wishes us, rather sardonically I think, a pleasant feast. Then I spend a half hour in semi-darkness putting Dick's automobile back together.

Then, trying to start it. Car theft was a forum I missed in juvey, due to my early release for good behaviour. Finally it whoops, coughs and splutters just like dirty Dick Turpin himself. But doesn't catch. Exasperated, I go back around to the front of the hostel, then all the way down into the bowels of The Block. I have oil, grease and shit right up to the elbows and I am less than pleased – a car cannot flood with only 200 mills of gas in it. Ah yeah, Dick says, shoulda told ya – you gotta jump the cranky old bitch.

Jump it? I say, like I've never heard the words before.

Aye, c'mon, I'll give ya a push, if me knee'll hold up.

I look at him incredulously; what kind of a fucking gangbang is this? But off we go, the Jo'ster and Dick pushing the heap o' rust up the street while I 'pop' it.

Not fucken third! I hear Dick holler. First, ya twat!

Shit, must they do everything arse backwards in this country?

It catches in first, very reluctantly, and when it does catch, it belches out a tailpipe full of unctuous grease that almost chokes Dick and the Jo'ster. I'm not worried about the old bugger, but my poor bewedded! Jesus H. Christ, if she has a mush like a coal miner my arse is grass as they say in the high country. Jump in! I tell her abruptly while we still have forward momentum. We gotta get gas!

She is mighty pissed, and even more so as I consistently fail to navigate this maze-like one-way system. It is like being lost on the way to the Mad Hatter's tea party and I am certainly late; all we need is a fucking giant white rabbit in the back seat.

There! There! Turn there you fucking moron! she berates me.

The needle on Dick's fuel gauge is flickering dangerously under the 'long way past reserve' level. In fact, it has passed the pump icon and is now indicating that we need a well instead.

I crash onto a forecourt and notice the Perspex-ensconced attendant reach for the silent alarm. Angrily I pump gas, traipse in, pay for it, climb back aboard, turn the ignition key and ... yeah, baby, the thing is as dead as a Pharaoh. That is when I begin trying to rip the whole dash from its mounting. Fucking piece of fucking fuck fuck fuck fucking shit!

Jo says nothing: nada, zilch, not a dicky bird. Eventually she calmly alights the vehicle and slams the passenger door so hard that Dick's radio unit falls out of its mounting. Hey, where ya going? I ask.

The fucking bus stop, she replies.

But then, just when all hope is lost, a big gas-hungry 4x4 rolls up behind us, and from within its depths the tiniest woman in the world emerges. Thumbelina, no less. I can hardly see her face but I hear her asking if I need a push ... at least, by Christ, I think that's what she said. But ... hang on, there is some ogre-like fiend at the passenger door, a Cyclops who looks capable of picking this piece of Japanese tin up and putting it under his arm. Hubby'll help yer, the little woman says, and to be sure Goliath has the strength of the All Blacks front row. Within seconds we are back in action, and I honk merrily at my beloved as she leans against the side of the bus shelter looking dangerous.

Dick's map is completely useless. Had he by some over-sight been in charge of operation Desert Shield, they'd still be looking for the road to Baghdad. We are lost, driving around roundabouts in a funk of bad navigational skills and

blasphemous language. This is my fault – I am not concentrating as I ought. My mind is fully committed to circum-
venting hot-tub bathing protocol, lathering myself up ready for
a command performance. We spin off the exit in a screech of
already bald tyre rubber and fishtail up the unlit street looking
for a giant sign, like the kind that proliferate along the highways of A-merica. This one isn't for 'Bubba Joe's all-you-can-
eat crawfish buffet', however. If it were I'd be as happy as an
Irishman on St Paddy's Day. Nope, this one is for The Manor.
You can't fucken miss it, the old weasel had said, sign's as big as
a fucken house! Well maybe so, in broad Canterbury daylight
when you come hairin' around this blind bend, junked up on
happy tabs only to be met by the dazzling white smiles of Jim
and Tammy Bakker staring down on you from on high. That'd
rattle your bones for sure, a sight like that, but not now, not in
pitch black when you've already realized you've gone 30 ks too
far into the wild beyond because your host, your employer in
fact, is too goddamned tight to floodlight the bloody billboard!
I do a fourth gear U-ie, which ain't advised for those of you
without advanced driving skills; those of you who haven't driven
through Beirut at rush hour looking for a barber's shop. Dick's
old pile of filler only just holds together, although I hear
chromium bouncing not far away as I accelerate back up the
deserted highway.

The iron framework of the sign glints in the moonlight and
there, just beyond, lays a small gravel track – again unlit. I shoot
up there spraying grit and chippings everywhere, a hundred
thousand pockmarks all pebble-dashing Dick's already battered
paint job. That'll teach the old codger to loan me his wheels.

We round the bend too fast and almost skid straight into
the artificial lake. A few swans shoot up to our left. Ahead, as
the driveway opens up onto open tundra, we almost take out

two madly shrieking peacocks. I am as demented as all hell. I do a sharp handbrake stop and a slew of gravel almost decapitates what looks like, in these murky shadows, the hunchback of Notre Dame. Sweet Mary, mother of God! I cry, as suddenly we are in the blinding glare of three 6000-watt halogens. That is some fucking security system.

The place is alive as bedlam on half-day closing. There are figures everywhere, scuttling about like aliens emerging from the Mother Ship. I have to shield my eyes from the immense brightness, and it is all I can do to reach out for the Jo'ster's trembling hand. The lights go off and we are plunged into a Victorian half light. I see the Doc, wearing his Polo™ casual attire, and I see that crouching fool, the Brother, although I have no idea why he is here ... There is another half breed I don't immediately recognize and Zsa Zsa, of course, all dollied up in her finery like Gloria Swanson. As the dust clears we are beckoned into the warmth of the interior by something resembling Lurch, a big dude dressed like a butler carrying three or four small glasses on a tray. He hands us one each. How very fucking civilized.

I must remember to keep an air of civility about me, and try to act fucking normal. The Doc shows us through to the bar, yes indeed, the bar, which is in the billiards room, wherein is a full-sized billiards table. No fucking fold-up half measures here, my friends. Would I like a few frames? he asks me. Maybe later.

You could get lost in here: there are at least six bathrooms downstairs, all with heated towel rails and soap dispensers. The dining room can seat 50 people, more at a push, and we are going to dine up one end of the Norfolk-pine table. The one adorned with three or four baroque candelabras. As I sit there, wallowing in the grandeur and looking out on the expanse of lawn through the French doors, the Doc tells me, just-as-casual-as-you-fucking-like, that they are bussing up hostel trash to dig ditches for under-soil heating. I cannot forget that back in town there is a big damp building full of health and safety infringements which is obviously financing this whole rort.

I am infrequently overcome by speechless bewilderment; the last time was at the Taj Mahal. The Doc can sense my awe and as Lurch lurches about with canapés, he suggests we go outside and get some 'air'. Lurch flips on the garden lights – well, flood-lights, I guess. As I take in the landscaping, it becomes clear you could hold a three-day event out here with a small boat fair on the side, or a couple of games in the rugby world sevens. The man I do not recognize comes out holding a stubby of beer. He is the greenkeeper, I understand now, and all of this is his craftsmanship. Well, him and 200-odd bussed-in wetbacks. It is a massive piece of construction, and it is, I am assured by my host, a long way from completion. There are still the grass courts and the nine-hole golf course to complete. And why the hell not? It is all very … what? Sometimes – not often, you'll understand – words fail me when I need them the most.

Below the surface of my calm and interested veneer I am seething at the injustice of it all. Not the injustice of a mob of backpackers being short-changed every summer, but the injus-tice that we are working our tits off in inclement conditions to finance this luxury for guests with more cash than conscience.

So what? This isn't a book about the rich and the poor; screw those people. Me, I'm only interested in the short-term investment, the non-interest-bearing one that I've made with Jim and Tammy. At least I've seen it now, witnessed it with my own cool blue eyes. I know now that any novel ideas for upgrade and upkeep of a sleazy hostel will almost always cer-tainly fall on stone-deaf ears. The Doc is a man of honeyed words, and the sting to those words is right here, right now. Comatose in that knowledge I am resigned to the fact that our six months will be exactly that – these people are not the kind to let hired guns over-winter on the slate. I swig down my beer and watch as the hunter-cum-gamekeeper-cum-groundsman, the one with the high-powered rifle slung over his shoulder, leads us to the conservatory. They have some kind of exotic plant affair going on, for rainy days I suppose, of which there are a lot in this neck of the woods. They have imported large boulders from Death Valley to add to the ambience, probably even a few death adders or sidewinders, who knows? It is humid in here, as sticky and cloying as midday in Jakarta.

The Brother meanwhile, is as hammered as Boris Yeltzin at a KGB function for war widows but the Jo'ster is doing her best to impress, imprisoned as she is in the 5-star hotel-sized kitchen that Zsa Zsa is showing her around. They are going to cater for receptions from this kitchen that could easily fit the brigade from the Sheraton. It is dinnertime, thank god, although the Brother should have 'Nil By Mouth' written on his chart as he is barely coherent and badly affected by the laws of gravity. Luckily, Lurch is at hand, and he eases the jibbering wreck into a seat with armrests – which is a good fucking move, as the Brother saw the remains of this particular day off long before the sun departed for Stockholm. The Hunter, however, is into the juice big time, sucking hard on the neck of any and every opened bottle within his vicinity. After dinner, he announces in a slurred Botswana brogue, he will take us on the Tour around the grounds. I nod encouragingly because the Tour sounds one hell of a lot easier to handle than the hot tub – a matter that mercifully hasn't yet been broached. But perhaps that's only because Zsa Zsa has been slaving the entire afternoon over a roast ostrich and enough spuds to feed the west coast of Ireland.

Zsa Zsa refers to this bird, a bird with more stubble than Lily Savage, as Sweetpea. Most likely this fucker was still carefree and gay yesterday, out on the faux savannah, before that brute of a Hunter pumped it full of buckshot. That'd explain the feathers all over the verandah and in the Brother's wispy tufts of hair. When Zsa Zsa finally totters in with the gigantic bird it almost slips her grasp before it reaches the table ... but Lurch does what he's paid for. Zsa Zsa precedes to whip a mean 40-inch carving knife up a rusty steel, then calmly announces: And after tea we'll all decamp to the hot tub!

I grab a stray beer from the Hunter, knock it back hard and, stifling a belch, say, Oh Jesus, I'd love to but ...

Oh, no buts, dear! she says, picking out shot from the bird. We've got a trunk full of bathers for those who forgot their cozzies!

I shoot a furtive glance across to Jo who receives my mental Morse even though she has an ostrich leg in one hand and a bottle of suds in the other. No, I can't, I had minor surgery this afternoon! I respond gaily, and everyone, including the Jo'ster, goes as quiet as a Sunday night in Nelson – except for the Brother who is sliding forward into his mashed pumpkin while making death-throe gurglings. After his head is snapped backwards by the Hunter, quiet reigns as the throng hangs on my next utterance until ... the phone rings. The Doc is up quicker than an Afghan camel rider. His face peers at mine. It's for you, he says, amazed with the notion.

It is that crooked car saleswoman Helga, all befuddled over some extra-blanket deposit screw-up. She has inadvertently saved my neck by ringing now, while also giving me an opportunity to impress with my diplomacy. I concentrate on looking serious, managerial in fact, and from what she is babbling on about I ascertain that it's been my balls-up. So what? When you have a hot-tub session at the forefront of your mind you cannot be expected to stipulate whether someone has paid for an extra blanket or not. I dig my way out of that situation only to be immediately faced with another – like this fucking ostrich, I suppose.

I could drop Helga into the shit bog right now but I see no point, so instead pass it off as just another cock-up. Which leads Zsa Zsa to a long-winded explanation of how she became the Madam of Mercenaries in the backpacking industry, and why she still owns the best little hostel in town. Sweet Jesus, what a bunch of sanctimonious bullshit. But whatever, it is all using up valuable time, as will the consumption of this much white meat and metallic-tasting stuffing.

We tuck in while the Doc slyly brings the conversation round to my forays into day-surgery techniques. I think on my feet, well, my butt actually, telling them I had to have a rather indelicate tattoo removed from my, uh, nether regions on account of my beloved's angst over me having another woman's name on my person. How very interesting, Zsa Zsa says, as she sucks up a few more feathers, and what was the name?

Good Lord, is so much data really necessary? I feel myself redden slightly, even L'Oréal strawberry blonde can't stop you blushing. But then my offsider, on my wavelength as submariners say, pitches in with: Zeta. What the?

Was she Russian? Zsa Zsa asks. I am watching the Brother slurp gravy straight from his plate without the use of cutlery, fermenting as he masticates.

Uh, no, Belgian actually, I finally reply. This white-hot lie is scalding my English-rose cheeks.

Well, Zsa Zsa says at last, can't you wear a waterproof dressing?

For the love of Beelzebub, I have to end this madness now.

She was a cheap whore anyhow, my Jo Buck says, now rather enjoying the deception.

Who? Zsa Zsa asks.

Zeta, that's who.

This woman is purely a figment, you understand, dear reader. There is no goddamned Zeta and there never was, all there was down there is what God, in his twisted way, ordained to bestow upon me.

I don't think you're supposed to get them wet, the Doc says between mouthfuls of whole-berry glaze and bird feet pieces.

Zetas? Zsa Zsa replies.

We all look at her, and then everyone but me looks at me. No, you can't, I finally say.

It ain't what's down there that bothers me, that can take care of itself. It's what's up top. And I'm sure it would bother them too. Anyway, the ruse has run its sleazy course and I am excused bathing duties ... but not Jo. These people are mad for flesh and cleavage, as inscrutable and insatiable as Hugh Hefner. Thankfully the Doc don't wanna double dip either coz he is full to bursting. And besides, there's still the Tour.

We do inside first, which is a relief. It means stairs and exercise, and after a meal that size it will certainly aid the digestion, get the old wind tunnel working if you know what I mean. We all go up apart from the Brother; he is still between the flags slowly drowning in his own gravy.

Morticia is explaining that each guest boudoir has been decorated in a distinctive theme. That way, she assures us, as the Hunter lets go a thunderous anal expulsion that any rhino out on the veldt would be chuffed with, guests can select a room to suit their moods.

The first room is King Tut's tomb – so realistic that Howard

Carter himself would be hoodwinked into believing it was the real deal. Where the hell did they find all this shit? The Marie Antoinette room is some kind of French bordello with enough chintz and swishy satin to satisfy every cross-dresser's fantasies; and even a mirror on the ceiling. Further along we are in a Disneyland Jungle Room, but it contains more than the bare necessities of life; the bed cover is tribal and the four-poster has vines entwined around it, just the right environment for that pantless bear Baloo and his jungle boy to get more deeply acquainted. And then we're in Ali Baba's den, the Arabian knights kasbah, all cushions on the floor and Bedouin tenting. If you're feeling like a filthy thief, this is the place you'd want to hang your caftan for the night.

I am mentally exhausted after this whirlwind tour de force through opulence, as brain-funked as a peyote-smokin' Mexican, and while I can appreciate the extent of these facilities, it's the lack of faculties governing them that's gnawing away at me. But yowser. There's more. We are still required on the grounds tour. We wait on the verandah while the taped sounds of jungle beasts echo from the wall-mounted speakers. I can understand why the Knights Templar got in a sacking kinda mood. The Hunter turns up driving a buggy, like one of those golf carts but with a huge spotlight on the front, and everyone climbs aboard the ride except Zsa Zsa who is staying behind to whip up a bombe Alaska. Jo sits reluctantly in the back clutching an ostrich bone as we head off, at 5 ks an hour, like Bob Hope at a pro-am golf tournament. I'm hoping some bug-eyed wild cat will spring from the undergrowth with fangs bared and for the Hunter to leap from our barely moving buggy and grapple with it a while in a beast-versus-man-epic-tug-of-war scene. But no, alas, it is like driving Miss Daisy, only Miss Daisy would be far more entertaining. When you have seen one water feature you have pretty much seen them all, any connoisseur of water sports will tell you the same.

The whole notion of budget accommodation is being wantonly debased up here on the savannah. This is a refuge for over-monied types tired of slumming it as an aphrodisiac. Up here they can buy whatever they please, probably whomever they please, and that kind of business always leaves a leadish taste in my mouth – or maybe that's just from the buckshot that was still in that fucking bird. I cannot overindulge any longer, not on the sights or sounds of unabashed wealth or pistachio ice-cream richly slathered in meringue. Not even the pyrotechnics can lift my pecker; the drugs have pretty much seen to that I'm afraid. I am overwhelmed with joy when it is time to leave, and as I grab Jo and sprint to Dick's waiting limo I can still hear Zsa Zsa bemoaning the fact that we didn't get wet together. What with these grounds, these rooms, her fetish for water sports and the size of her baked dinners, the Chippendales would make better dinner guests.

I turn the key and nothing happens; there are no warm fuzzy lights of communion on the dash. Feeling seditious, a warm rage dropping over me like a kimono, I begin to wind up some choice expletives – when suddenly the Doc is at my window smiling his televangelist smile.

Need a shove? he enquires in the gloom.

I do not need to answer because the Doc goes on to explain that this old piece of crap was his very own Love Wagon for many a hot summer … Dick got himself a real bargain. Keeping it in the family is better – which is what Charlie M espoused too. The Doc, Lurch and the Hunter give us the big heave-ho and I pop first, there is life in the old girl yet. I am in fourth before the native-bird enclosure, as high-octane and lead-footed as any rev head on a Saturday night. We hit bitumen again within record time and the old car swings across the oncoming lanes before I wrestle it back into a legal driving situation. We say nothing on the bad acid trip back, not a single word. It has all been, well, it's hard to fully explain just what it has been. The one thing it hasn't been is boring.

You cannot say, among all the things that you could say, that these people are squares. No, sir, in Kiwi land they breed 'em ostentatious, yeah, shagadelic, baby. We rumble into the back lot with enough juice to splutter into Dick's 'reserved' bay. I turn it off and rip out a handful of cables which I plonk on the desk for Helga to deal with. If Dick ain't quick she'll have flogged 'em before sun-up.

16.

Bouncing Balls, Broads and Czechs

All is quiet in the Hood this morning and I have checked out the god squad. They are off to the nether regions to continue the good fight; two-up on rented choppers. But other strange shit is occurring; the hostelling industry hasn't gotten where it is today by squatting on its arse.

We are expecting an invasion of 30-odd assorted Czech firefighters and police, in town for the world Olympiad of police, firefighters and other assorted public servile types. Many, I am sure, will be looking for defection as well as alloy-plated medallions. And good luck to them. I have considered defection, maybe to a country where you queue for potatoes and vodka once a week. Instead I am stuck in the middle of god's country, shepherding a flock not even the dumbest of shepherds would consider tending. Will I ever find someplace to call home? Will I always be at the beck, call and mercy of other people? Like this cute girl beside me on the stairs who young Jo has taken a dislike to, over nothing at all – apart from the fact the girl asked to talk to me in private.

Think about it a moment. What on earth could I get up to? I really don't see how a person born male but who became a woman and is now acting as a man again (to stop from starving to death on the cold streets of Christchurch, NZ) could get into anything but serious trouble with an unnamed girl who may, or may not, have designs on me, sexual or otherwise. This girl presumes I'm a man. I figure she'd be mighty surprised if we got to fondling someplace out of the way, like the old linen room, and the first thing her hand found was a breast. That's what I said to Jo a few days ago when I laughed it off the first time. But there is no such thing as common sense when a relationship contains four tits.

If I ever had male privilege then I didn't appreciate it and now I have no privileges whatsoever. All I have is strapped-down tits, a bunch of keys jiggling on my hip, a wanton smile, and a lover who thinks I'll hump anything with a pulse.

I have to make excuses to the girl on the stairs today as I'm afraid CCTV footage might incriminate me when Jo rewinds and watches and I'll be forced to defend a conversation caught on tape that could be misconstrued. It's embarrassing being on the stairs in close proximity to a young, far-from-home traveller of the fairer sex, when I'm of that sex myself but in the throes of deception. I smile at her, but in a manly no-nonsense way. God knows what the poor bewildered girl is thinking.

There is always something happening in the world of budget travel to draw your mind from grappling with dilemmas concerning physical attraction. There is news straight off the mojo wires from a desperate goon up the road. Somewhere on the South Island of New Zealand there is a busload of well-manicured Japanese looking for beds. They are here to whale watch, maybe do a spot of harpooning, grab a movie and a couple of Maori geishas, and get down and grubby with the local fauna. Their previous booking has gone arse over tit through incompetence. Before the Doc can hit the Emergency Reservations button, I am already waist-deep in musical beds.

I see that it can be done; but just because it *can* be done doesn't mean that it *will* be. To get something as intricate as this to work you need all hands on deck, and you need to be able to rely on those hands to put into practice your well-versed theory. The hands I have at my disposal are not best served re-arranging dorms, or, indeed, whole landings. They are idle mischievous hands that spend more time hauling booty to unwarranted vehicles than turning beds. I explain this to the Doc, in a roundabout sort of way. You know I have 30 Czechs arriving any goddamned minute, I say, and – don't forget – there are five Canadians and quite possibly a delegation from Slovenia.

The wayward girl turns up and starts leaning seductively on the counter making eyes at me, or maybe the Doc? Nope, it's me.

Do you know her? the Doc asks me.

Hell no, I tell him, as she asks the Doc if she can talk to me in private.

I brush her off and turn my attention to my master. He cannot expect me to show a busload of hungry Japanese down to the half-lit delights of subterranean living, can he? Those Japanese might well be used to living in plastic tubes high above the ground in Electric City, but when they are abroad they expect the very best the West has to offer. Which, even at the best of times, ain't one hell of a lot.

You were made for this job, the Doc tells me excitedly. You hijack the cleaners and round up Dick and the Brother, Jo can man the desk and we'll all pitch together.

Well, fine, I tell him, but I'm in charge, okay?

Beds are being stripped faster than you can say, Pass me that bug killer, and all is going well. I have the Czechs pencilled into the third-floor rooms so they can all be together when they alight onto the mean streets and head for the NZ Immigration

Service. The Japs I'm gonna put in the second-floor annex, crammed in like a bait ball dodging hungry dolphins. I see that my shadow has returned. This girl is beginning to give me the heebies.

I walk around, jangling keys. She follows at a safe distance, pouting.

You know her? a cleaner asks.

Hell, no.

I am a born organizer, goddamned Martha Stewart on amphetamines, apart from when some screwball chick bursts in on my life and I fall apart. Now my problems are multiplying. When I first sight Zsa Zsa I think it is merely another after-dinner hallucination. I have been suffering them a lot since that chow down. But no, she is here, in situ as they say at NASA, in all of her heirloom and divorce-settlement finery. Why, oh dear god, would she choose today to impose her overbearing split-personality on me? I know what is going to happen even before she does. When Zsa Zsa is around, you can bet your last rouble your dreams will go to shit in a spin-dryer faster than in Harare on Election Day. She has some flouncy dog loping along behind her like a wolf that's eaten one too many hippies and has picked up the vibe. This New Age capitalist is all love and peace, incense-burning after-life and you-get-what-you-give karma. I know her type; she wears beads and sandals and never shaves under her arms, she is a hundred-per-cent kosher vegan and has two dozen stray cats to feed. And, for the love of Krishna, she is carrying what appears to be a very large pack of permanent markers as she touches the flimsy walls here and there for kinetic experiences and she has instructed Dick to locate faux shrubbery.

I am becoming disorganized. Maybe I ought to just grab that girl's hand and drag her off to an unoccupied room and …

Zsa Zsa is in a lather. It could well be that the scene up at the mansion, or should I say, the non-scene, has turned this madam of hostelling off me. When I start to sneak away I spy the Doc on hands and knees like some grovelling pig dog. Jesus, these people are weird. I glance at my watch – okay, the watch I found in the kitchen yesterday – and even though it is still on Seoul time I can work out that within the half hour the Japanese will be rushing into reception taking a hundred thousand photographs of the Brother for the record.

I slip unnoticed into the safe haven of the laundry. Occasionally I spy palm trees sliding past the doorway, on their way to reception. I hear the hippy, with all her tinkering bells it is like being in pixie heaven. I discover folding laundry is remedial. It has a calming effect on even the most jittery of nerves and the heat from the tumble dryers is soothing. Zsa Zsa storms in and discovers me buried in an avalanche of sheets. She says she's found me help. How odd, I think, that Zsa Zsa would bother if I had help or not. Then I see that my help for the morning is the girl who is always asking me to talk in private, who whispers seductive words on the stairs.

When will the rooms be ready? Zsa Zsa asks me. It's my guess there won't be rooms ready by this afternoon when the Czechs arrive and start bouncing. But I don't tell her that. I tell her they'll be ready soon now that I've got help.

An hour later I hear shrieking. It could be anyone in a place like this so I'm not unduly perturbed. Then I see blurred shapes running here and there, one I recognize as the Doc. Next, to my complete surprise, a smiling Japanese man appears in the laundry doorway, flashes me a toothy white smile, takes my photograph and bows courteously. What the fucking hell? Then, the Doc is back, white as bleach powder.

Where is he? he asks breathlessly.

Who? I reply.

That Japanese man, you seen him?

The little guy with the pearly whites?

Him. Which way'd he go? he demands. I shrug and he disappears. After this, I don't hear or see anyone for around an hour judging by the shadows on the laundry wall ... although I can smell permanent marker and hear those bells.

The Jo'ster appears, chomping on a hot dog. How's it going out there? I ask her. She starts to speak, then sees my new friend and she's gone. Ah shit. There goes my goddamned lunch.

I'll go buy you lunch, the girl offers. At least if she goes to get lunch she won't be in here making things hotter than they already are. Off she goes, cute arse that ... At least I get lunch, and a smile.

Think I'd get a job here? the girl says.

Not if I can help it, I reply.

Two hours later, back in the Hole, the register looks like Hirohito's map of the Pacific in 1945. There is crossing out everywhere, and the Doc is hunched over it like an imperial idiot savant desperate to pinpoint just exactly where it all went wrong – although I doubt that even John Nash himself could figure this one out.

Half of the hostel still doesn't have made-up rooms, and we are only twenty minutes from zero hour number two. All we are left with is the what-might-have-beens, and about 30 fake palm trees Zsa Zsa had brought that make the place look like Bangkok Airport. I don't know what to do next, where to start cleaning up this carnage, and I haven't seen Dick since eleven bells. There are Zsa Zsa's happy slogans daubed on every wall. Those pick-you-up ditties that are supposed to improve your mood, like, Every cloud has a silver lining. Shit like that, oh, and from what I saw at least three yards of the second-floor landing carpet has been ripped up and laid back down in an unsafe manner. I do not pry, these are no longer my concerns; all I need to know right now is who is making up all these fucking rooms?

And I find out straight from the horse's mouth. I am the prize prick just delegated that filthy chore because the Brother is half-cut in the TV lounge, Dick is in the sack with a cruciate ligament injury, the cleaners can't be called back in under in-house rule number 408, and the Doc is required at an urgent accountancy meeting. Meaning Jo will have to run the desk, leaving only yours very fucking truly with idle hands.

That's almost thirty fucking rooms! I tell him angrily.

Well, just make up enough to cover the Czechs and try to do as many as possible between now and the end of shift. Leave the rest for the cleaners tomorrow. Besides, you've got help.

And with that the Doc is off, satchel under one arm and the abacus under the other. I wait ten minutes for Jo to arrive, and she does so as casual-as-you-fucking-like. She has dyed her hair jet black – very Japanese. She scowls at me, inscrutable, and rips open a bag of cheese puffs she's just half-inched from the shelf, and says, Have fun.

Oh sure, I have to go make up rooms, I tell her disconsolately.

Tough life, eh? How's your friend?

How should I know?

She got a name?

I never asked.

Well, off you go then, Mother Theresa.

Oh, very funny, I'm sure.

Making beds with a girl who has designs on your body, or some small part of it (and in my case it would be a very small part), is challenging, but finally it is done. I walk around opening doors and closing doors and being philosophical. I am so philosophical I ought to run my own cult somewhere out on the Plains. You can get a lot of chicks that way, I hear. At last I make my decision and go and find no name in the laundry to tell her there can never be anything meaningful between us, only why did I use the word meaningful? That could be misunderstood. She says she knows that but her motto is, If at first you don't succeed ... I stop her there. I'm familiar with the saying.

What about a kiss for old time's sake? she asks.

What old times? I say.

She shrugs. Just one, just so I'll know.

Know what?

What it is like to kiss you, stupid!

No tongue though, okay?

Okay!

God, what a day. Everyone has the shits with me and all I did was get up. The collateral damage of life is like scattered debris after a high-speed head-on. I'm going down to see young Jo and grovel about on all fours just like the Doc was doing earlier when I laughed at him. Who would want to be a man? I ask you.

17.

Reindeer Games

So, this is where they hide it all ...

I am in the inner sanctum of the cleaners, clutching the keys to everywhere, and only now am I discovering just how many doors they open. There are more sunglasses here than you would find in the cloakroom at an Ibiza club. There are all manner of pilfered paraphernalia, not so well concealed, just waiting to be removed. Cleaning house is a lucrative business. This box here marked 'Detergent', is actually half full of small electrical goods: personal fans, electric razors, dildos, travel clocks, Walkmans, headphones, the whole gamut of discarded personal accoutrements from those in a hurry to catch a big bird. Over here is a boxful of personal travel diaries and around there a stash of pens, combs, hairbrushes, clips and hair ties – various hues of hair still attached. There is a laundry basket crammed with socks and jocks, lots of half full packets of rubbers, enough pharmaceuticals to start a crack lab, and all manner of other shit stacked and packed every goddamned where. But alas, insofar as I can ascertain, there are no actual room-cleaning products.

I mean to take this up with certain people ... or maybe I don't. Maybe I'll just gatecrash this sticky-fingered menagerie of crooked cleaners and pilfer straight from the pilferers –

I mean, they could hardly lodge a formal complaint, huh? I am interested in these locked doors and what they hide but my most pressing concern is the doors that are still wide open awaiting the gentle touch of a cleaning genie. I cannot waste more time ferreting around in here, I have a whole night shift to do that; what I need to do now is backtrack to Dick's cupboard and lift his bucket o' supplies and grab me a few perfectly folded sets of sheets and do the hustle, baby.

On the way down I am rudely accosted by an American girl – or at least she looks American and somewhat deranged, as is customary for Shermans abroad. She is keen to manhandle the first gook jangling keys she can find. I do not recognize her so she must be a new arrival in the Land of the Long White Cloud and I shall do my utmost to quell any feelings of anxiety she may have – until, that is, she opens her cake-hole. She does not even say excuse me. No sir, she is obviously from the East Coast, maybe Boston or some other pilgrim town of the Union, judging by her caustic accentuations. If I am understanding her correctly, it would appear some light-fingered arsewipe has swiped the braided cord she uses to keep her glasses about her person – although, that begs the question of why the cord and glasses were separated in the first place. I ask where she last saw the cord and she says in the restroom – she has obviously been well-schooled. Maybe you flushed it accidentally? I suggest, and she shoots me a look. In her own black-eyed-pea way she sees herself as the quintessential seasoned traveller, although between you and me, I would have no hesitation in laying off bets that she has never been further from home than Wal Mart. Still, that does not infer that I should treat her as a numbnut, no indeed, for all I know she might have already circumnavigated the globe eight times in a kayak; although when I spy the braided glasses cord around her neck, I seriously doubt it. I point out this fact to her without indulging in gloating; we can all make the silliest of mistakes when we are disoriented.

She has the gall to accost me. What about the goddamned spectacles, huh? The ones that cost six hundred dollars.

You mean those ones, on your head? I reply. And still she does not feel the least bit stupid, she is in fact blind to the obvious, which is that she is making a spectacle of herself.

I do not have the time or the patience to partake of any further hostility; the girl is quite obviously a few stars short of a spangled banner and it is amazing that she has made it this far without being murdered. So I leave her there, the American psycho, contemplating yet another Cosmo light-bulb moment. Jesus, and they say we blondes are dumb.

I go back upstairs via the other route, just in case the Yankee poikilotherm is still crawling on the stairs waiting to entrap me. The day has been full of drama and I am now content to scrub shitters badly and unblock en-suite drains. Making beds, by the way, is fucking hard work, and struggling with fitted sheets that never quite fit onto two-up bunks is even more of a freaking struggle. Nevertheless, against staggering odds, I begin to make progress.

But hell, it has been the mother of all of the days we have endured so far and it still has several spleen-bursting hours to run. After three rooms my mouth is as dry as Bostonian humour, and my back aches more than Atlas's. Good Christ Almighty, I cannot be this out of condition. I carry on, heaving, groaning and blaspheming anything and anyone, and, as I struggle with a dodgy leg on a double-bed base that refuses to screw back on, I am rudely interrupted by my newly acquired American stalker. This time it is the goddamned heater in her dorm. She has turned it on and now the thing won't desist from rendering her rented abode a furnace. It'll turn itself off after five minutes, I tell her, just don't touch it any more.

But no, simplicity is not her way any more than patience is mine. Reaching boiling point, I let the bed drop and frog-march her to her dorm. How many times have you pressed this button? I ask her, as sweat bubbles on my forehead like some chemistry experiment in fourth form.

Jesus, she shrugs, how should I know, about fifty maybe.

Fifty? I ask her. Can't you read? I point to the sign below the wall heater that states that for comfort and efficiency, the button should be pressed just once, or as many times as is required to facilitate the desired duration of heat. Each press equals five minutes. Fifty fives are 250 minutes, over four hours of overbearing heat – no wonder they refuse to ratify Kyoto.

Look, buddy, you already know I lost my spectacles.

They were on top of your head, for Christ's sake, didn't you look in a mirror?

I already told you – I lost my spectacles!

Okay, okay, this'll take a while to cool down, I tell her while pointing at the heater. I think it automatically shuts off after thirty minutes. How long's it been on now?

Since I arrived in this mangy joint.

Which was?

Hell ... six, seven hours ago.

Bear this in mind, friends: I clearly remember telling the Yankee girl NOT to open the window in her dorm because it was awaiting repair. She called me a doofus, and I've no idea what that means, but I told her to take a walk in the fresh spring air, clear her mind – maybe her veins too – and when she got back the heater would be off and the dorm would have a pleasant, homely kind of ambiance. That's what I told her ...

Downstairs it is all very *Inspector Rex*. There are six men of uniform height, same pallid complexion, wearing 70s sunglasses and cheap suits. An interpreter woman is leaning on the counter talking to the Jo'ster; she looks like that Rusky chick out of that Gere and Willis re-make of *The Jackal*, the one with the scar. Just outside the front doors are 30 rough-house types dragging heavily on aromatic cigarettes. They look like Czechs to me. I go into the Hole and the translator, who speaks better English than that American I've just been dealing with, is listening intently to the book-in procedure. The only part she fails to grasp is the part about MONEY. Apparently the Czech team has been whisked straight from the airport to our door without stopping to exchange either currency or welcomes with the various meet 'n' greet committees. Maybe they can book in, grab a shit, untape all those US dollars they have strapped to various parts of their anatomies, find a place that sells good red meat and cheap women and settle up tomorrow?

Who are *these* people? I ask the translator as I glance nervously at the half dozen Stockingers.

Don't worry about them, she tells me in a deep voice. They're here to see that our team completes its mission.

Its mission, huh? Well, okay, but no one's told me about an extra half dozen bodies that require accommodation. All becomes clear when a black car arrives and the Stockingers leave our fine hostel in unison, first glancing this way and then up and down the street. After this, Team Czech crowd around their interpreter and begin assailing her with throaty queries, which, even in a foreign tongue, resonate with an accusatory tone. Me and the Jo'ster move back from the counter and let them slug it out, there is no need to become involved in some kind of diplomatic incident.

You broke a nail, Jo says to me.

Yeah, making up fucking bunks, I respond.

After a while it seems they are finished; or maybe they've only just started. If they do not get a move on I will have to hand them over to Marlon and then Christ knows what'll happen. I intercede as politely as I can and tell the translator that, really, we ought to be getting this tedious but necessary booking-in procedure started. Dar, dar, she tells me, then tells her charges the same thing, only louder.

I do not know who the Czechs loathe most: the Slovaks, the Russians, or their gatekeepers. They are more than a trifle perturbed over this 'handing over of documentation' procedure and yet I cannot allow them to roam about the joint when I don't know who is who and who is in what bed – Czech-ing up, I guess. It is therefore a surly and long-winded procedure that takes me well past the time Marlon arrives with a side of pickled ham under one arm. He cannot get a berth on a ship outta town until his papers are updated – which is akin to the problem many of these disgruntled Czechs are experiencing.

Finally, give or take a few stragglers who have gone to tramp the streets looking for superior accommodation, I have allo-cated rooms for them all. I am glad to pass all this crap over to Marlon, to be shot of my obligation to serve. I am halfway up the stairs when who should I bump into, or more correctly, who should deliberately bump into me, than an aggrieved American with a chip on both shoulders.

Her window, the one I asked her not to push up if you recall, is now, of course, jammed and her room is cold enough for a polar bear cub. I tell her brusquely to turn the heater on, that'll even up the ambient temperatures. She looks at me with a blank expression as if she has not the slightest notion what the word ambient means.

I have three female cousins who grew up in America. All three, left alone with a globe, a compass and a magnifying glass, could not make their way from A to B in a direct line. I do not know why – the sons and daughters of a nation that is so fond of invading other nations cannot seem to find their way to the ATM from reception. Sooner or later you will be stopped by a disoriented American with no clue whatsoever to where he or she is.

This one knows where she is, or so I'm presuming, and she has decided that she will just carry on behaving the way she does when summering at the Hamptons or wherever she goes. Maybe she thinks I'm the janitor or some other lackey just living to be at her beck and call? I tell her to go downstairs and see the hairy brute manning reception, a monster with hands like his won't need to fetch a stepladder, a hammer and a jar of Vaseline to fix this problem. She has an unzipped sleeping bag wrapped around her, like a big American quilt. I refuse to go through this charade. I am so tired, fatigued to the point of a complete nervous breakdown, grinding my teeth and nibbling skin from my fingertips. This is not how I envisioned this gig panning out, and it ain't even high season.

Her mind is set on filling out a guest complaint sheet (not that we have them) and she takes herself, her bunny slippers, her cup of Gatorade and her bumbag down the stairs to entertain the monster lurking behind the wire mesh. When she first catches a glimpse of Marlon gnawing on a leg of ham she'll probably flip, think that she's stumbled into some Tarantino world of cutthroat madness and, hopefully, she'll CHECK THE HELL OUT!

In the morning the Doc is out back counting cash, licking his finger as he flips through bank notes while keeping both eyes riveted to the two-way mirror. The Doc sees everything; he sees all evil, hears all evil and hears people thinking evil. The Doc is the good young prince of Camelot and maybe he can smooth the American's ruffled feathers. By the time it comes to handover I have still not seen the American girl nor a sign of the Czechs. I am sure that any minute now the Doc is going to slither out from the backroom and ask me about all of these entries that have blank spaces next to them on the register – the spaces in which you usually enter amounts paid.

Jo arrives and I hand her the highlighter, glad to be the hell out of here, but as I'm about to yank open the door I hear some kind of stampede coming from the restaurant, like the first tremulous sounds you hear as the mob flees the bulls in darkest Spain. And talking of Spain, I have not seen young Pedro in quite a while.

It is a charge of the Czech brigade and they are on us before I can make a clean getaway. I find myself dragged back into the milieu like a sinking liner drags down her passengers. Jesus H. This is pissy luck, a streak as odorous and as aureolin as yesterday's ablutions. And talking of those, I wonder if Marlon got to do the shitters this morning? God, I hope so, who knows what those Czechs were eating last night . . .

There is money everywhere, held up in clumps like bidders at a whore market, and the Doc can smell it. He is out of his swivel chair like a district attorney, the V-neck sweater that was seconds ago stylishly draped about his shoulders now just a crumpled heap on the floor. I still plan to make my escape from this mayhem but too many Czechs are leaning against the other side of the door as they struggle to stuff cash through the hatch. This is a blue-collar scrum, ex-Soviet manhood attired in tight, white muscle shirts and regulatory blood-flow-restricting state-issue navy-blue shorts. They all have large moustaches too, as if they have been bred specifically for the purpose of keeping moustaches en vogue – and only Gorbachev knows what potato hour in Prague must be like.

The Doc, a skilled auctioneer, as agile and alert as any ring-master at a circus, is soon in control of the pandemonium. Now for my getaway, I think. I want this goddamned door open. But no, there appears to be new consternation among the Czechs. Something to do with cleavage.

It must be Jo and her black hair and, oh, that rather plunging top she's wearing, the one that accentuates the fact that she is over-stacked up top. The Czechs have stopped prof-fering cash to the Doc and are forming a civil and orderly queue in front of the Jo'ster. This alleviates the strain on the door and I somersault through into the reality of life on the opposite side of the counter. At last I am free, free to flee, to slip away like a thief in the night and deploy my talents to where they are better suited: opportunistic scavenging.

This is my game plan today, to get myself involved in the daily ritual of acquiring lost property for my own ends. Why wait for it to turn up in reception and be labelled and then go through the Doc's '30 days' procedure before lodging a claim? Why indeed, why not just source your goods at the source, go wholesale as they like to say around at the cash 'n' carry.

To do this you have to be where the action is, and between eight and eleven in the mornings the action is above ground floor. It strikes me, as I mosey on upstairs, that on night shift you start checking folks out as early as five in the morning. The cleaners never arrive before eight, which leaves a good three hours – sometimes even more – when a judicious, if not some-what bent, hostel employee could get the jump on his or her colleagues. Well, hello, Teri Louise, welcome back from wherever you've been ... And what is the busiest turnover morning, the day with the greatest rush for departure and early flights, buses, trains? That's right ... Sunday bloody Sunday.

Oi! Dick says to me as I sneak stealthily around the corridors among piles of sheets and split rubbish bags. You seen that Yank broad? Dick is all for picking up foreign tongues.

Nope, I tell him gladly, as I start eyeing up a kill.

She's looking for you, he advises me. She drove Marlon to the brink of insanity all goddamned night with dumbass question after dumbass question.

I shrug, That don't surprise me.

What'cha looking for? he asks suspiciously.

Nothing in particular.

You hear that Marlon found a wallet stuffed full of cash?

Again? How damned freaky is that? I suppose he's handed it in?

Of course he has, Dick tells me. Marlon is as honest as the day is long.

And the days here are fucking long, eh?

Must be from one of those Czechs, Dick decides. Made one hell of a fucken noise last night when they got back from the taverna, singin' the polka or whatever it was.

I never heard them.

Well you wouldn't, not up there in the penthouse.

Say, what is it you actually want, Dick?

Nothing, just keeping you abreast of the news. 'Abreast' get it?

Get what, exactly?

Nothing. Say, your missus is pretty well stacked, huh?

Fucking hell, Dick, don't let her hear you saying stuff like that or you'll be one ball short of a ping-pong set.

He quickly changes tack. She knows a bit about computers, don't she?

She's techno-literate, yeah.

She couldn't teach me to surf could she, ain't that what they call it?

Not when I tell her you've bin perving on her chest she won't . . . the only surfing you'll be doing after I tell her that is on morphine to ease the pain up at the ICU.

Nah, c'mon, I didn't mean nothing . . . she's sweet as, your missus – a real diamond, I'm always telling the boss that.

I bet you are, look, I'll ask her, but for now, piss off, okay?

The thought of Dick ogling my babe's top shelf has distracted me. And then there's fucking 'Las Vegas Marlon' with more good luck than a whole commune of Buddahs – Jesus, what a fucking gyp. All I've found on night shift is a pool of puke. This shitload of monster mash gives me a tom-tom-like headache, so I go lay down before I whittle away too much of my allotted break getting nowhere fast.

On the register I see that Jo has been indulging her passion for art; there is a hammer and sickle by the Czech's dorm, a moose that must signify Canadians, and another moose . . .

That's not a moose, she tells me, that's a reindeer. There's two Laplanders up there or at least there were. No one's seen nor heard of them for two days.

Probably absconded already, I tell her, like Pedro. You seen Pedro lately?

I think he checked out, gone to live with a guy in Maryvale or someplace.

How'd you know so much?

I study, darling, that's what I do.

Well, you've got the time, I suppose, down here in la-la land, I reply as we watch the Doc vanish into the hailstorm, plastic bag over his barnet, sack full of cash under his arm. These Kiwis don't let the wrath of Allah deter them from their rightful business. Anyhow, I tell her, maybe you ought to attire yourself more adequately. Up top.

What?

Well, it's just that your, uh ... well, babe, your décolletage is causing hallucinations with the men folk in this joint ...

Who's been talking about my tits? The Doc?

Jesus H., no. The Doc don't have time for those kind of indulgences. The Doc is a thigh man, I'd wager. Nah, let's just say you got fans in all the wrong places, okay?

It's that sleazy old pervert Dick, isn't it? That old bugger'll get a knee in the date, that'll cure his wanderin' eyes.

And talking about sleazy perverts, and Dick, the old sod wants me to ask you if you'll teach him how to surf?

Surf what?

Well I doubt it's the fucking Avon!

Do you really think someone like Dick ought to be let loose on the www?

Personally, yes. Or in the WWF.

I am alone, an unchained melody, working under instructions left on some kind of FAQ manual for guests, which seems like an okay idea, or at least it would be if all of them could read. I have my head down and cheeks up, afraid that any minute the American will come down with some new deadbeat request. As I work I find the wallet, the one Marlon 'discovered', and it is Czech property. That driver's licence is straight out of the KGB's most-wanted archive. And, good god, there's something like 700 greenbacks stuffed in it, which makes me ponder how come travellers, and especially just-freed ones, are so loose with their bread and ... what's the go here? Say it ain't claimed, what's the deal?

There is always much to ponder, like this wallet, the merits of low-slung tops, why I'm sitting here staring at the CCTV while it plays nothing but white noise, when *I'll* be able to wear low-slung tops again instead of four layers of polar fleece to hide my curves. All of these post-it notes every damned where. Dick stalking victims in cyberspace, Marlon with his flukey streak of cosmic interference ...

Another fierce shower of hailstones shatters my meditations, and then the phone, which I pick up although I'm sure it's wise not to answer phones during severe electrical activity. It's the Doc keen to know if anyone's turned up for the very wallet I'm fondling.

No, I tell him, and before I can delve into the claims procedure, the line goes dead – maybe the Doc has just been struck down with a golf ball-sized hailstone outside the quick deposit slot?

That'd be Czechmate for sure!

18.

One Indian Doesn't Make a Summer

Oh ye of little faith, this is no time to abandon the good ship sinking fast. High season looms like a ghoulish spectre in the night and those with a piss-weak disposition are ditching overboard. In the hostelling industry, this means part-timers or, as they so adeptly call them around these parts, casuals.

After our two days off cruising pubs and vintage fash stores, we are plopped back into the giant toilet bowl of hostel life with a vicious expulsion of flatulence. The Doc is edgy, like he always is at this precarious cusp of the seasons. Some of his staff or, more accurately, his ex-Soviet staff, have vanished into the funk. First Helga, after she was nabbed by consumer affairs and charged by the fraud squad, and then Marlon who has finally secured a berth on a Latin American-registered transport on its way to the far-flung reaches of the Rim. It is all lavatorial jibes today, my friends, like cisterns, U's, rods, crap, lids, rims and Delhi belly.

We have Indians in town. When you receive your first Indians of the season, you can be assured that the vast mob of filthy travellers isn't too far behind, rosary beads jangling, crabs biting. Indians herald spring in the hostel trade, they also prelude what is known as the Time of Risky Business. I have had occasion to partake of the visual and aromatic delights of the Subcontinent myself, and I can tell you that the old adage of when in Rome bears no relevance whatsoever to when in India. You can be hassled and hustled into an early grave in a place like that, even if the spicy bacteria don't consume you from the inside first. There is no such thing as peace in India, not the kind of tranquillity or room to breathe or deliberate that we First World folks so admire; no, sir, India moves along at a pace that would frighten the living shit out of most people. Even if you are fortunate enough to survive extended hospitalization, if the beggars don't fleece you of everything bar your soul (which the voodoo men will pick up cheap anyhow), if you aren't struck by a runaway moped or a charging steer with its nuts hog-tied in rubber bands, the public transport system will all but see you off.

It is worth bearing this in mind when the first smiling Indian face appears at the reception window to complain vehemently about the not-quite-perfect sewer system. It would be no surprise to some more travelled types if I was of a mind to tell this jerk to take a hike – having myself been once made to squat over a hole in the ground in rural India. But alas, with the Very Reverend Dr Good Intentions leering through the two-way, I have to be more circumspect. So, I'll see how we can help, sir.

Don't forget, there is no more Marlon with his big red hands – all there are now are rods, a whole Indian family, and five Canadians who look as if they have recently undergone some off-the-record suction-cup treatment performed by an unlicenced natural therapy practitioner, the kind who has a large but empty waiting room with one of those pre-war radio sets playing nothing but EVPs.

I might have some empathy with the Canadians when their turn to gripe arrives, having spent yesterday in the boondocks at a medical centre getting my half-yearly hormone implant for less than the cost of a good milking goat. This is what I like about New Zealand, among many things. Over here you can just rock up with a referral and your friendly GP will have no hesitation in slicing you up for the sake of womanhood. That is the way things ought to be done in a civilized world. Okay, so I needed three stitches, but that is a small price to pay for such service.

I am in some pain around the groin area, however, and must avoid all strenuous tasks, except for verbal ones. I mean to ask the Doc about that wallet, but first I have to speak with our friends from Calcutta. They've blocked up the shitter in their room and, seeing there are eight of them, I can't even begin to imagine what kind of hell that looks like. After I calm their jittery minds with the assurance that a registered plumber will soon be up there with 50 metres of good quality New Zealand tubing – to shove their fetid waste out into the pristine waters – I turn my attention and my aching nether regions to the red-welted Canadians, who are all the build of a stereotypical lumberjack.

I am no trained physician and can't be sure what's caused their sudden outbreak of hives, but as a hostel manager I am aware that foreign types can be unduly affected by all manner of local parasites and nematodes. Just as I am flipping through the Yellow Pages to find a nearby surgery the Doc summons me quietly to a back room, where he whispers he has been studying my performance for training and customer relations purposes. While he has no complaint over my handling of matters so far, he does wish to impart into my brain that past experience has shown him how to spot an outbreak of bugs. I think he means flu and suchlike, but no, that will come later. The bugs he is referring to now, in a church voice, are the ones that crawl.

As I prepare to shriek, he clamps one soft hand over my

mouth and drags me further back into the organizational hub of our fine hostel. Don't let on to those guys, he whispers in my ear, and my silent nodding allows him to let me breathe again. He puts one finger to his own lips and tells me almost in cipher that this kind of problem is quite common, all that's needed is to find a ruse so we can relocate the Canadians then ring the Bug Man, who knows how to deal with these outbreaks discreetly. I am to engineer the ruse and my boss will make the Call from a secret line. I had never realized that hostelling and working for the CIA had so much in common.

I have received my orders from the top dog and I am expected to carry them out. This is what the world of employment entails: complete subservience to the greater good, or parts thereof. So I go back out and smile at my scratching Canadian friends, who will be somewhat disadvantaged in today's games at the uptown Olympiad. Hell, what kind of a yarn can I spin these woodchoppers? I am still smiling gormlessly, as my mind suddenly goes as blank as an Etch-a-Sketch that's been shaken one too many times. They are all staring at me suspiciously, the cent is about to drop I'm sure . . .

I am saved by the rude interruption of a girl from the eastern seaboard of the United States of America who, like the rest of her country folk, has no time to waste waiting for Canadian wasters to get to the crux of the matter. That has always been the way, even when Trudeau was prime minister.

Good morning, madam, I tell her cheerfully, and she is momentarily taken aback by the warmth of my servility. She has lost her room key, and before she can start laying into me big time with a whole honey pot of lame excuses I have quelled her anxieties with a quick call to the Doc out back. Look, I tell him, I have to let this young lady back into her room – you couldn't handle things here a mo', could you?

In an instant I have grabbed my keys and am off. Sweet Mary, what goddamned good providence. I let the befuddled one back into her abode away from home with a pleasant 'you have a nice day now' to which she has no response. Then I decide that as I'm upstairs I might just as well take my fucking time going back down. So I do. I walk around whistling a few bars of some Bryan Adams' tune – he was a Canuck too.

There is still the shitter, however, the one blocked to the rim with torn-up newspaper and bogus identity documents, not to mention very pungent subcontinentel droppings. I can smell it here, fifteen rooms away, drifting through the place like cow shite on a sultry afternoon in downtown Calcutta. I detour knowing full well that the last time this joint saw a licensed plumber was in the great flood. With any luck that halfwit the Brother will soon be dispatched up here with a set of rods and a stupid grin painted on his face; and why the hell not? He is doing nothing but moulding that reception sofa to the contours of his rather sumptuous derriere.

Today is like a game of chess and I am undoubtedly a pawn. The Brother of course is the rook, given that he can only move in a straight line, and El Dick is a knight, even with a gammy leg he can leap his enemies whenever he chooses. The Doc has to be a bishop as that fits in nicely with the religious angle we're peddling in this memoir, and Zsa Zsa, well, she's the queen. As a pawn, my sole purpose in this game is to strike down as many pieces as I can en route to the end zone, where not only will I have then scored a touchdown for pawnkind everywhere but, as in all good fairy tales (or even real-life tales of the gender confused), I shall receive my just desserts and be made a queen myself! Yes, it all fits, I realise and finally wind my way back downstairs via the block and I see her, the queen.

The van is in the backyard, its rear doors wide open, and through the filthy glass I can see the hobbling hobbit deep in animated conversation with his mistress. Now what the fuck is she doing here AGAIN, and just what in the hell is that cranky old bastard whispering into her shell-like? Well, it ain't sweet nothings. How I wish I was deaf and had learned to lip read, a skill like that'd come in real handy in a profession like this. There's some other goon I don't immediately recognize, and then him and tricky Dicky start hauling something outta the back of the van – something all wrapped up in polythene. Ah, Jesus fucking Christ, and me with a half hour of my stint still to go . . .

Back in the hole the Doc is under artillery attack from the Canucks. They have sensed he's trying to pull a flanker, their hackles raised by that idiot Aussie who is still hanging around like cheap scent on a discarded fur coat – although I'd guess for not much longer after he's blundered into the cross-counter shenanigans and dropped the B-word. The mere mention of the B-word sends everyone into a state of agitation, and especially Canucks – those folks aren't hot on bugs of any kind. No sooner can you say flapjacks, than they are all downstairs with maple-leafed rucksacks slung in a very YMCA manner over their broad shoulders, demanding adequate compensation. The Doc fights on gamely though; pound for pound he's gotta be one of the best fly-by-night-weights in the hostelry business.

I listen in as the Doc tries to explain in his calmest tone that bugs don't necessarily originate in-house, that they're more commonly brought by travellers. That don't wash with the Canucks, the insinuation that they're hauling critters as well as phobias around.

As they troop out, Dick and the other goon I spotted in the

backyard crash through the front doors hauling something bulky. Lady Zsa Zsa of the lamp is just behind them, full of instructions as per fucking usual. Dick almost goes arse over tit in the plastic plant display and only just remembers to silence his cursing about the moron who put them there – because that same moron is right behind him. Finally he gives up the ghost and collapses in the foyer gripping his knee and moaning like a just-whupped dog. Everyone rushes to his aid, apart from me.

I know exactly what is coming next – and that is me on one end of a brand-new sofa bed that has to be heaved up to the first-floor TV lounge; it is item one of six. This'll rip my stitches out for sure. Within nanoseconds I'm wedged into the landing alcove by Einstein's theory of relativity, the dumb brute strength of the idiot on the other end and by my own doing. Then I see the Jo'ster. She is less than happy with the fact I am doing man's work. Fucking-A, me too, I gasp at her, but the muscle-bound lump below me is still shoving like a demented elephant. We have quite a crowd now on the small dog-leg landing. There is yours truly, Jo, the American girl chomping on a brownie, and now the Indian patriarch who feels this is a proper time to accost me again about still-blocked shit holes. Then I hear the tomcat-like cries of Zsa Zsa from below, telling me in no uncertain tones to shake my tush. Above me, at last, I spy at least ten Czech firefighters in white muscle shirts and tightly tailored shorts. I am free to breathe again, before Zsa Zsa can abuse me further. I broker a deal with them and suddenly my sofa bed-moving dilemma is flushed away. Which only leaves Gandhi and his non-flushing problem, oh, and the big sweating guy with the breathing apparatus and the two heavy tanks strapped to his bent back.

He is the plumber? Gandhi asks me.

Sure, I tell him, don't worry now, okay? He nods, reassured, and leaves.

That's not the plumber! the Doc tells me. That's Jean Claude the Bug Man.

Well where's the fucking plumber? You did call one, didn't you?

Of course he didn't, not with overbearing Imelda on-site. The Doc would rather spend the rest of his morning waist-deep in excrement than risk the wrath of his mistress for forking out dough to solve a problem she already pays him in kind to remedy. That is how those kinda set-ups work; one minute you're on top and the next you're on your hands and knees grovelling around like the Gimp. Who cares? I'm legally off, and as I go I see the Doc fishing out his trusty rods and elbow-length rubber gloves from under the desk.

Me, I need to know about bugs, thus I am off to assail the bug man with a whole plethora of dumbarsed questions. The time taken to answer them, he can put on the company tab ...

The bug man is a Frenchy. He resides in that Edelweiss-state-of-mind hamlet over the hills, I forget the name of the joint. There are a lot of them down there growing snails and riding around in blue-and-white stripe Ts, wearing berets for the whole atmospheric tourism thing. He is the size of giant puffball fungi and geared up like John Goodman in *Arachnophobia*. He is standing on the landing, chewing on a cheroot, mad as all hell because these gin joints never ring for preventative measures – only cures.

I nod sympathetically; it is the same philosophy the gender confused apply. Still, from now till Easter he will make enough bread to see him through to the shallot harvesting season, maybe even right up to the ritual crushing of the grapes and de-flowering of virgins. He will be at it hammer and tong, spraying and spraying until the cycle has been all but eradicated.

You gotta get ze fucking eggs too, oui? he tells me. Fortunately I resided in Paris many moons ago and am familiar with Franglais. But zeese creeps, he moans as he switches the stub between sides in his mouth, zeese creeps never want ze full job, non, Monsieur – all zeese creeps is too tight, n'est pa? You see, your bug, Monsieur *Cimex lectularius*, 'im 'eez resilient to chemicals, like ze roach, oui? – Monsieur *Blattidae*. Spray, zey say – but, non, ze spray it only kill adult, not larvae. Need special shit for zat, kid, ze big fucking H-bomb, eh?

Can they fly, these fuckers? I ask him.

Fly? Sheet, no! Your bug 'ee's a crawler, 'ides 'ere zee, in ze fold of ze mattress, too small to see 'im, but at night, when 'ee feels ze warmth, then voila! Out 'ee comes for – 'ow you say? Uh, to drink ze blood!

Sounds fucking disgusting.

But of course! Ze bug him like ze piranha, you know zis fish? 'im like zat, 'ee takes one, okay, maybe two bites and zen 'im bloats up like zis …

Urgh, that's fucking 'orrible, that is.

I tell you trick. Get clean sheet, okay, zen put it in dryer sirty minutes on 'igh – ze bug 'im don't like it too 'ot. Wash don't drown 'im – but 'igh 'eat, oui, that sauté 'im.

Sure, thanks, but how's it get here?

Ah! Zat's ze best bit … 'im not 'ere, 'im carried 'ere from ozzer place, okay? In filthy sleep bag, on case, any way 'im can, like immigrant. You kill zeese ones today zen you put creep in 'ere tomorrow and 'im unleash 'ole new cycle!

Shit, so the Doc was right – who'd have guessed it, huh? You learn something new every day, in life or in hostelling, if you just know where to look – or, where not to look.

I leave Jean Claude to his spraying and sidle back down-stairs – where I hear grunting coming from a room with a log-jammed shit hole, and polythene being ripped just a few steps below. The joint is certainly crawling with life today. On the way back to my room to check for uninvited creepy crawlies, I bump into Miss Spelling Bee Massachusetts 1999, and since I've let her back into her dorm with civility she has dropped some of that bourgeoisie Bostonian attitude. She wants to know who the masked crusader down the hall is, like, is there an outbreak of malaria or something?

You had your shots didn't you? I ask her.

Gee, sure, but . . .

Then you've nothing to trifle yourself over. All of that's just routine precaution and in your best interests.

On that uplifting note, I retire to my hovel. The one stacked with pre-loved vintage fash and bags full of still-to-be-rummaged-through booty. But then I think, hang on, maybe those bags are full of bugs? So I haul them to the dryers and drag out some geek's still-damp Kathmandu apparel and drop it on the floor and bang the dial up to max, high heat as Jean Claude had said.

What are all these for? I ask Dick. He is in the former upstairs TV lounge, now a makeshift overflow dorm.

These new beauties are for all of those poor souls who'll find 'emselves bed-less, come high season, due to their own lack of planning and the airline's desire to drop people into the chaos at goddamned four in the morning. Where can you get a decent kip at four in the morning?

What about the airport floor?

Fuck no, that place'll already be as jam-packed as a Woodstock crap house. This is the answer, he says proudly, pointing to the six just de-polythened sofa beds. Two to a bed, maybe three, shit, if they're the kinda folks that don't care much for bed partners you could even go four at a push. Feel these beauties, huh – that's posture fucken pedic, that is! No inward sag on these babies.

Well, maybe so. I think better of engaging Dick in a deep and meaningful conversation about trifling matters like fire regulations and suchlike. Four to a bed, eh, that'll certainly spice up the place, and give the bugs a whole smorgasbord to feast on. This room resembles one of those boy's-home wards, what with these beds regimentally spaced for minimum privacy and optimum cash return. How are we expected to keep tabs on how many goons are up here at any one time? And what about sexual deviancy practices, opportunists, washing facilities and shit like that? No, sir, it'd be a dumb wretch of a fool who'd wanna part with good moolah to bunk down in a four-to-a-bed makeshift dorm – a fool, I tell ya, it'll never work …

19.

For Whom the Bells Sound

Dick has been rounded up for a few extra night shifts while the Doc surfs through a hundred or so websites that avail the Western employer of dirt-cheap Eastern hands. This is how he gets night porters: mail order.

At least with Dick you know no psychotic creep is going to pass himself off as a paying guest and then go methodically from room to room hacking up anything the bugs haven't already devoured. But then again, it does seem that when Dick's on night patrol something happens.

Tonight it is bells, not the ones at the cathedral, no, this bell is a continuous, shrill, eardrum-bursting shriek that you cannot ignore unless you are already dead, and even then it would raise you. I fumble for the digital clock radio I only yesterday lifted from the cleaner's cave and the red numerals tell me it is 3:05. What is that crazy son of a bitch up to now?

Still the bell toils, or is it fucking tolls?

Get up, I tell Jo angrily, and she tries to lay me out with a king hit. Fuck off, she grumbles, and pulls the covers up higher.

It's a fucking fire. Get your arse up, baby, okay?

Next it's the hotline, and I know damned well who is on the other end. Get up you fucking idiot! Dick screams at me the very moment I lift the receiver. And get your missus down here to watch the cash, I gotta roust up every shithead in this place!

Dick has a length of pipe in one hand, a smouldering dog-end behind one ear and a look on his dial like the Joker. I am out in the hallway. There is no smoke, but there are pill-heads starting to appear, sleep and dope still ravaging them. Then, suddenly, there's a dozen or so fully togged-up fire-persons breathing heavily through big masks ... some have axes and they're ready to chop ... and now there's a few Czech firefighters, in their X-rated communist Ys, tackle bulging and moustaches quivering. Wuh wuh wuh? one of the local crew says to me through his facial apparatus.

Huh? I say.

Wuh wuh wuh fucking wuh?

Some words are decipherable, but mostly it's just wuhs. Another one rips off his mask – where's the fire, darling? he asks. Darling? I think, and realize I'm not quite attired for middle of the night shenanigans, that I don't have my ... daywear on.

Dick is looking at me queerly, licking his dry lips. I fold my arms quickly and strike a macho pose. I don't know anything about a fire, I don't know anything about anything ... I'm just the girl next door.

There is no fire, no smoke, nothing untoward. All is quiet and eternal, and no one, not me, not Jo, not all the firefighters, guests and recently appeared non-paying wasters, have any-thing to be alarmed about. That bell's shot to shit, one fireman says to another. No point keeping coming here if they won't upgrade the fucking system, he responds. Let it fucking burn.

You girls okay? a big brute already stripped to the waist asks Jo and me as he spits on his axe and shines it on his tree-like leg. We nod, and then I'm dragged back into our boudoir by Jo and given a stern dressing down over my negligence in respect of public appearances. Those guys were ogling your fucking tits, she spits.

To be honest, I don't know what to say. I just forgot, you know . . . I mutter.

You forgot you had tits?

Well, yeah, it just all happened so fast.

I fucking bet, you cheap little whore.

What?

Did Dick see 'em? she demands.

Uh, I dunno, I don't think . . .

Yeah, there's your problem, girl, you just don't.

It's a bad night, well, what's left of it is bad, and made worse by visions of Dick telling all and sundry that I've got a real beauty of a pair . . . Ah, Jesus, maybe we should just pack up and run, get the hell out of here before I have to face some kind of back-room inquisition.

The following morning the Czechs bounce right out the door, and they leave that still unclaimed wallet behind. The Doc is as mad as Khan on a bender, irate about the false fire alarm, the attendance fine, our sloppy procedures and the written rebuke he's reading from the relevant authorities. There is no mention of my tits, not even from Dick who must have thought he'd just imagined it. For now, it seems, I am free of further investigation on the chest front, but not the fire front.

Dick has grassed everyone who could be grassed, and plenty more besides. He must have spent what remained of his shift laying out charges for dereliction of duty. Of course, I do understand the regulations, like I've told you, I'm fire savvy. But, Jesus, we hadn't even had a fire drill and . . .

Right! the Doc says angrily, we're going to have a drill, a mock-up. I'll arrange a time so the fire brigade are aware and I'll tell you guys the week, but not the exact time; there'd be no point in that, would there?

I guess not, but let's just pray the fool doesn't do it next Saturday night when the place is booked to the rafters with pisshead rugby fans. Christ no, the Doc wouldn't be that cruel, surely?

Night shift:

Some crank keeps calling the 1800 number, you know, the freefone thing they have at the railway station and airport, and every time I answer the damned phone, he just goes wuh wuh wuh.

Oh, maybe it's one of those firefighters? But no, this is just a kid's voice, some stoner at a juvey party randomly going through free calls just for kicks. Brother, the kid is really starting to wear down my patience.

By three am, my *Play Misty For Me* caller is unconscious, or dead, and finally the place is quiet – apart from rats scratching around here and there, and a few gooks out on the dark streets searching for Jehovah. I like sitting in the darkness of the old bar, which is now the rumpus room, and watching the streets. There are a lot of students driving around fast in big flash cars, others stumbling out of the karaoke bars around here; there are small gangs of thugs and drunken couples who have just met looking for a bed. Many of them will ring my bell, and I will tell them to take a hike in universal sign language. There are drunk-as-a-skunk women stumbling up the sidewalk while a car, registration partially obscured, slows to a crawl to investigate. There are the yellers and the bangers, those who can't stop yelling and those who can't stop banging on every door and window they pass; and then there are the projectile vomiters and those who defecate. Our doorway and our outdoor plant tubs are usually full of puke and shit on a Sunday morning – you can sit in the shadows of the bar and watch some rat-faced son of a bitch take a dump right on your doorstep. But hey, why go out and remonstrate? Drunks are the most dangerous beasts of all; they feel neither shame nor pain and I do not get paid enough to tackle a drunk who wants to shit on my doorstep, whether he has his pants about his ankles or not. Anyhow, this is obviously what the Brother is for, that numbnut lives to shovel shit.

This is how the city lives under cover of dark and I am not averse to it. I would rather watch this stuff than go spook hunting, being quite content to let the dead frolic among themselves until the day I join them, but others, such as Dick, a bona fide psychic in his own little universe, are of a different mind. Dick is adamant that some demented old hag dragging a ball and chain stalks the downstairs corridors, and that sometimes he goes down to the restaurant in the voodoo hours, after it has been padlocked as tight as Brinks Mat, only to find all of the chairs and tables re-arranged, occasionally even built into a pyramid.

Personally I think Dick has been hitting the meths too hard, either that or his brain has been spun out by ogling too much teenage porn on the www. Dick is a voyeur, albeit a clumsy one. Tired of pay per viewing, he is still sniffin' around my woman for some hands-on chat-room tuition, and wants to get down to the business. Well, maybe it'll do the old bastard good. That is what I'm thinking as first light creeps along the sidewalks like a still-stoned hophead. I go open the restaurant and there is no pyramid, just split vinyl chairs and sticky rubber tablecloths, and while it looks about as good as it's ever gonna get, within the hour it will look like the chow hall in Sing Sing.

I do not care, within hours we will be free again for a couple of days; free to hit the Irish bar with its roaring faux log fire, Brendan Behan open sandwiches and lovingly pulled pints of the black stuff, yes indeed. Liam already knows us down there, by sight at least, for we are renowned big spenders, and we like the craic. On Monday, I believe, we are booked to partake of the eyebrow-waxing talents of one Miz Ruby, ex-Singapore; she rips one hell of a strip but always does it with an anecdote or two, which makes a difference when the bill is thrust into your hand after you've been chemically re-peeled in the cucumber lounge. As you can tell, I get down with the girl stuff on my time off – me and the Jo'ster hit the shoe shops big time, and that is why our room resembles Al Bundy's workplace.

Back in the hole:

The Doc is going away. Again? you ask. Yes, indeed, the Doc likes to see how the other half live and then install those very living conditions back here. He and his wanton lover are off to buy another hostel in Oz, or maybe a butcher's shop, they can't decide. Whatever, I am happy, any time free of that scrutiny is good time, and with Dick ever eager to enter chat city I will be free to instigate my great removal plan. Just look at these fools, sitting there on the couch, totally unaware that within hours their lives will be taking a sharp turn for the worse. The lesson that shit travels downhill is a true one. That is where they are headed one and all – down the hill. Dick is about to get some new neighbours on death row, some new shower buddies, if you will, and by god I hope he's got a fair stock of tinea cream at hand. Why, you wonder? Well, I'm jumping on board the train of thought expressed by some former high season guests of the fairer sex, that $18.50 to sleep in a mixed dorm with geriatric perverts is a bit fucking rich.

I tend to agree. The most prominent complaint is about our long-term residents and their sleeping habits, or as the case may be, their lack of such. If I were some supple goddess new to town, desperate for a bed, only to find myself surrounded by seven pairs of bloodshot eyes and sheets that seemingly can't keep still, I wouldn't return either. Therefore I have decided, decreed as it were in my capacity as the chief, that all ye with pop-up genitalia and twitchy fingers shall at the dawn of the new morn be taking a ride downtown.

Oh, and by the way, I have just found that wallet. As empty as an oats canister in bear country. All of the greenbacks have vamoosed. The Doc has a sleight of hand that would have stood him in good stead in the Wild West.

I will keep you informed of developments, rest assured.

20.

A Very Kiwi Christmas

This is what's happened in the preceding month – yes, a month! The fire drill went off without a hitch and now I have one gold star racked up next to my name on The Chart. I have not been able to pin down the Doc over the whereabouts of a certain 700 of Uncle Sam's bills; he is very cagey about it all. I did the vagrant shuffle and there was much gnashing of dentures, flaking of dead skin, wringing of spider-vein-riddled hands and a general air of disenchantment. I tried to sack a cleaner but it didn't work out – that is the way of the world in the low-rent end of town. My other half has begun tutoring Dick in the finer protocols of chat-room etiquette and it is obvious we have unleashed a beast; every night in the still hours, you can find Dick hunched over a flickering screen, cackling madly to himself while he abuses some desperate housewife in the back-woods of the South. A new night porter arrived whose command of basic English is inadequate for the position to which he has been appointed. He is exceedingly competent with U-bends and rods, however, which more than compensates for the fact his register looks like something out of *Kindergarten Cop*. My American stalker, Brenda was her name, finally checked out, but not before asking me one of the dumbest questions I have ever been asked, even dumber than, Are those tits real?

I was on parade, doing my sworn dooty. She arrived all rugged up like a New York mugger.

Say, she said, can you help me with one last thing?

Sure, I replied. She proceeded to rustle out a guidebook from one of her numerous bags. Finally she spread it open on the counter – it was a Rough Guide or, as they have in the US for US travellers, a Very Rough Guide. I presumed she wished to find some two-bit shantytown to hole up in, but no – she had far grander plans.

This is where I want to go, she said, pointing.

Where? I asked. I read the word indicated by her chewed-down fingernail: Aotearoa.

What? I said, dumbfounded.

Yes there, that place, how'd I get there?

I had to handle the whole thing tactfully. Uh, yeah ... how can I say this? Well, see that door there?

That one? she said, turning to look at the main entrance.

Yeah, that door, that's right, just go out there and turn either way. Or if you feel like it, just cross the street.

Sure, and after that? she asked, bemused.

After that just keep on going any which way – it's all good.

I don't quite understand?

I know, but the thing is, this place you're so keen on going – you're, uh, standing in it, see?

I don't get it.

No, but you will, I'm sure, one day.

And she left, one chick who could definitely use a dick, because, by Christ, that girl needed something to rely upon, and there's nothing more reliable than a dick – that mother always points due north.

So, what else? Ah yes, one day last week my boss turned up, you remember my boss, don't you? That's right, the frisky bellwether who leads our raggedy flock. Lady Zsa Zsa of the lamp. She arrived in her usual grandiose manner, arms flailing, lips smacking, cheap plastic jewellery rattling – you know the kind of woman I'm painting here don't you? She had on these big Christmas earrings, trees they were, with lights that twinkled on and off and, no, I didn't want to know where the battery was – the thigh is certainly the limit.

It was not sartorial splendour, nowhere near it; but she did bring a 49 per cent fire-retardant synthetic Christmas tree. It came in fifteen pieces and she and Dick – the Elf – spent a whole afternoon buggering about with it, dragging it hither and dither until finally they put it back in its original locale. Then they roped in the Brother to wind fairy lights about it, and himself, and that was basically that – oh, apart from the fairy right at the top, the one that if you studied it long enough, looked eerily like Dick in drag.

Yep, and they put up this poster near the bolt hole:

Celebrate a Genuine Kiwi Christmas!
Lunch $25 per Person
Book at Reception!

I was dubious about it right from the start.

That's a fucken good feed, that is, Dick said to me as he lent on the counter giving some podgy Caucasian woman the evil eye. Fucken good value for twenty-five bucks.

Really? I replied, and what'd you get for your twenty-five, bro?

Dick gave me a sly wink. You'll see, cuz, he said. I was sure I would, but whatever Dick was selling I wasn't interested in buying. Before we knew it, the clock would strike one. This was no place to spend Christmas; it was all but empty bar the hard-core types and cash-only workers readying the bar for Big Kev's New Year's Eve opening spectacular. Sally Lim had shipped in a whole container of Taiwanese fire crackers just to make the whole thing go off with a Whoosh!

The Big Day arrived – just like that. Most of our resident dead-beats had opted for the more enticing celebrations being held at the city mission, and the watch-house, and all that remained were me 'n' young Jo, a just-arrived family of Swedes who looked as miserable as Bjorn Borg when metal rackets came along, a couple of smack johnnies bagging up for the deals ahead, and the first stragglers from the Big Island who'd grabbed cheap flights. Dick was off to the big house for his feed, the Brother too, and all we had to do was sit it out.

Festivities commenced with the Doc and Zsa Zsa bringing us, at seven in the morning, the great Kiwi Christmas lunches that had been ordered. There was nothing hot. What the great Kiwi Christmas lunch entailed was a grim collation of cold cuts cunningly garnished with greens. Not even any fucking salads? How was I going to placate the starving when they saw they'd paid real money for this platter of pie in the sky? The Doc and his missus handed me and the Jo'ster a box of wrapped Christmas gifts and with that they vanished into the mist of cheap perfumes they were both liberally doused in.

It's not usual to be given gifts by an employer, but our bosses were kind-hearted, although it was just cheap white and a couple of pirated videos, nothing to write home about. So there we were, marooned behind the mesh, trapped like a couple of paperhangers on parole. And then there was that Kiwi lunch, that problem still had to be solved somehow. Having been a chef in another life, you'd think that I of all people dumped in such a mess could find a way out.

Well, Jo said to me, better haul your sweet tush down to the 7Eleven. Pick up a few nibbles to get these goons in the mood to imbibe.

Like what?

I dunno, she shrugged, some cheese balls, a bag of ready salted, a tub of nuts, crap like that. There's still plenty of jerky here so we can bung that on too, and they can have this wine, that oughtta do fine, just like a home away from home. What d'ya say?

I didn't say much, not that I can remember, and as I made my way to the exit armed with a crisp 50 who should I bump into but Big Kev?

He wasn't much on Christmas either, he told me, what with the bitchin' and moanin', so he brought around a bottle of rather fine Scotch, not that cheap muck they give you on Air New Zealand either, the real McHaggis.

That lifted my spirits, and before you know it I was standing in the queue at 7Eleven alongside a melee of other weary types clutching my sundries for the Big Day. Back in the hole Big Kev was telling my other half all about his new bar. It's called the Bye Bye Bar, well okay, it isn't – but I can't give you the actual name, so I'm improvising. Anyhow, it ought to be called that, what with it being quite expensive; the kind of bar where travellers might spend their last few dollars before they head back to whatever dunghill they came from. That's Big Kev's hope, that most of these rubes will hit the sauce big time on their very last night in the garden.

To perk up Jo, I invested some of the hostel's cash on a four pack of Guinness; she is a woman renowned for liking the brown, or the black, and this small offering might go some way to alleviating the pangs of present-less-ness she is currently experiencing.

So there we were, deep into it as they say on the boxcars, down and dirty and in no mood to take Christmas queries by the busload. Alas, there is always one, and on Christmas Day it was some late-rising juicehead from far away who was in reception examining the red welts fast appearing all over his otherwise pasty skin. Ye gods, I knew those signs, the telltale tramp stamps that are Mr Bug's calling card. There was no point ringing Jean Claude, he was already triple-chin deep in chestnut stuffing and most likely as plastered as a Greek ferry captain between islands. I knew damn well that Jean Claude was leaving for France a few days later and that he wouldn't return for another month. I feared that come Waitangi Day we would be as infested as a public hospital waiting room. I took a swig of Scotch, it hit the spot, then slurped some Guinness. It is a good combination that has served far better men than me in times of crisis.

Fortunately my pasty friend had never been bitten by a bug before, especially not in his own sleeping arrangement, and believed he had caught the clap from that whore he spent his last rupiah on in Bali. I don't need this fool making more of a fool of himself in reception on Christmas Day and, thanks to Big Kev's Scotch, before I knew what to do I had already done it. To allay his fears I gave him the keys to his own double room on the house, and that spontaneous offer of customer service rocked him back on the balls of his bare, grime-encrusted feet. Momentarily he forgot he had more bites on him than a virgin in Romania. Jesus, he said, all misty-eyed.

Forget it buddy, I told him. It's Christmas. You just haul arse straight to your new digs and I'll have the porter bring your bags right along.

There's no need to ...

Au contraire, my good friend, there is every need. Now up

you go, and don't worry – just jump in the shower and hit the hay as they say in Kansas, and how about a seasonal tipple on us?

Are you stark raving mad? Jo hissed after he moved on. What porter?

Look, that chump probably carried those critters in here with him and if we let him take that bug-infested swag of his along to another room he'll just infest that one too.

And how're you gonna stop it?

You just keep him plied with cheap booze, okay?

Jesus, bud, the kid in the 7Eleven said, I see some strange shit, but eight cans of insect killer and two rolls of duct tape on Christmas Day? You guys must be havin' a choice kinda party.

You'd better believe it, bro – and how much are those Asian flu masks up there?

Two hours later I had let go all eight cans in the bunkhouse, the one with the windows sealed with duct tape. I couldn't see a goddamned thing and my eyes felt as if they were being casseroled. I sprayed the kid's gear too, even inside his sleeping bag and his boxer shorts, and that is shitty fucking work on any day. I crawled out of the haze, groping for the door frame. Unwilling to let one of these mother-fuckers escape, I slammed the door behind me and started taping, then I hung the poison gas sign on the door handle, and with what spray I had left, sprayed my own shoes. Lying on the very thin carpet, one of the tacks Dick didn't hammer back in correctly jamming into my shoulder, I ripped off the mask. As my sight returned, I saw the Swedish family standing nearby looking at me oddly. It is not usual to unload eight cans of insect killer into one room, and certainly not wise when you have already been on the malt and the brown. Add that to the fumes of the industrial adhesive they slather that duct tape in, and you will realize why I was about as high as a kilt on a blustery day in Inverness.

Shit yes, weird Christmas Days are my bag – and I had a feeling that this one was nowhere near finished ragging my butt.

Hey! the Swedish guy said to me. He was very tall and had long blond hair plus obligatory beard – chuck in a tin hat with horns and a menacing-looking sword and you have the essential ingredients for rape and pillage. Hey, I said back, from my horizontal position. The Swedes use the same word for hello and goodbye, thus I had no idea whether they were about to go or were just arriving back from wherever they'd been. I guessed I would soon find out.

Do you need a hand? the man asked.

Nah, I'm fine thanks. Just a spot of uh ... housekeeping.

Is bug? the woman asked. She had long blonde hair, like that Abba chick, the one with blonde hair.

Bug? Jesus, no, ha ha, bug indeed – shit, no, I said as I tried to get up, but what's left of my senses started doing the foxtrot backwards. No, no, just a spot of illness, never pays to be too careful, eh? So, hey, where you guys from in Sweden?

I am nothing if not sly.

An hour or so later the debacle of the Kiwi Christmas lunch had been forgotten courtesy of BK, some Viking-like Swede with a half-dozen bottles of schnapps and a jar of pickled herrings, some no-label chardonnay and a fair few bottles from Dick's private slush fund. Everyone was deliriously up-beat.

But happiness is a state of mind, and in the world of hostelling it can never last. You know when it is about to end, you see the signs, and these signs were ominous when the Doc and dirty Dick Turpin came back through the front doors loaded up with potato salad and cold sausage rolls at five in the afternoon.

Oh, so sorry, the Doc said, we took the salads home with us – did you get many complaints?

Shomplaint? Wot schomplaints? I slurred at him.

Swedish people, as is their wont, were running about half-naked. There were empties scattered everywhere and the house videos were in the TV lounge being pawed over by a well-pissed pasty-looking kid covered in huge red welts. And there was the distinct odour of insect killer.

What's that smell? Dick asked me.

Shmeel? What schmeel?

Well, it looks like you're all having a ball of a time, huh? the Doc said dryly, and before I knew it he was in the hole counting cash. I have no recollection of what happened, but Jo says the Doc told her to tell me (which is the roundabout kind of communication we have in operation here) that Dick had one too many ports and couldn't drive back down for his night shift. Our instructions were to man the bridge until four, when the Doc himself would relieve us.

Wot fucking shoor? I said to her.

04:05 Boxing Day

I was sober, and my head ached. I had done the cleaning and washed up the debris from the great Kiwi Christmas lunch. I spent two hours talking to Sven the Viking, about life, the high cost of beer in Sweden, and how to make a Viking ship – I told him I saw one being built before, up Auckland way. He couldn't sleep, someone was moaning and wailing upstairs and there was a strong smell of chemical. I told him I would look into it all – sometime.

05:05 Boxing Day
I was asleep on the old bar counter in the rumpus room, or at least I think I slept.

05:56 Boxing Day
I heard someone entering through the front door. I waited – there have been many false alarms but this was not one of them. My leader had arrived, all scrubbed up, shitted, shaved and showered, as bright as an elf the morning after a night on Santa's knee. First he wanted to run through the register with me and given that we had only 30 guests it was as simple as simple can be.

Have you done the banking? the Doc asked me.

Yes, I've done the banking, I told him.

Have you reconciled the deposit books? he asked me.

Yes, I've reconciled the deposit books, I told him.

Have you checked the ladies' room? he asked me.

I've checked the ladies' room. Been in there all night.

Are there any wake-up calls? he asked me.

No, there are no wake-up calls, it's Boxing Day, I told him.

Is there anything else I ought to know?

Yes, I told him.

And that is? he queried me, even though I had dutifully written it all out in the captain's log.

There are bugs in room six, a bug-bitten kid in eighteen who used to be in six, eleven petty-cash receipts in the petty-cash tin, and all of those bottle tops in that plastic bag over there are for Sven the Swede in room three – the one with the shitter that won't flush properly. Still.

And that's it? he quizzed me.

Yes, that's it, I told him.

Well, goodnight. I'll see you in – he looks at his Rolex – one-and-a-half hours or thereabouts. Enjoy your sleep.

Thanks, I told him.

And, hey! he said to me before the lock clicked shut.

What? I replied.

Merry Christmas.

Yeah, thanks for nothing, I told him, but he didn't hear. He was counting coinage.

It was 06:39 and our new shift started at 08:00. As I pass the laundry I heard something bouncing around in the tumble-dryer. I was so tired but . . . I flipped on the light. Inside was a pair of sneakers even though there's a sign on the wall here that says: **Guests are reminded never to leave baggage, documents, their morals or their fucking room key unattended!**

So I stopped the machine and juggled the hot sneakers. I threw them away when I was back on shift 69 minutes later.

21.

Shalom

You go to sleep on Boxing Day night and when you wake up on the 27th, you are living in a kibbutz.

Overnight, there have been several planeloads of Israelis disgorged into the brave new world, and all bar a half dozen or so of them have selected your roach-pit as their accommodation of choice. There are many reasons for this: they are barred from every other joint in town; we have the slackest check-in procedure on the Island; their comrades have provided detailed instructions via Mossad on how to infiltrate the place; and because we're dead cheap and ask no questions.

We need cash and they prefer the relative anonymity that squalor in the low-rent end of town affords. They can flout every rule in the book here, do pretty much as they please – as I am about to find out.

The men arrive first. They lay the groundwork, so to speak. We argue with them, question them, eject them and take them back again after they have proffered the humblest of insincere apologies. Our day – that fifteen-hour stretch at the coalface – screams by. The majority of that time is tied up with constantly re-doing the register. It is not normal procedure to have to completely rewrite your register six times a day, but when you have serviced the fickle whims of 60-odd Israelis hell-bent on breaking you in the first 24 hours of combat, you quickly learn that it is either re-do or quit.

Many in seasons past have opted for the latter, and I can see why. To have to go through 40 days of this, before the jarheads move south en masse to ruin some other poor bastard's life, is the ultimate test of endurance. Forget those corny Japanese game shows where some smiling fool stands in a bucket of iced water with electrodes attached to his nuts trying hard to control a bloated bladder; buddy, that shit is a walk in the garden compared to this gig. There is no time to piss on shift, bladder control is a pre-requisite. You cannot leave this mob alone for a minute, not unless you want to come back and see nothing left but the carpet tacks. These bastards will lift anything – not a half hour into my first encounter with our friends from Tel Aviv and I am already biro-less. I am down to the pencil, and it is not a piece of lead designed for this much work.

All of the brochures have gone, though most, I see, have been made into paper aeroplanes and are now scattered along the hallway. Four of these new guests have the hot drinks vending machine upside down, pouring the last dregs into the open mouth of one of their smiling colleagues. The plastic shrubbery Zsa Zsa put here a few months ago is out on the sidewalk, and they have ripped the coin slot from the pool table so they don't have to go through the annoying procedure of queuing for change. They have a desert thirst on them and the grog is flowing, despite it only being fifteen degrees Celsius. Did you know it was a Swede, Mr Celsius no less, who gave us that scale? I must take that up with Sven ... But, anyhow, despite the temperature inside, many of these Israelis are bare-chested, even bear-chested, and ready to rumble. Any piece of rump that is foolish enough to wander through the front door is fair game, even androgynous boys. These brutes have been starved of good action on the Front.

I have seen nothing of Dick, come Yom Kippur he has been dipped in invisible ink. There is not even a sniff of our erstwhile boss, not even a cipher-like e-mail. It is left to me and Jo – if she ever finally arrives on deck. Given the amount of testosterone in the air down here, I better tell her to rug up. Jesus H., I am having enough strife myself fending off sexually explicit questions from these animals.

Next I know they are in the communal chow hall wreaking havoc; they have re-arranged all the tables, including those that weren't available but suddenly became so, into one long last supper-like arrangement. They are all crowded around with maps and mug shots spread out. At least it has given reception a break and I can start counting cash. I don't like to, what with so many agents about the joint.

Jo comes down, blissfully unaware of what she is walking slap bang into the middle of. I grimace and she looks at the register, which is already a mess. Where are all the fucking pens? she asks me. The phone starts ringing – and it will not stop, not for another 30 days, maybe more.

We quickly decide that our normal routine won't suffice. We cannot leave one or other of us alone for a couple of hours trying to handle all of this so we'll do this shift together through to the bitter end, just like Thelma and Louise. That is why girls will always be closer friends than boys.

There will be no time to buy food either, or to cook it for that matter. We will have to order in, stay hunkered down and eat on the go. This is going to be one bitch of a month.

Where's the hot drinks machine gone? Jo enquires. I fancied a hot chocolate.

Fucked if I know, it's probably halfway up the street by now. Forget it, that's my advice, forget everything we've been taught and just go with your gut instinct, okay?

It can't be that fucking bad, can it?

I raise my eyebrows, the eyebrows Miz Ruby ex-Singapore has only recently worked on. Suddenly there is a dreadful noise, like a far-off herd of water buffalo charging full bore in my direction. I give Jo's hand a quick squeeze then grab the pencil sharpener – without that I'm all butt fucked.

They swarm on us like a mass of bees. I feel like a tail gunner in the Battle of Britain. There are bandits everywhere, attempting to overrun staff by sheer volume of numbers. Gut instinct might work too; I have used the same ruse on the mean streets of Cardiff, but this is not deep in the valleys, this is paradise – and in paradise there are no pieces of slag laying around to hurl at the onrushing mob. Here there is civility, oh yeah, and servitude, that might work – and if it doesn't there's always Dick's mace …

We continue to double team. These people are used to getting their own way, normally at the barrel of a gun. But Jesus, if rudeness were some kind of international competition, your average Israeli grunt would be right up there next to the Yank. No explanation, no matter how rational, appeases these people, and it strikes me that I am simply wasting my time and vocal cords. I can already feel the abrasive signs of wear 'n' tear, I am hoarse – as they used to say on *Bonanza* – and if I have to fight one more good fight today, in the name of reputations, ethical business practices, consumer affairs legislation, international hostelling and bi-partisan fellowship toward all of mankind, I think I will take to hard drugs with a vengeance. But still they come, many for the umpteenth time. I am beginning to recognize faces now, but not names; the names are far too complicated to remember.

Jo is making a far better fist of the whole scene than me due to the fact that she does not bow to international law; she does not believe than we should respect our fellow man, unless that man is the respectful type himself. Many of these nomads are receiving a very short shrift – and the most surprising thing is, they like it.

There is still no trace of Dick, the Triangle has claimed another victim; but there is news from the Doc over the mojo wire. I've been ringing you all day! he says to me, exasperated, and I tell him the phone is so hot we have to keep dunking it in a jug of mineral water. You can tell he's happy – happy to have no part of this initial high-season insanity, and happy to look forward to the cash windfall awaiting his tender lovin' come sun-up. Anyhow, he has some 'prior engagements' to attend to, and we will have to muddle through as best we can – oh, and try not to disturb Dick, his lumbago is giving him gyp again.

Fucking lumbago, the only thing giving Dick gyp is the fact he can't get to the liquor store without me seeing him. So I hang up. All communication ceases thereafter; this is a manual ride and there's no point flipping on the automatic pilot.

Cloudy day turns to stormy night. At around six there's a lull, which affords us enough time to straighten the furniture, but then they pile into the internet lounge, seven to a terminal, messages on hold, pay later, maybe never at all. They have this jive down flat. At around ten I catch my first glimpse of Dick, who is hobbling around like a vet, not the animal kind. He is trying to get to chat-room city but there will be no joy tonight – there isn't a free monitor, and won't be until February.

I am thinking that soon I will be able to hand over to the newest night man: let's call him Freddy, huh? That warm fuzzy feeling is disturbed when I catch a glimpse of a shock of bright-red hair drifting through reception like a toxic bloom. I know that hair, and those freckles, and, by god, that smell. Tommy is no fool, he plays the game well and knows that even his pungent bodily aroma can be masked by the mingling aromas of 50 Israelis fresh from the West Bank. But he has come up short on this occasion – one of the benefits of overloading your system with large doses of oestrogen is a heightened sense of smell, and Tommy's is a parfum I would recognize anywhere, even in a shitbog.

I'm on the scent, eager as a bloodhound that's just taken a couple of big nostrils full of still-warm underwear. I follow my nose to the TV lounge or, as it's now temporarily referred to, Gaza. A shock of red hair nestles in a beanbag in the far corner; as my nemesis senses my approach he sinks deeper into the polystyrene beads.

Well, well, I say, how's things, Tommy lad? Which room are you booked into tonight?

Tommy's face goes as red as his hair, and he is up fast, full of apologies – which is what I like about him. I escort him to the front entrance and see him safely onto the street – that is two-nil to me – watch him go as I watch another mob of jarheads come. They bustle in through reception like a cloud of gas; when their scent clears I see several plastic shrubs sitting forlornly up the street.

Say, lady, one of the jarheads starts, and then stops. He can tell that I'm in a foul mood, he and his 30 dirty cronies. The small musty room adjoining reception that was once a flash travel shop, in times when travel was still the sole domain of the well-heeled, is now our overpriced internet 'lounge'. There are six computers, two of which only serve a diet of hard porn due to tampering by some Swiss who are still in residence. I shall get to them later. No one, not even the Doc's techno-nerd pal Nigel, has been able to shift the filthy screensavers those Swiss downloaded. Some don't mind it and when I think about it, they're in the immoral majority. I have more concerns right now.

There is a behemoth standing in reception, a huge grizzled specimen wearing a rumpled suit and loaded up with money bags. He looks more than a trifle miffed, so much so that even my front-line jarheads are giving him a wide berth. His shadow soon dwarfs me, his odour not far behind. The guy smells like a dairy hand come morning tea. Good Christ Almighty, there is no bed in this joint capable of holding a brute like this, and certainly not a fucking bunk bed. Chuck a monster like this in a mixed dorm and you'll have an accidental death on your books by sun-up. No sir, a situation as large as this requires very delicate handling, and fortunately I have very delicate hands. The brute's tag is Wolfgang and he is as surly as all hell.

This Teutonic titan has gigantic hands, ones that'd do well shoved down our U-bends. But what in the name of Walt Disney is a freak like this doing in a joint like ours? How did he get here? I mean, pity the poor fools wedged in next to this sweating beast on a long-haul charter flight! I have to think fast, which, when you have been verbally assailed most of the day by ex-marines looking for meat to hump, is no mean feat. The German slaps something on the counter and all my remaining pencils fall to the floor. He demands a safe to deposit his valu-ables in. I immediately oblige. And just while I'm considering tacking on some kind of bed levy to cover the damage a monster like this will do to a hostel bed, who should I spy with my little eye other than King Rat? He is back hoping for a seat on the Porn Express but, alas, our friends from the Wailing Wall are still there in numbers sending messages home. I cannot be expected to keep track of six computer terminals charged at two bucks per fifteen minutes, respond to constant requests for more high-glucose beverages, *and* check in a Hercules like this man in front of me. I could ask Dick to help ... but before I can, he has scuttled off to the house bar like a ferret. The Brother is nowhere to be seen, his roost having been taken over by the grunts from operation Hostel Rout; in fact, the last time I saw the Brother he was in the upstairs lounge giving himself a sponge bath.

Wolfgang is dragging me down big time. He has a zillion questions, all centred on seedy sexual encounters, and there are no such adventures in the hostel's portfolio. The closest is naturist paragliding, but there is no chute in existence that would keep Wolfgang airborne for more than the time it takes to scream back to Earth. Whichever room I give him will be out of service for a considerable time to come, so I give him the worst one available. That makes good sense, and I'm sure my leader will concur if I ever see his smiling pearly whites again. Wolfgang grunts, gesticulates and heads off, his ample butt filling the CCTV screen. I heave his money bags to the vault. This guy is obviously loaded, all those Germans are.

My last chore is to book in some other sleazy-looking waster loitering around reception with his hands stuffed deep into his pockets. I ought to tell him that the only opening I have is to share a bed with that monster who just left reception, but I do have a few beds spare and my mission, which I've already agreed to take as you'll recall, is to flog sleeping space. When the guy saunters up to me I realize that he's German too. What a fucking coincidence! Maybe him and the brute are in cahoots of some kind, up to some dirty abduction plan that involves taut flesh and baby breasts? This guy wants to pay by cheque? Like, as if! I have a clearly defined protocol when it comes to pieces of paper with imaginary monetary amounts scribbled on them, and that is to shake my head aggressively. I can take some stuff in lieu of payment, stuff like a passport. That might seem like a kosher rule but it don't explain why there are at least six current foreign passports in the drawer. Now, why would you leave without paying eighteen bucks and sacrifice the most valuable document you hold? What kind of numbnut would think that kind of exchange is good value? My own rule is to forget the passport deposit – you no pay, you no stay, that's a better fucking rule. Sometimes we take foreign currency, but only if that currency is a Euro or a US dollar, those are the only two languages the Doc understands. One for one, that way the Doc is always ahead.

This new addition to my fast-growing multicultural menagerie is giving his name as Gustav, and he is paying me in good Euro currency. Last high season my fool predecessor booked in a party of twenty who paid by cheque and were never heard of again. The Doc offloaded that shithead on the spot, after deducting the outstanding debt from his pay. I am no one's fool, although both Gustav and the behemoth already upstairs will do much to tarnish my already tainted reputation. But I do not know this now.

What I do know, is that it's time to knock off. That my head is a cloudy funk of half-caste ideas and raw fantasies. That my feet are like two pounded beef cuts, that I haven't trimmed my nasal hair, shaved my legs, or had a facial for far too long. I cannot go on like this without falling into a heap someplace; either that or go on some crazed spree that culminates in me hacking some innocent bystander to death with a steak knife. I can smell burning too, and with this many numbnuts in residence it is surely only a matter of time before we are all evacuated in the middle of the night dead or alive while flash-bulbs go pop!

I give Freddy the news, he takes it well. Freddy is studying for his matriculation or something, and he's hoping there's a computer free sometime.

Try number four, I tell him, if those bizarre sights don't push you toward a steely resolve to get educated and avoid pornography, nothing will.

22.

Artificial Highs

Jo has sold more tickets for bus trips than Ken Kesey. I don't know how she does it. Maybe it's that cleavage. The Doc is rolling in filthy cash, and fifteen per cent of the price of each trip goes straight into his pockets – not one cent of it ends up in ours. So adept has Jo become at selling trips to wasters that each bus company is showering her with freebies to induce her to flog its line. There have been wine, flowers, chocolates, sex toys, all manner of sleazy inducement, but this latest one is really upping the ante. When I crawl into the hole she is perusing the contents of a large, gold envelope.

What you got this time? I ask her.

Tickets for lame-brain crap like rides and shite.

Here, let me see.

I ain't going on any of them; I hate speed, heights, any kind of motion. Even a waterbed makes me queasy, remember that one at . . .

Sure, how could I forget? I say, as I study the freebies. There are tickets for jet-boating, paragliding, quad-bike riding, and a balloon trip. I hand them back to her. Maybe you could flog 'em on to someone else?

Non-transferable. What a crock, no horse riding or spa treatments or movies. What kind of a shithead wants to get up before the sun and climb into a basket attached to a giant balloon with Chinese nylon?

Not me, babe. Better luck next time.

She throws the tickets on the desk and we resume our messy business. The Doc finally arrives and plunges straight into a pile of cash. After a half hour he summons us to the back room. Whose are these? he asks, holding the wad of tickets. I tell him that if he looks closer, he'll see that the tickets have a name on them. The recipient's name, plus guest.

I think you ought to avail yourselves of these, he says. It'll be good business for the hostel.

How so? I ask him.

Well, it shows that we can sell trips with the best – and, not only sell them, but enjoy experiencing the products we're selling.

So why don't you and your good lady go?

Oh no, we've done all this before. Besides, this kind of trip is a young person's caper!

Would we get time off on top of our rostered time off?

Well I don't think that's . . .

Fuck it then, Jo says, and saunters back to the desk. I am left looking at the Doc while he considers the various scenarios and ramifications. If it's so good for business, I tell him, those two extra days ought to go on your time, not ours. Some time later, he reluctantly concedes the point.

Jo is adamant she is not going on anything that moves faster than her. She is still berating me when the courtesy bus pulls up three days later. We climb aboard and some wobbly chick gives us three plastic ducks. What the hell are these for? Jo asks loudly.

Those are your duckies, the guide says. If you lose your duckies, there are consequences.

What consequences?

Oh, you'll see!

Jo lobs her ducks over her head and puts in her earphones. As far as she's concerned, this is the trip that never was. The smiley lady grimaces at me. I shoot her the finger. It is a bad start.

We arrive at the quad-bike track about two hours later. The other grunts on the bus – various hostel trash – pile out gleefully. Me and Jo clamber out reluctantly. We are both duck-less but, so far, there have been no consequences. The other jellyheads put their ducks in a puddle for some reason, and we all set off behind the vibrating arse of our erstwhile guide. Jo stamps at least three ducks down to flat yellow squares as we spend time listening to safe quad-bike handling instructions. Then we are given helmets. I am quite looking forward to it. Jo refuses a helmet and instead sits on a rock with her earphones in. She don't drive *and* she gets motion sickness, I tell the guide.

By the first turn of the track marked out with hay bales, I am already well in the lead, gunning the shit out of that bike – my wheels are becoming airborne when I corner or hit a hump. Each time I pass Jo I give her a wave and she gives me the bird. By the end, I have lapped a couple of goons at least three times and run some greasehead straight into the stack of tyres on turn two. I dismount, rather chuffed with my expertise and go sit with Jo. We climb back on the bus and head off to the jet-boating place. We don't participate on this one. Both Jo and me sit on a bench watching the tedium, scheming how we can abscond when we get to the lunch stop.

Luckily for us we are decamped in some tourist town for the night. The rest of the fools are off paragliding but Jo and I have already declined. Instead, we find an Irish pub and decamp there for the remainder of the day and most of the evening, getting happily smashed on the brown. When we turn up at the hostel accommodation arranged, we see it's a dump, even worse than our own. So instead we hike up the road and find a decent hotel.

The following morning, at four thirty, we are the last on the ballooning bus. Somehow, I have talked Jo into joining me on the balloon ride. It is a beautifully clean and crisp morning. As Emile the balloon pilot speaks, his words are shrouded with vapour. He is saying something about not leaning out over the side or making unexpected movements, I think. A lot of the bus goons have cried-off, are still blotto, or in the sack with some piece of rough located only a few hours earlier in a gutter. It is just Jo and me, the guide lady – arse and all – and two Americans in matching lime-green shell-suits. If we come down unexpectedly at least they will see us from the spotter plane. There is also a tall German going by the handle of Franz. We are not a happy crew. Once in the basket Jo starts grabbing at me madly and blaspheming all and sundry. It is the Yanks who've started her off, crapping on about all the joy-flights and near-death experiences they've had over the Rio Grande, Niagara Falls, Stonehenge. I tell the pilot not to be alarmed if I have to smack my bitch.

Vas? Franz asks, his junkie-eyes widening. Smack? Ist gut?

The guide sighs, disgusted, and huddles up with the Yanks. Emile does what balloon pilots do so that we gradually begin to leave the earth. At about eleven feet Jo goes for me like a wild woman, flaying and trying to bite my nose off. Emile quickly drops us back down. I get a hold of Jo and tell her sternly to quit it. She is spouting wildly and Franz is still sniffing around for any good dope she might have. Finally, I get Jo under control and tell Franz there is no smack, only this kind, and show him my clenched fist. Die Englender! he moans to the trio cowering in the opposite corner.

The Yanks now introduce themselves as Chuck and Betty. Perhaps they feel some kind of informality will help Jo over her bout of jitters. With Jo placated momentarily, Emile lets rip and up we go, as quick as a dodgy tikka. Jo doesn't even have time to shriek, but she does have time to grab my arm so hard her talons penetrate my three layers of polar fleece. Chuck, presuming that the pre-flight nerves have calmed, starts babbling on about the time him and Betty came perilously close to being lion food on the Serengeti. Must have been a flamingo that flew into the balloon, he's saying, because I swear to God that I could see down that lion's throat.

Zip it, Chuck, I'm saying.

As the plains spread out below us I spy Franz emptying a vial of white substance onto the back of one hand. It's about then that we hit a thermal and everyone is thrown about like sneakers in a tumble-dryer. I hear Franz cry something like Shizer! Jo instinctively thinks that we're on a one-way spiral back to Earth and goes for me like a champion jelly-pit wrestler. With the basket swaying and her weight on top of mine, our combined momentum almost tips Emile out. He is the only fucker that can fly this baby so I shoot one hand out to catch him while I arm-wrestle Jo with the other. Franz drops his vial and, just for a second, we are all inhaling what tastes like Columbian gold. I am sure that Betty is praying – because it ain't Jo or me – and I can't believe Jo is so god-damned heavy. I must have missed all this extra poundage she'd gained. It is then I realize that the big-arsed dame is on top of both of us, wriggling about like a hippo and shrieking like a jackdaw. Franz is on his hands and knees trying to finger up any dope that's settled, and Chuck – well, I don't know where the fuck Chuck is, maybe he went over and that's why Betty's reciting the Lord's Prayer. So long as I have Jo, and

Emile, things are still okay – though, talking of Emile ... where the hell is he?

Squirming out from under two well-stacked broads ain't easy, but my athletic prowess comes to the fore. Upright, I see that it ain't Franz scrabbling around sucking up dope flakes, it's Emile, the goddamned pothead. I yank him up by his collar. I can't even see the earth below – we are almost in fucking space. Pretty soon we will all pass out and at a certain altitude the balloon will shred and the force of gravity will bungee cord us back to earth, most likely dead before impact. I smack Emile around his bright-red face. Get a fucking grip on yourself you dirty junkie! How'd you ever get a pilot's licence?

You don't need a fucking licence to fly these babies! Just a doctored CV!

Leave that shit alone and take us down!

What about that bit? he whines.

Where?

Look, there! he points. On the Yank's coat sleeve!

I'll get it. You fucking fly this thing!

It isn't dope anyhow, it's snot. In-between praying, Betty has been wiping her nose on her sleeve. As we start our descent, everyone is vertical again, even Franz who is yelling at the red sky and shaking his fist. Chuck is still there too, retching over the side bringing up his over-easy eggs. Betty has stopped praying, but she has a big snot bubble coming in and going out of both nostrils. The tour guide is back up too, albeit on wobbly legs. She is looking daggers at Jo and me. Emile is babbling some gibberish about investigations and well-paying jobs. And Jo? Well, Jo has found a strip of jerky in her pocket and is merrily munching away, as if nothing untoward has occurred.

It is a nice view, innit? she says to me.

A nice view? Is that what you said, you crazy bitch?

Yeah, look at all da sheep!

Sheep? Those aren't sheep, you fucker, those are houses!

Woah! How high are we?

High as in altitude or high as in artificially?

Either.

I think about slapping her. No one up here would so much as bat an eyelid if I did, in fact, they'd probably all want a go. I ask Emile how high we are. He laughs wildly and tells me that if we go much higher we'll dock with a fucking space station. You fucking hear that? I say to Jo, but she is oblivious. Indeed, seeing as how she's hyperventilating, maybe she inhaled most of Franz's shit. She is, to use a cheesy metaphor, as high as a goddamned kite; no, fuck that, she is as high as a smackhead balloon pilot. Even I am giddy, and have no idea what the safe altitude for hormone addicts is.

Finally back on land, some distance from where we took off I might add, the balloon ground crew rush to our aid. With the balloon safely tethered, they subdue Emile with a stun gun and duct tape. Fucking right too, I tell one of the ground crew. That crazy son of a bitch is a fucking menace, has he been drug-tested recently?

I am escorting an incoherent Jo away from the whole debacle. She is babbling on about the Velvet Underground and how Nico was in the balloon. Sure she was, I reassure her. As we pass the lard-arse guide, I hear her whinging on to the Yanks about it all being our fault and how she forgot to release her ducks. Chuck goes to say something but I don't listen, he is attired in lime-green and his whole 'great adventurer' thing has been shot to hell. I lead Jo away to the waiting courtesy shuttle, and when we have made it back to town I take her on a hostel crawl where we abuse other hostel staff, indulge in malicious bogus-bookings calls, and get totally rat-faced.

We are let back into our hostel by Freddy. It has been a surreal couple of days on the company tab and I for one never want to go on any kind of adventure tourism gig again. Running this shit hole is about all the adventure I can stomach . . .

23.

Filthy Lucre

Neither of us sleeps well after the ballooning caper. All night long there are sounds of shrieking. We don't know how Freddy fared, even if he fared at all. Maybe he just upped and quit around four, took the day's takings and fled north. I wouldn't blame him, I've considered it myself, even sketched out getaway routes. Jo, a dab hand with middle bacon, pork sausages and black pudding, is rustling up a good English breakfast in our wee kitchen. There must be Scottish in her somewhere.

Has Dick said anything about your tits? she asks as I munch on a piece of black pudding the size of a door wedge.

Nope, but he keeps looking at me kinda queer.

What about the Doc? she asks.

He's not even fucking here half the time. I think Dick just thought he'd imagined it all.

I wouldn't bet on it, honey, Dick's a sly bastard.

Don't I know it.

Downstairs, Freddy is still aboard ship. He tells me it's been a fucking rough night; I say it has been upstairs too and ask just what the fuck's been going on.

A new gang of Swiss turned up early this morning, he says. They booked in then demanded internet access.

You didn't let 'em, did you?

I had to, they saw Dick in there!

Dick was on-line?

Cackling away all fucking night, abusing some dirty cyber-woman someplace.

I am surrounded by cash, like a Great Train Robber at that farmhouse the morning after the night before. The booty is spread out on the Doc's desk, and in-between morning question and answer I have to somehow get all this filthy lucre into banking order. I have to balance the ledger, check the till receipt, add up discrepancies and explain them, count up the key deposits, tally the shop tin, balance the float, and count and itemize every trip sold yesterday in a separate deposit book. Haven't I told you someplace else that I loathe financial machinations? All the credit-card receipts have to be tallied and the cleaners shepherded toward rooms just vacated for ultra-quick turnarounds. I have to goad the Brother into forward motion with a pig stick, re-book and check-out, start a new register underneath yesterday's, and ensure that the two create a running commentary that even a moron could follow. As you can see, it's pretty easy work!

If I am unlucky, the cans will be blocked to bursting, some piece of bulk-bought kitchen equipment will malfunction, some meathead will miss their bus, train, or plane, and a dozen shuttles will arrive at my door full of dopeheads and mass murderers-in-waiting. I am a very lucky girl, blessed in fact, no girl could want more. Shit, yeah.

I am struggling along by rote. By now, I can count cash and tally figures just as quick as my erstwhile boss, maybe quicker. Sometimes Dick sits on his stool in the corner of the back office and watches me count with one beady eye, while watching the CCTV with the other. He'll sometimes tell me

I'm a whiz with cash, that he don't know how I do it, that I ought to have been a pit boss, that the sight of all that hard cash occasionally gives him a real boner ... What do I care?

Most mornings Jo'll arrive after I've waded through a couple of hours of mayhem. Immediately she'll evict Dick, eat something she's grabbed from the shop and listen to my handover instructions. But today when she turns up I'm chatting with Goran the Israeli pacifist. He's always lurking around here, buying trips and excursions he rarely seems to go on. As soon as Jo arrives he vanishes, like the morning mist.

Is that fucking creep hanging around again? she asks me.

He's okay, I tell her. Quite intelligent for an Israeli.

You know he's after you, don't you?

After me! Don't be ridiculous.

How many guys do you know who compliment 'other guys' on their bracelets?

Gay guys.

You fool! He knows exactly what you are, sugar, that's what's grinding his beans!

Get outta here! Shit!

Despite what you think, you can't fool everyone. The longer we're here, the more obvious it becomes.

What becomes?

Go stand in front of the mirror, babe, even through all those clothes I can see your tits! Whatcha gonna do in a week or so, when summer breaks?

That's a good question, one I've been pondering during my fleeting down-time; just what in the hell am I gonna do? The more sparsely attired I am, the easier it is to spot the obvious ... even a money-mad fool like the Doc won't be able to miss cute li'l jugs like these.

Summer arrives late here, much like everything else. The further south, the nearer you are to the pole and as yet it's only topped 25° C. That is not hot weather, not by the Australian definition. So what if the Doc is in shorts and an ironed polo shirt? The Doc is an immaculate conception. I'd bet that even while him and Zsa Zsa are at it, his hair stays in place. But maybe Jo's right. Maybe I'm this far south to avoid having to confront myself; to hide, keep it all under wraps? I've gone from boy to man-made woman to drag king in fewer hops than it takes a toad to find a place to shit. Maybe I oughtta buy one of those stick-on moustaches?

Only a few days ago, three Israeli chicks who, I might add, had rather fine moustaches of their own, started questioning me about my gender. You're a girl, aren't you? one of 'em asked point blank. We've been betting each other.

That had caught me off-guard. Maybe I even blushed, I don't remember, but she kept on: Why do you have nails? What about your eyebrows? Are you wearing eyeliner? I am wearing eyeliner, technically, because I can't take it off, it's kinda permanent.

Today is for other matters, however, as I'm about to find out. There is a cleaner in reception who cannot gain entry to two rooms. It takes me a minute – oh yeah, that's where my German friends are. I tell her not to worry, neither of them want to be disturbed as they have endured an arduous journey. She shrugs and goes on to tell me that there are bad smells coming from both rooms. Smells like what? I enquire. She tells me it smells like death from one, drugs from the other. I let it slide; she has an over-active imagination, another wannabe writer.

A one-armed Swiss is at the counter, not that there's any-thing unusual about a one-armed gunslinger checking in here. He's a nice guy but he wants to send an e-mail home. I don't see the problem. It takes him too long to set it up and write it, so can I help him?

Jeez, I'd like to but ... But, Jo is suddenly volunteering, and that is not like her. So he dictates while she types, and I watch. After they finish he fishes in his jacket pocket and produces a large silver coin. It's like 50 francs or something, totally useless, but a nice gesture of appreciation I suppose. By month's end Jo will have about twenty of these coins.

The Israelis are preparing to leave. They are buying up unwarranted second-hand cars and the back lot is full of them – oh Helga, look what you're missing! All this action gets me thinking about wheels, maybe me 'n' Jo oughtta invest in a mode of transport?

There are more room problems. The Swiss gang in four can't be budged, the cleaner tells me. She asks me to go up there and find out if they're staying or going, it's way past checkout time. I go, reluctantly, and after knocking on the door for ten minutes finally use the master key. This is what it's for, immediate access. It smells pretty fucking malodorous, like warm Swiss chocolate, beer and contraband narcotics. There are four, no, five ... okay, hang on, six ... seven of the fuckers in a four-person room. Fucking Freddy. I start kicking feet, opening the curtains, sliding up the window. Eyes flicker open, muscles stretch, private parts zoom into view ... good Christ.

I throw bedding over the offending sights and start telling these clowns that it's re-check in or book-out time. C'mon, buddy, move it or lose it! One of 'em gets up unsteadily, as naked as a water spout in Geneva, rummages around in a bag and hands me a wad of cash, then tells me to fuck off.

How very nice.

Look at this, I tell Jo, handing her the bundle of notes.

What'y going to do with it?

Fucked if I know, I don't have a clue whether those goons are staying one more night or what, but a quick tally and conversion tells me I've far more here than is required. I have every stoolie's dilemma and that vanishing 700 bucks is still front and centre in my thoughts. Surprisingly, I cover one day's accommodation and put the rest in a safe place. I'll decide later. The day grinds on. The Doc calls me to ask if I have done the banking. I tell him I'm on my way.

Sunlight falls on my pale face. Outside the city has had an enema of adventure tourism shot right up its filthy arse. All the cafe tables are overflowing, buses are pulling up or leaving. Everyone is on the move or getting ready to move. This is New Zealand in action. But my world doesn't move, I am the centrifugal force around which everything else spins out of control. I am the pole.

I do the banking. They know me there, understand I'm just this year's Ms Thang. I walk back slowly. Where are all these people going, where did they come from?

Soon there will be no beds. Time is moving faster and faster and the days blurring into each other, creating a pastiche of haze and hue that is barely, if at all, recognizable as life. By the time I have banked, booked tours, supervized the laundry and signed out the cleaners, I have already missed lunch. Shuttles arrive constantly, spewing out the rank and file of the travelling army, a sloppy parade of long-hairs, easy lays, and lice-riddled potheads. After a week of this insanity I even stop seeing them as individual human beings. All I notice is a sea of sorry-looking faces smeared on vacant heads attached to worthless hunks of human meat. There are no more people; all there is, is money.

Shiteloads of it, but money don't buy me love. I realize that I too have jettisoned my identity, sold it into bondage for a handful of coins, a free bed and a VCR. I am nothing, not he, not she, not anything the world could recognize. That is the price I'm paying for gainful employment, as Jo so rightly keeps telling me over jet-black Guinness aside the fire. Even there, in the bar, I'm all but invisible. Only Miz Ruby, ex-Singapore, really knows who I am. Her, Jo, and the heroin girl who books in and out of here when she's got enough bread for a bed. She knows, because she saw me in the salon. She was shoplifting and I was with Jo, getting a wax.

That's why I check her in, despite her being barred. She's a desperate soul, tired, bedraggled, totally uncaring about what happens to her body. You see the grunts here chatting her up now and again, during the fleeting moments she appears humpable, when her hair's been washed and her clothes changed, and she'll always oblige them for a drink in the bar afterward, a bittersweet sip of normality.

In about four weeks I will be in trouble for booking her in again, and then having to call an ambulance as she almost chokes to death on her own vomit on the TV lounge sofa, while three or four backpackers stand about and do nothing, apart from moan about the obnoxious stench. Jesus, these people really stick in my craw and as each day slips by like a jet stream, I'm more and more inclined to adopt my boss man's philosophy that they deserve to be taken for every red penny they own. Why the fuck not?

Afternoon becomes evening and the travellers show no sign of wishing to alter their ritualistic lives. They drift back from wherever it is they've been – taking photos, liberties, someone else's anal virginity, who the hell knows – and they stampede into the kitchen to wreak havoc. They crowd the bar, the pool room, the TV lounge. Whinge about the choice of in-house videos, the cost of laundry tokens, the blanket charge, any damned thing, and it all goes straight in one of my hairy ears and out the other. I no longer care, I am as immune to deceit and deception as these people are to unprotected sex. I start to overcharge for no other reason than I get a kick out of it. I have ceased being a diligent manager of the young and the hopeless and am now just another cynical mercenary who doesn't give two sloppy fucks for customer service. I am rather rude too, nowadays.

Before I would have civilly asked people to desist from speaking over the top of me; now I just tell them to shut the fuck up. Sure, it gives me problems, like when those two hot-headed Brazilians offer me the opportunity to go man on man out back to settle a key deposit dispute. In another time, in another place, I probably would have. I'd have grabbed up Dick's trusty length of industrial chain and strapped those mothers for their impudence. But not any more, these days I just laugh it off. Silly little Latin boys. I ought to have some empathy for them, I suppose, the Brazilians and the Jews. Between them they've given me two-thirds of my DNA, my genetic composite. Anyhow, where's my fucking boss? The Very Reverend Jimbo Jones.

Night falls, chat-room city is buzzing and even Dick's got a pew for the porn show. They're all in there tippy tapping away: Dick, a few Swiss, and a gaggle of Israeli chicks who smell like ether. I am finalizing my daily tallies. I am a de facto bean counter. All is steady, there are no icebergs that I know of loitering in my shipping lane, it's full steam to handover. I hear dripping first, but that is not an unusual sound. This place leaks like a Soviet attaché. Then, all I hear is a terrific

WHOOSH! as if the tide's racing out before a tsunami rolls in. For a few precious seconds, there is nothing but silence, and then ... there's Hades.

Not only can I smell smoke, I can see it, pouring from computers, thick, black and choking. People are wet; Dick is absolutely soaked, his nipples erect. Someone is screaming about having been electrocuted, and as I peer up at the ceiling in the internet room I am amazed to see that it is no longer there – just a very large hole, out of which water continues to gush. There are pieces of ceiling everywhere: flaked paint, hunks of plaster, dust, water, crap, and as people begin to yank themselves from sizzling mouses and keyboards I hear water sloshing.

What in the fuck was ... some geek at reception starts to ask me, but before I can respond Dick is past me and clawing madly at the fuse box. Everything goes dark, just like that – and then, the dim nicotine yellow of the back-up light flickers begrudgingly to life. Jo arrives, drops my cocoa and stares fascinated at the scene. The fire alarm goes off, deafening everyone within earshot. I tell Jo to ring the big house, ring fucking Houston and tell them we've got a fucking A-grade problem ... Then there are flickering lights outside and togged-up men with axes are hacking randomly at computer stations.

I am boggled by the magnitude of it all. Jo passes me the receiver; it is Lady Zsa Zsa of the lamp, spouting gibberish. She doesn't want me to call anyone. Has the power been isolated? Is Dick okay? Are the fire brigade there yet? Do I want to splash in the hot tub straight after work? There's no way I'm gonna be handing over to Fabulous Freddy on time.

A crowd has gathered but not one of them is interested in assisting. It is left to me and King Hobbit to ferret around for an old tarpaulin to bung over what remains of the cyberspace portals. Freddy turns up, then Zsa Zsa, followed in quick procession by the Hunter, who is wearing shorts and sandals and carrying the biggest monkey wrench I have ever seen. Behind him is that idle lump the Brother, carrying a bucket. How in the hell does he get up there and back? Zsa Zsa dismisses the fire brigade then tears the tarp from the terminal terminals. She wants them totally waterlogged, wet beyond repair so the insurance assessor can see exactly what's what. I get it straightaway, coming as I do from a family of Brazilian Jewish cockneys who wrote the book about dodgy insurance scams.

The Hunter clambers up through the hole in the roof with the wrench stuck between his teeth while the Brother sets about splashing more water everywhere, except into his bucket. Dick is quickly wrapped in a blanket by his surrogate mammy. I feel, deep in the pit of my empty gut, that somehow this latest mess is gonna be pinned on my notice board; I made a fatal error of judgment by not getting in that fucking hot tub when I had the chance. Once I've grasped this there appears no point in hanging about like a spare prick, so I grab Jo, give Freddy the keys to heaven and, before Zsa Zsa can accost me, I'm gone.

Did you see Dick! Jo laughs with me when we're in bed, must have thought he was being punished from above!

Maybe he was, maybe we all are, babe.

24.

Stripped to the Bone

The Doc is engaged in a poignant soliloquy when I stroll into reception. He is up to his recent chin-job in hard cash, so deep in moolah that one day they'll put his mugshot on a 50-buck note. What remains of the internet room is a goddamned mess. There is a jet heater blowing and some kind of industrial suction device wedged under the carpet. John Hurt would be right at home in here. I expect a team of white-coated techno-boffins to burst in at any minute, armed to the teeth with new technology.

But, as you know by now, I am the eternal optimist. The Doc tells me that the whole mess is a write off, but not to worry, Nigel is coming around later . . .

Nigel? I query my esteemed leader.

That's right; Nigel'll get 'em all working again!

We're not getting new ones?

Hell no! This is good stuff, A-grade equipment, a drop of water won't destroy these beauties. The Doc is patting the computers fondly while he regales me.

What about the insurance guy?

Oh sure, he'll write them off, but we're cleverer than that, huh?

Tighter you mean.

Pardon?

Nothing.

What a rort. That's what Jo said to me and of course she's correct. Anything to save a cent. Look after the cents and the dollars take care of 'emselves, eh? Shit yeah, I tell her, those Swiss upstairs would do a better job of fixing these crashed computers than that bifocal-wearing ...

Are you talking about Nigel? the Doc says. He has materialized out of thin, dust-laden Christchurch air.

Me? Shit no.

Anyhow, I need to speak to you about your ... uhm, manner.

My what?

Last night, you were overhead abusing a guest.

That wasn't a fucking guest, it was that deadhead, Tommy!

Look, that's what I mean, your language ...

So fucking what?

Really, you've got to cut out the attitude. Remember, our job is to serve, okay?

Whatever you fucking say, chief.

I am a bowling ball heading straight for the gutter. Life goes from bad to very bad too quick for my taste. The cleaners are here bemoaning the fact that they still can't get access to those two rooms that stink. I feel my spirits dip further; those wacky Germans will be the death of me. I start to move but the Doc stops me. I'll go, he tells me firmly. How very odd, the Doc leaving me to count cash while he does the real hands-on dirty work? Has he, I wonder, felt a few stabs of remorse?

Ten minutes later the in-house phone rings and I see from the small switchboard that my call is from the cleaners. What? I say.

Call an ambulance! the Doc orders.

What? I answer politely.

There's a guy dead up here, call an ambulance!

I dial 999, nothing happens. Hellfire! Then I dial 000, nothing happens, double-damnation, rat boy! What bloody country am I in? Dick strolls into reception, an expression of congenial idiocy on his face. I am gripped by panic. Why, I don't know. I understand strange deaths.

What's the emergency number? I scream at him.

Why? Dick asks, as he spreads out the racing form.

Because there's a stiff upstairs, that's why!

Jo grabs the phone and hits speed dial, me and Dick race upstairs – and yes, Dick can race when he has to. In the room where I put Wolfgang there is a very bad smell. Two cleaners and the Doc (who, it turns out, isn't a doctor at all) are standing there with lockjaw. Partly obscured by blankets there is a huge mouldering lump and that lump, we see when Dick yanks back the sheet, is naked, naked and blue. Fucking oath! I hear Dick say, and the next thing I see is Dick giving this podgy blue stiff a bit of tongue. Oh my good god, this can't be happening ... I can't be seeing this, I am scarred for life. Dick is sucking tongue, gurgling like a bear with its snout stuck in a soda can, mouth to mouthing a fat dead German in a sleazy hostel.

Suddenly, the German kicks out. That's no back-to-life spasm, I tell the Doc, but Herr Chancellor is indeed alive, back from the brink of blut und boden, no less, and all due to the eager tongue of our very own King Rat, the life-giver. I am nothing if not amazed. Remember that St John's course we made Dick attend? the Doc reminds me smugly.

Now some people, when unexpectedly resurrected from the dark beyond, are exceedingly happy. Their mood is tranquil, their thoughts pure, forgiveness radiates from their again-beating heart. But not this specimen. He grabs Dick in a headlock and starts yelling Germanic obscenities. Shizer, I think, did any one of these fools check this guy's pulse before they unleashed St Dick, patron saint of French kissing?

Was this guy in fact, technically, clinically, dead? Judging by his reaction, I am figuring not, maybe this fat lump is just a very heavy sleeper. What are those bottles of pills on the bedside table? Oh shit, this is a real mess, and still no one has leapt to Dick's aid. Soon it will be the old sod himself who needs a pair of lips attached to his own, and you can count me out of that gig, thanks very much.

I look at the Doc, he looks at me, we communicate telepathically, and then I begin to untangle Dick from his betrothed. The paramedics turn up; it is a ghastly scene. The German is irate, Dick is clutching his throat and wheezing for breath. Just what the hell are they going to write in the report?

It is not the large German who is stretchered out, no indeed, it is Dick himself. How many more medals does his Tweety Pie chest have room for? Sleeping pills, the paramedics tell us, prescription. The guy doesn't travel well and after a long flight he sleeps for like, 70 hours. It's not unusual. Didn't we check for a pulse? I look at the Doc; they are asking him, not me.

Well, that was a close shave, he finally says to me.

Too close for me, I reply.

Right, the Doc orders, let's go up and sort out this other mess. C'mon. So I follow the Doc upstairs: those shorts are a size too small for him. But what if, I think, what if that German had snuffed it? Jeez, there's far more to this job than I'd first thought. What would I have done if it were just me and Jo here, no Doc, no lip-sucking Dick? Would I have mouthed that ugly mush? Would Jo have let me? Would I have let Jo? Would I have just quietly closed the door and left it to some other fool?

Probably yes. Good grief, I am no Samaritan, no Saint fucking Christopher, hell no.

Christ, what's that pong? the Doc quizzes as we near the next fatal door. I dread to think, but if it's another stiff I'm outta here. I say nothing though, not a twitter. The Doc slides in the key and pushes the door. Nothing happens. What the? Here, help me shove, he orders.

Shit, this is much closer to my boss than I feel the need to be, hugging him while we both grunt and push together, more homoerotica. The door budges a little, it's obvious that the dopehead in this room has barricaded himself in. What in the name of the Reich is wrong with these people?

Keep shoving! the Doc demands like some queer pirate at a sleaze ball. It gives enough for one of us to squeeze through – and fortunately for me the Doc has a waspish waistline, so in he slithers. I hear furniture being shifted, then the door is sufficiently ajar for size-twelve me to enter. Good god, this room has been totally wrecked: the window is up, so is the carpet, ripped up and stuffed into the shower cubicle. There are cigarette burns on the bedclothes, the mattress, the dresser, the curtains. There is a pile of crap in one corner and saucers, plates and filthy cups among mouldy pizzas, half-eaten burgers, and a few mung beans, still sprouting. And, alas, there is the filthy detritus of the junkie: spent syringes, torn strips of sheet, blood, piss, little neat piles of burned residue. This is a crack den. The TV is gone, probably already pawned I think. What a . . .

What a bloody mess, the Doc sighs. I nod agreeably. In fact it is more than a mess, in any fool's language it is an unmitigated disaster. We both stand there, deep in thought . . . my, the Doc does have tight buns.

I tell Jo all about it later, after the Doc has left with the cash and the cleaners have begun the arduous task of stripping that room barer. How do you do it? Jo asks me as she watches some lunatic talk to himself by the faux shrubbery.

Damned if I know, but I ought to have known, bloody Germans.

Oi! I'm one of those bloody Germans! She is too, madness is in her blood. At least that shithead paid. And what about my Swiss?

They checked out, I tell her, all but one.

The one-armed one?

No, Adolf wasn't with them.

Adolf? Are you yanking my chain?

I kid you not, sweet cheeks, that's his name! Jo shrugs.

So, who stayed?

Some guy called Franco Fux.

Ah c'mon, quit it!

Straight up, I got his passport. He wants to sell you a car.

I bet he does. Franco Fux, indeed.

But that was his name and, friends, Franco and I would soon be solar plexus deep in dodgy car sales. But what comes first is night shift. The night shift is long and boisterous. BK's bar is doing a roaring trade, what with the free drink vouchers he's handing around like plugs of dope. Hell yes, I have enough on my hands trying to lock the front doors, chain up the kitchen and stop people using the tumble-dryers. We are selling phone cards by the hundred and I'm walking around with a dozen or so in my back pocket – the ones fools buy and leave in the booth having spent only a third of their value. I am a phone-card scalper, it's a good screw.

I have to roust the dregs of society out of the TV lounge, try to heave shut the connecting door to the bar and keep ever-vigilant for potential killers who shouldn't be in my joint.

That ogre Wolfgang is down here every 30 minutes demanding his money bags then standing at the hatch counting his bread with one podgy thumb. Each time he completes this chore he roars, Who has been stealing my money? Each time I tell him to count it again or lodge a complaint – I need eight sets of eyes and at least three pairs of hands to keep a lid on this chaos.

By the time Jo arrives at sixish I am as buggered as a plains sheep come sun-up. I have spent the last three hours of my five-hour stint counting and re-counting cash; I could be held up at any minute and it is starting to unnerve me. Having done a half-decent job at cleaning up the carnage in the kitchen, I have checked the fire-escapes for wannabe Boston stranglers, booked in yet more middle-of-the-night arrivals, de-bugged the phone booths, and kept Dick away from the two PCs Nigel has brought back to still life. I am the consummate pro.

On Sunday afternoon, when we are finally reprieved and weekend passed, we get absolutely blotto in some bar. After this we go to the video store and haul home an armful of films we won't have time to watch. Later, we go out to buy burgers then lie in the bath taking a few randomly selected tabs we've found hidden in the discarded prescription drug box in the cleaner's room. Mixed with the booze and the MSG the whole experience is very *Naked Lunch*. The following day I have a head like the Elephant Man and we have to drive out to Whoop Whoop to see my quack. Franco Fux has kindly lent us one of his fleet of ex-CIB Sierras as a sort of road-test. It belches more tar than a power plant and the clutch is nonexistent, the kind of car at least three seasons of speed freaks have humped to

Invercargill and back. There are more miles on the clock than at Chernobyl.

My doctor, after she's studied my blood tests, says, Shut, Turri, your livils are all ever the shaw! Whut the hill is going on in your leaf? That's what she says slipping more vowels than my clutch plate does gears.

Luts git you up on the bid, she continues, and obediently I climb up on the gurney. She has my pants off in a flash – god that woman has nimble fingers, and cold ones too. The next minute she has my sack in one hand and is asking me to cough. Jeez. Jo is sitting in the corner looking at me angrily until she discovers the plastic head you can flip open and slide the brain out of. Dr Sweetlove is still holding my balls while she counts to ten: win, two, thre, fir, fauve . . .

I am thinking I'll tell the Doc that a Ritalin dispenser would be better than a hot drinks machine in reception . . .

I thunk we shud lup these off, heh? the doctor says oh so casually, as if she's disgusted by them.

What? I ask from my ceiling-gazing position.

I thunk your problums all stim from these luttle beggars.

I think she is right. Jo thinks she is right, though she also thinks it's about time the doctor let go of my tackle. I agree.

Rit than, up you git. Jesus, finally. I feel about as grubby as a defrocked pageant queen in Trump Tower and as flat as a deflated weather girl. She hands me a script for something, listens to my chest with her equipment, gets me to blow in the asthma inhaler, slaps my arse twice to check my blood flow and gives me a referral to a veterinary clinic that does cheap castrations. Shit, yes, give me a good old-fashioned country doctor any day of the damned week.

You enjoyed that, didn't you? Jo berates me when we are back trying to roll start Franco's love wagon.

Don't be ridiculous, I tell her, it's just a medical examination. Christ, what kind of a sick freak do you think I am?

Did she have nice hands?

How in the hell should I know?

I bet if she grew up on a farm milking cows she'd have soft hands.

Can't we just leave it? Haven't I been invaded enough for one day?

I bet she thought you felt just like one of those udders, all squirmy and soft.

You're making me feel queasy!

It's Jo's idea that we go shopping for lingerie, just to keep our hands in, and it's a noble gesture. Not so many moons ago I was pretty blasé about being in the lingerie department and waltzing past the change-room frau with an armful of something lace-trimmed and flouncy. But not today, today I'm all flustered and over-dressed in my disguise, very decently exposed. I feel like a liar in there amid the perfumes and the finery, as the retail chick gives me a frown.

I simply can't grasp the core concept of who I really am and slowly but very surely that hostel is erasing me, rubbing out the me who arrived in this fair land almost a year ago with high hopes. I even scuttle away while Jo pays for our choices, which makes me feel even more a coward. Over a beer Jo tells me I ought to just rock up to work tomorrow in full make-up, a boob tube and a micro skirt, and see if they'll sack me on the spot for fraud.

It's a fine rebellious idea, right up my street, but somehow I just don't have the balls for it; those things are still in the hands of Dr Strangelove.

High season has arrived, in its summer fash. You cannot walk casually past reception en route to your humble lodgings because there are bags everywhere, many with bleary-eyed grunts laying on them. This is a flesh fest, planeload after cargo-hold full of ditch-hoppers all ready to round off their once in a lifetime OE. It's the big time, baby, time to separate the men from the boys.

You're sick, Jo tells me, but she doesn't mean sick in the head. I am sick. It has come down on me overnight and I do not just feel bad, no, I feel as if I have one foot inside of death's waiting room. I think I must have caught something up in Whoop Whoop, some kind of cow disease. Worse than colic as overnight my lungs have contracted and I have more phlegm at my beck and call than the mob at a punk gig circa '76. There is no way that I can get through fifteen-hour days feeling like this . . .

There is no provision for sick leave in the covenant, however. We studied it by candlelight last night, even the small print written in lemon juice. Me no work, me no get paid. It has been another wretched night full of screams; another night of unrequited advances, forced anal penetration and lustful thoughts. This place is like a colony of Barbary apes trying to work out the magical angle of yaw. This is Rings country, hobbits, gremlins, ogres and fair maidens stripped buck naked and tied to trees in moonlit forests. They are all stark raving mad, and especially these ones here; five to a pull-down sofa bed in the upstairs TV-lounge-cum-overflow-dormitory; even this pill-head, sleeping in his roll by the bin. I kick his feet deliberately. What a bunch of good-for-nothing wasters.

The whole joint smells ripe, ready to breed.

25.

Peek-A-View

Here is how one day looks from our vantage point, our little window on the world of the backpacker ... There are two Nordic-looking girls attired very unseasonably. They are straight from the big southern land, all blonde hair, white teeth, brown skin, micro-micro skirts and bulging vulvas – bona fide penis fly traps. I am groping for the mace that was confiscated from the American girl who left this morning refusing to pay her bill – just in case I need it. Two more travel-weary types enter the fray, take one look at the carnage and quickly do an about-turn. I don't worry – this is high season and they'll soon find out that there are *no* other beds available within a 50-k radius.

I book in the Nordic girls, they are good for business, these walking, talking Barbie dolls will draw a crowd and that crowd will spend up big in the bar; that is our brief. I turn away two dodgy types who look like career criminals; they have no luggage or ID and sound as if they come from the big smoke on the North Island. They are opportunists, drawn to the ritual mugging season like iron filings to a magnet. They are polarized and ready to rob.

The police arrive. They are on the hunt for an absconded dope fiend wanted in eight countries. They show me his mug shot and my heart plunges downwards like a hot turd in a septic tank about to be eaten alive by anaerobic bacteria. I recognize the face, once you have seen it, you could never forget it, even a mother couldn't love something as brutal as that. I do my civic duty and give them the room number and they tear upstairs. Just when I think it can't get any worse, all hell breaks loose in the communal kitchen over rights to a house wok. I should go down there but I value my life more than a hostel wok. That is good sense and why I've survived as long as I have on this crazy chunk of molten rock we call home. Dick arrives and wants to know who let the Kiwis in.

What Kiwis? I ask.

These. He shows me five drivers' licences with ugly snapshots.

What's the problem, we've got their ID, ain't we?

And that's all we've got! Those bros stripped this place bare last night, took everything that weren't bolted down. Even the fish tank! I've got to spend the day compiling an inventory!

Over on the table by the sofa is a rectangular space in the dust. All of this raises puzzling questions: Why take an empty fish tank? If the place has been stripped bare, what on earth is there left to add to an inventory?

Now, what about this dope fiend, huh?

He sure looked cruel, a fact attested to by the picture on the front page of today's paper, the one I'm looking at right now. Jeesus, that guy is butt ugly. And famous to boot, if this press beat-up is anything to go by he's the most-wanted crim on the islands. Who'd have thought, eh? What drama! At least I didn't check that mug in.

I'm still looking at the photo, thinking I'll clip it out for the hostel's rogues gallery, when I glance up and – lo and behold –

the same toothy lopsided grin is leering at me in techno 3D. Ye gods! I step back warily before spotting the accompanying plain-clothed cops. Reassured, I study him closely. This crim has more jewellery than a cheap transvestite, not to mention several tattoos and facial piercings – I mean it's hardly a look designed to blend, is it? The cops here must be slack as, oops, keep it to yourself, Teri Lou, cops have long memories. This joker wants his sunglasses, one of the cops tells me. It's an odd request. En Zed's most-wanted wants his sunglasses back? And the police seem happy about it. I'm not sure what they want me to do, although I'm certain I'll find out any minute.

We go upstairs, two cops, the rogue, and yours very truly. I am not under arrest, a fact I state to a couple of numbnuts ready to gloat. I think we are going to the dorm this fiend was in yesterday, all four of us – but no, the two cops plop down on the upstairs-landing sofa to ogle some foreign flesh wrapped in a towel heading for the mud bath. Take him, will you, they ask me, see if his bloody sunnies are there or not, he's been bitching about those glasses ...

I'm about to say, Do you think that's wise? But I never get the opportunity. Me and the crim go into the dorm, where the crim lies on the bunk he'd occupied and fiddles about in the slats of the bunk above – the guy is obviously jailhouse schooled. He produces his sunnies, cheap yellow plastic, two bucks in any variety shop, and about four wraps of something white, 75 a gram on any street corner. Shit, I think, maybe I ought to ...

Say, bud, the fiend says to me, smiling his graveyard smile, I forgot to return me key yesterday, here. And he chucks the key at me.

Thanks, I say.

You wanna pair of sunglasses too?

Won't you need them?

Nah, too obvious.

Choice, bro.

Say, is that the fire-escape out there?

I look out the window. Uh, yeah …

Spot of luck, eh? He pauses while he considers his next move. What say you count to ten, nah, say twenty, and then walk slowly back and tell those two dumbass cops you went for a piss and when you came back … He already has one leg outside, what could I do?

As he scuttles off, I go downstairs the back way – no point getting those cops, that'd only incriminate me. At reception I check out the fiend's key and discover, shit, he didn't bother to collect his key deposit, which means another twenty in the Doc's tax-free slush fund. I busy myself with the register, waiting for the fall out.

Fifteen minutes later two plain-clothed cops tear past reception, then race back in.

Where is he? they yell at me.

Who? I say.

Who! they cry in unison. Later I give my side of events to a WPC, who proves sympathetic to my situation. Those are way nice earrings, she tells me between taking calls on her walkie-talkie.

You should see my cool yellow sunnies, I reply.

A week or so later, when me and the Jo'ster are relaxing in our abode, who should be on the Sunday night current affairs show other than our good friend Mr Absconded. Jesus, yes, he had made it to Fiji or someplace, and there he is basking in his own exploits, sipping a cocktail with a little pink umbrella in it and fondling his new twelve-year-old spouse. I almost choke on the wishbone of the pull-apart chook we're devouring, when he raises his glass to the good guy at ... Oh, Lordy.

And now to this 'indecent' assault business. I can't recall how it all began, but I'm pretty sure it caught alight in a mixed dorm. Those places are nothing more than brothels really. Six bodies in a room with anatomies exposed. What do you expect, sister? What assault *isn't* indecent?

Anyhow, the lady in question turns up at the Hole claiming to have been indecently molested for eight straight hours.

Eight hours? I am not unsympathetic but somewhat sceptical. There were four other people in that dorm, two other chicks, what did they do? You are sure it wasn't consensual? I have to ask.

Hell, no! she shrieks at me.

Unfortunately I've been here before, the cops too, and just like me they're sick of filing false reports. Maybe this girl has been assaulted, but surely not for eight hours. Grab a Ritalin and settle down, okay? But no, we're going all the way on this one, in-house line-ups, swabs, fingerprinting, paternity tests ... another fine advert for budget travelling.

I call the fuzz on the hotline through to a makeshift desk at The Station, the one set up each summer for these kinds of hijinks. Someone will call around later, yeah sure, and in the meantime I'll be left babysitting this probable nut job. I am thinking she is a nut job because now she's bringing back the free phone card I just gave her to call home with, complaining that it doesn't work. I have to go with her to the booth, yank out some waster ringing escort services and dial the number for her, whereupon it connects first time. Bing! Hello!

Next, one of her roommates-for-the-night is down here telling me the numbnut in that phone booth there caused havoc in their dorm all night, verbally abusing people, claiming they'd stolen her hairbrush, nits, hymen, cold cream, any damned thing. She demands a refund. I agree with her but explain that I am charged with an onerous responsibility and must take all complaints, no matter how ridiculous, seriously. Phone girl comes back and straightaway accuses the other girl of wearing her T-shirt. Good Christ, this is becoming intolerable, even for a person with a patient streak as long as mine. They start arguing then fall into the harem scare'em cat-fight routine, right there in the middle of a high season backpacking reception. What can I do? No way am I gonna waste a manicured nail or risk a stray claw scarring me for life by getting between these two klepto kittens.

I could do with Jo and her Doc Marten's right now but she's off buying magazines. The Brother is next to useless and Dick's taking inventory. Why are none of these people around when I need them? A crowd gathers, congeals and starts yelling and baiting as the two sisters of the apocalypse go at it hair root for hair root. Why? One of these girls is a certified nutter, probably some escapee from the funny farm, and the other is a real jaw-breaker. Wham! That was one hell of a swing, unorthodox, no trainer could teach that shit. I couldn't have done it better myself. Jaw-breaker lays the nutter out flat, no point counting to ten. And that's definitely assault of some kind . . .

The uniforms arrive and I have to give yet another statement; they have my signature on a lot of documents down there. Anyhow, just like in Borstal I claim I'm blind, deaf and dumb, no point in getting all catty about it. It'll all pan out in the rinse, no one is innocent and everyone is guilty of something. But, hell, that was some punch.

You remember the rough-house Aussie and the jilted mail-order Danish bride? Well, here they are, engaged 'n' all. From heartbreaker to heart maker. The guy is happy as a moonbeam on vacation, tells me they're having a ceremony down by the river tomorrow and how'd I like to be best man, seeing how it was me who ... He must have caught my eyebrows arching. Oh shit, sorry, luv. This place is real queer, innit?

Queerer than you realize, friend.

When it's way busy like this, even we run out of floor space and when that happens we have to go through the pointless exercise of phoning other hostels to appease fraught, bedless guests. The whole business is a charade, achieving nothing more than a chance to chat to others in your vocation. Other fools grafting for a pittance and a bed. Today by some weird cosmic fluke, I've rung Puppy Love, the boutique backpackers.

I get through to some slack-jawed geek and we have a conversation. Hi, I say, you wouldn't have any ...

Not a chance, bud. What are you, new to town?

Ho ho ho. Say, shithead, you guys still got that rotunda up there, the one with the fancy sunnies on?

Hell, no, that thing was gone in sixty seconds!

How's the Krishna canteen?

Brother, I've chowed nothing but lentils since I've been here!

Good-o, nice to hear another voice!

Same. Say, any vacancies up there on the job front?

You know what, kid, give it about six weeks.

Ta, bud, watch out for a fat German with money belts.

You got him up there now?

Shit yes, had the paramedics here last night, thought that monster had snuffed it!

Ho ho ho.

Some days, this job is sweet as. I take a call from the Doc. Watch out for strippers, he tells me.

Strippers? What the hell is that guy chewing? Strippers is all I need in a rat pit like this.

Any dramas? he asks before he checks into liposuction.

Dramas? F –, hell no, everything's tickety-boo, boss, ticking along very nicely.

You're doing a great job.

Click.

26.

In the Summertime

The heat is on. Radiant heat, friends, and I'm right in its glare. I told you I was feeling unwell. Well it's gone beyond that stage. I am wheezing worse than Dick after his first roll-up of the day and I have lungs like blocked drains.

Besides this, I am now in the used-car business; New Zealand's answer to Arthur Daley. Stand on me, my word is my bond, all that cockney shit. I've got it down pat. Somehow I ended up sinking too many pints of BK's finest ale last night, secreted in a corner with that Swiss hit man, Franco Fux. That guy was loaded, he had more cash than Thomas Cook himself. Look, he told me, I have to get out of town real fast. There's some kind of mess with immigration over fake passports. Only, I've got all these cars, see? He did have too, the car park had quickly become Franco's lot. It seemed like a good idea at the time. Franco would fly home before he was extradited to some-place hellish, and I'd become his de facto partner in unwarranted vehicles. Here, he said, sliding me a sheaf of registration documents and a bunch of keys bigger than St Peters. What else could I do? Forty per cent is good business, and all for flogging unroadworthy motor vehicles to gullible straight-off-the-plane cripples. Shit, I ought to change my name to Helga and just be done with it.

On night shift I ignored the jobs list while I ripped other folk's 'cars for sale' notices off the in-house board and covered it with my own little beauties. The Doc can smell a rat as soon as faxes headed Geneva Prison begin spewing out of his mojo machine all hours of the day and night. Good old Franco.

Can't you stop that crazy guy faxing you all the time? the Doc demands. It's jamming our lines of communication! And when are you gonna move all those cars out of our lot, it ain't your personal playground you know?

Where in the hell am I going to put a dozen cars? I have to slash the prices, and I tell Franco that in a stern fax written in BOLD.

Fuck you! he replies.

Aren't you hot? the Doc asks me, on at least ten consecutive mornings. He is down to a G-string and a singlet, all very blue-collar man-about-town. Even Dick has taken the callipers off his pins and slithered into a pair of khaki cargo shorts. Those legs of his look like two albino praying mantises. The Brother is on the sofa in his muu-muu, like a fat Arab waiting for a blonde day tripper. Each new wave of disgorged travellers is wearing less than the mob preceding them. Cleavage and butt cracks are all the rage, stomachs and vulvas are in vogue. Whole landings are vibrating to the rhythm of the night. But not me, the only vibrating I am doing is caused by the regular spasm attacks that bend me double and send my face crimson. Snot runs from my nose in an unstemmable torrent. My arse is so open and enflamed you can park a Mac truck up there. Each and every muscle, already wasted from my savage doses of oestrogen, tries to gnaw off the sinew attaching it to my skeletal frame. A big band percussion section has set up a squat in my head, and they play some Fat Boy Slim combo on loop. And still the temperature outside rises, and still I can't get warm.

And then I do get warm, so warm I am overcome with a gripping urge to rip off my eight layers of clothes and sprint buck naked to the communal showers. Hormones and bronchial infections aren't compatible bedmates. You boil first, then freeze, your eyes feel like they're hanging out of their sockets on small bungee ropes and your tongue doesn't fit your mouth any more.

Still, this flu is letting me off the undressing hook, the one the Doc keeps hammering home like a crooked nail. I'm in no state to walk around undressed, surely he can see that much?

I am hacking my way through another night shift, the front doors are shut and the restaurant padlocked. Jo is still with me helping with the cleaning, bless her little bobby socks. I have every mother here, all 156 of them, according to the official register, on a very short leash. None of those meatheads fancies a face full of infected spittle should they dare to remonstrate over any of my spur-of-the-moment house rules. Such as: Get off that fucking couch right now and either hit your bunk or the street.

There are a thousand sticky plates and dishes down in our kitchen that I'm not touching. The health and safety department has just turned up unexpectedly with warrants to enter and peruse. This is what you dread the most, except for an outbreak of fire. The Doc fears it and Zsa Zsa lives in absolute terror of it. If *it happens*, I'm to stall and ring the hotline IMMEDI-ATELY. For what? Petty officialdom isn't interested in lame excuses, they're in and you're done, that's the bottom line.

I traipse around wearily behind the posse of inspectors, nodding in agreement each time they stop and berate me.

Jesus, yes, smoke detectors, well ... Why is that fire-escape door welded shut? Shit, that's a good question! Emergency lighting tests? Passageways too dark? Bins overflowing? Kitchen appliances not earthed and still-smouldering cigarettes in that trash can. Really? The last time we did a full drill was ... Oh, a list of violations, thanks. Twenty-one days to fix and repair or vacate? Swell, don't worry, boss, I'm on it ... Oops, yeah, mind that live cable there. I'm not doing well, these boys are all for boarding up and plastering 'Condemned!' notices everywhere.

There are no more rapturous epiphanies about upgrades and modernization to be heard. There is more bullshit in this place than out on any stud farm. The spin-doctoring Doc and his heathen mistress have just been spun out. I am left with a sheaf of evil-looking paperwork, much of which has large, red writing at the top. I plop it in the Doc's in-tray. This is not my business, I have four more cars to shift tonight at an incredibly inflated price and somehow I've misplaced Franco's Swiss bank details. Oh well, once smitten twice fried, as the Chinese say. I have at least 30 phone cards to panhandle and enough small electrical gear to open my own discount store as compensation. Need a rucksack, roll, mat, hiking boots in size eighteen, ski poles, climbing spikes, inflatable vest, money belt? Then, sister, I'm your girl. Please step into my office right here. That's right, the ladies shithouse, that 'Out Of Order' notice is just there for my convenience. Clean? Hell yes, you could eat your noodles out of any bowl and live to tell the tale, my friend. Now, US dollars or Euros only, okay?

By morning's first light, those bar girls haven't so much as dirtied a fake nail touching that mountain of crockery. I am three cars to the good but still coughing like an asthmatic glue sniffer – but I am almost off. Jo will be here soon, then I can hit the hay and count cash. There is an odd ensemble of folks ringing my buzzer. One is a shady-looking guy accompanied by a gang of long-legged hookers. Fuck off, I mouth through the doors I haven't bothered to clean. In the light I can see they have more paw prints than a feed truck at the zoo. The guy is holding up something, most likely another warrant to enter. I move closer and read it; it's a forward booking receipt ... whoops, no beds at this inn, honey.

I buzz him and his hoes in. These must be the strippers the Doc alluded to but never actually pencilled in. They sure look like strippers; there's more latex on these chicks than at a fetish carnival, and they squeak when they walk. They've come straight from their first gig and reek of sweat and medically manipulated ovarian cycles. Even if I had a room, none of these girls could hold a pen to sign their name, not with nails that long. Hmmm, now, let me see, there'll be no room until eleven at the earliest. The greasy manager checks his wrist watch. That's seven hours away?

Sure, I tell him, but look at it this way, fella, if I were to book you in now you'd be paying a day's rate for six hours, huh? Why not just doss down in the smoking room there. You can hang a sheet over the door and I'll chuck in some pillows and a few blankets. Problem sol-ved!

How much? the guy quizzes me. Actually, I was gonna give it to him for free, but seeing I'll be back on the desk at eleven anyhow ...

Sweet deals in paradise. Welcome to the asylum. Free tuberculosis shot with every third night booked! No wonder I'm a golden princess, man, I could pimp my own mother in a joint like this, sell stale stools to coprophiliacs at a handsome profit. It's the Romany in me. I hand the baton of power over to Jo.

You look fucking dead, she tells me.

I think I have died, and come back.

What was on the other side?

The Department of Occupational and Environmental Health and Safety.

Crapola.

It is all getting far too much for me, and Jo is suffering twice as much. She is as near to cracking as I've seen, even nearer than when she tried to beat that poor kid senseless on the bus in Scotland. I ought to go easy on her; she's doing her best . . .

27.

Upstairs Downstairs

I return to work still feeling as sick as a pig dog with mange. I have been to my quack, but she was not pleased to see me – like that. Shut, Turri, she said, after I couldn't even blow on the machine that measures your lung capacity, we have old ludies here who ken bluw this thung like a Sully Army trumpet.

My lungs are shot to shit. I am a size ten and falling. She doesn't know what I've got, maybe asthma, maybe tuberculosis, only blood will reveal the truth. She gives me antibiotics, a slap on the rump to check my colour and a sick certificate, which I eat on the way back to the car.

And so, here I am, listening to my revered leader Doctor Benway inform us that me and Jo are going upstairs. Jo is with me, sitting on the stool, ripping more designer holes in the fishnets she bought yesterday. She shoots me a furtive glance of displeasure, her cute little mouth turned upwards and her dimples flushed with anger. I know that look. I smile at her and put one finger to my own sweet lips. She scowls, and as the Doc carries on with his fantastic story – the one about being under-manned and overbooked, about the cleaners being on the verge of physical exhaustion, and Dick being laid up crook – that scowl turns to undisguised fury.

After our next set of days off, the Doc tells us, we will be starting work at eight, upstairs, cleaning. I smile, like the gorm-less hormone-ravaged freak I am. Smiling is just about the only facial emotion I can manage these days, and hadn't my quack said that a smile a day keeps a slow death at bay? We will strip rooms, make up beds, clean shit pots, scrub showers, empty trash, run the laundry, get big into domesticity on an industrial scale, and after we've done all that, one of us will take over the desk at midday and our normal day shall resume.

I hate this fucking place, Jo tells me angrily after the Doc has scuttled off.

Me too, honey. But, hey, every cloud has a silver lining.

Yeah, and what's this one?

Plunder and piracy, my high-seas wench. If these fools think we're going to bust our butts cleaning rooms while their appointed cleaners sit outside and smoke grass, they have one big shock coming! Most vacated rooms yield up something useful, don't they? Thermal socks, toiletries, nail clippers, tweezers, eyelash curlers. Not squeamish about putting your privates in pre-worn undies? Don't mind buying your own batteries, or invading your personal space with another gal's vagina balls?

Some slapper's old vagina balls, yuk! She cannot be charmed. You can shove those up your sweet arse if that's what turns you on.

And what's that supposed to mean?

Though of course I knew damn well it means we've reached a critical point in the meltdown process and that the options, other than having it out, are absolute zero. I hate this stuff, but I'm the elder – I have a daughter only a handful of years younger than Jo. As the elder – but not necessarily the wiser – I guess it falls upon me to get us out of the messes I've gotten us into.

It simmers all day. The handover is tense and tetchy. I understand. I don't want to bust my balls upstairs either and, yes, we've been cheated, but we're so close to the end, and I'd like to explain all this and more to Jo over a beer or even after sex but there's no opportunity for anything as civil as that because it's just never-ending hours at the coalface. So instead, we just exchange grimaces and by shift's end I'm as het up as she is. I know she's waiting up there for me. But not like she sometimes waits. She's not in the fishnets tonight, just one bad-arsed mother of a mood. I climb upstairs slowly; maybe I can still talk her out of this bleak funk. I'll try, anyhow. I open the door and she starts: Where the fucking hell have you been?

I'm not even late, really. I remind her I had to do the handover.

Oh yeah, it's always the handover, the job, the roster, the money, the Doc, the shuttle, some skanky bitch hanging around the desk who maybe wants to fuck you or you want . . .

Hey! I say, trying not to raise my voice. Raising my voice isn't a good thing. Raising my voice infuriates her because we're supposed to be equals. Girl equals. When I raise my voice she thinks I'm talking over/at/down to her and that's such a shithead guy thing to do.

Don't you hey me, she says angrily. Why didn't you tell him to take a hike with his stupid fucking cleaning, I thought you were a . . .

Oh, she's stopped just short. I was sure she was going to say she thought I was a man.

You thought I was a what? I can't let it go. Her words have just slid on out, old habits still not dead after these past few years of trying.

I thought you'd stand up to him, for us. She scowls.

Why the fuck didn't *you*? I'm yelling now. We're equals aren't we? Why'd you expect me to do it?

You told me to be quiet.

Yeah, that's a nice pincer move – a real girl checkmate kind of move. Smack! I try to smile at her in a vain attempt to diffuse the situation but my smile comes across as mockery.

You always think you're right. You always tell me to shut up. You always wanna take charge then land us both in a mess. Her words come out rapid fire, rat-a-tat-tat.

I don't always think I'm right. It's just I've had more . . .

Oh yeah, more experience, that's right. Like, you've had oh so much experience of boring jobs and going home to your straight wife and yelling at her just like you yell at me some-times because you think I'm just a stupid girl who's never been anywhere or done anything and . . .

Just shut the fuck up, okay! There, I've said it. The immortal guy phrase. And the moment it's slipped the leash I'm regret-ting it, but we're both too far in to concede now. Some people might say it's the age factor, but not me. I don't believe in it. On almost every level, young Jo and I are compatible. Even in the sack, though, by god, when they're young and horny it can be hard to stay the pace.

That's right. Start with the guy bullshit, she chides me.

What guy bullshit? Don't dykes tell each other to shut the fuck up now and again?

Not like you say it. Not like the way you get so angry and physical with it.

Bullshit.

That's your answer to everything. I hate this place and these people and I wanna go.

Well, fucking go then, go on, grab a fucking bag and fuck off! Why don't ya!

This is getting way out of hand. I have no idea why I'm still going at it – perhaps because I've got a testosterone surge; perhaps because I've been acting the man here for too long already, perhaps perhaps perhaps – perhaps because I'm just an old idiot.

Jo jumps up, makes a grab for the suitcase on top of the wardrobe, almost ripping the top from it as she slings it on the bed. She starts opening drawers in the chest so hard that they come right out and lingerie goes everywhere. I don't intervene – much as I want to.

She is slinging stuff at random into the case. I wonder how far she's going to get with two dozen pairs of panties. I almost – almost – want to laugh at the ludicrousness of this situation, but I can't. So instead, I urge her on: Go on, that's it, run away little girl.

Ah fuck, I wish I hadn't said that.

FUCK YOU! She screams so loud that I'm pretty sure they'll have heard it in the lounge two floors below. I have the overwhelming desire to yell back, only louder, to really let one rip and use the old boom box I've struggled so hard to subdue these past few years. She keeps on stuffing more and more crap into the case so that now I can't even see the damned case.

You'll need another case, I say dryly.

FUCK YOUUUU!!

Oh man, even those guys in the motorcycle dealership up the street will have heard that one.

Keep your fucking voice down, for chrissakes!

Why? In case anyone hears us? Hears me screaming? Or maybe hears me scream something like: YOU'RE SUPPOSED TO BE A FUCKING GIRRRLLLLL!!!!!!!!!

Oh man. That one really registered.

Okay, okay! I say. You're right, okay?

Oh, I'm right! Well, so fucking WHATTTT!!!

Look, keep your fucking voice down!

NO I FUCKING WON'T!!

You crazy bitch!

Me crazy? Look at you!

C'mon now, it'll be okay, like it always is.

Fuck if it will! Go and tell those jerks you're a GIIRRLLL!!!

Stop fucking yelling, goddamnit!

I can yell if I want. I'll yell all day and all night and I'll yell that you're a girl not a stupid fucking guy!

Christ! Shut up you silly fucking CUNT!!!!

Oh fuck. That was a real biggy. A big, booming, angry slur of male indignation. Like a lion roaring out on the plains. She looks at me dumbfounded, frozen in fear, humiliation, shock . . .

That really ends the argument. And maybe it'll end it all. I am as dumbstruck as Jo with what just came out of my mouth. I fumble around, ashamed of myself. I need to say sorry, to rewind and erase, but that big C word is still resonating.

I have sometimes thought that we have these sporadic tiffs just so young Jo can indulge her penchant for make-up sex. She just wants things to be like they were not so long ago. Like when we used to put away a couple of bottles of red a night then pee in one another's glasses just to get that alcohol content too. Or like when we used to stay the night in swish hotels and make the room service boy come at four in the morning with cheese toasties and we'd be scantily clad and have a strap-on strategically placed. Or like, maybe, when we used to two-up in the ladies' change rooms in posh stores and fake sex so that the change room chick would have to come tell us it wasn't a dyke bar, you know? I know Jo misses all that bump and grind fun shit. Me too. But I have to remind her constantly that we're doing this shit because at the end of our season of pain there'll be a cash crop that'll allow us some freedom again. The minute we're out of here, I tell her, you bet your sweet arse I'll ditch this stupid charade and we can get back to, uh, normal.

You think anyone heard us screaming? she asks me.

Most likely the whole town, even the Wizard down at the Square most likes!

Oh, Jesus, what'll we do?

Say nothing, babe. And if you feel as if you must say something, make it a denial.

I go out to get booze. A few people look at me uneasily. I smile as if nothing's happened. The loser on reception tells me I've instructions from our esteemed leader, and hands me an envelope. Yup, that fool is off on another junket someplace and who really gives a flying fuck.

When I get back upstairs I give Jo the good news.

So when he gets back you're going to tell them we're leaving the day our contract finishes?

Or we'll flip for it.

But . . .

No buts, babe. If we're equals, which we are, then flipping is the fairest possible way to decide who does the dirty business, huh?

S'pose.

The last wave of the high season is about to commence.

28.

The British are Coming

The British are coming and they are a cinch for me, the minutiae of their lives and needs are mine too: sleep, shit, drink copiously, check the football results, read a rag, eat a late-night curry and start all over again.

No more Canadians with their hang-dog grimaces. No more Germans with their surly arrogance. No more Yanks with that air of superiority. No more Israelis with their aggressive stare-downs. No more Chinese with their cunning righteousness. No more Indians with their know-it-all demeanours. Now I can ditch the carefully scripted deceit of the hostelling industry – with the British, I can let it all rip. The Doc is offshore, Dick is recently engaged to a Tupperware tart from Austin, Texas, and the Brother's secret assignations are no longer secret. His wo-man turned up last night; I think she's real, a GG – genetic girl – unless she's so flush she could afford to have her Adam's Apple shaved and a couple of ribs removed.

She is a children's writer, or so I'm led to believe. Maybe the Brother is the subject of her next book and she is undertaking research. That kind of information gathering is above and beyond the call of literary duty. Today the Brother turned up all spick 'n' span, buffed up and bronzed. I hardly recognized him. And for the first time the Brother came to the hole and engaged me in conversation. He's not as dumb as I'd thought, or as I've painted him to you. The Brother has his head screwed on. He's shafting these rubes big time, with bed and board gratis for hauling a few dirty sheets to and fro. That Zsa Zsa is a sucker for a dumb brute. Well, good on him, he sure fooled me. He's been biding his time in the nuthouse waiting his moment. His act shouldn't get him too many openings, but didn't 200 women a week pen love letters to Ted Bundy on death row? Women are unable to resist flinging themselves hair first at a giant lump of hopelessness. Jesus, there's prospects for anyone, for any guy who presumes he'll be on the shelf till the slab and all he has to cling to for titillation is peeping through half-open blinds with his tool out. Women are strange creatures.

I stand there chewing the fat with the Brother. He is telling me about his days in Indo-China when he hunted down traitors for Mao. The guy is well travelled; well read too, he's reading Oscar Wilde. The Brother is the master of deception, much like my good self, I suppose.

The Brother's woman turns up again, this time in broad daylight and I see she's not bad looking considering her age. In another time, I'd probably have ridden her bare back. The Brother has scored big time with this catch; a landing like this would prove a winner in any angling competition. Off they go, hand in hand, like a couple of desperate housewives. Dick slinks into reception, big black circles around his snake-brown eyes. Hell of a night in space, he tells me tiredly while he rips the racing supplement from the day's paper. Dick has picked up the vernacular, and the blank facial expression that comes from long nights staving off an epileptic fit. The poor fool has most likely jacked himself stupid over some balding beer-bellied guy pretending to be a seventeen-year-old cheerleader kicked out of home for having over-active sex glands.

You ain't sent this woman bread, have you? I ask him, not that I'd give a dry hump whether Dick was being taken, but maybe I can impart some good funk into his head, after all, it was me 'n' Jo who got him into this ...

Don't be fucking stupid, he tells me, not until I get something in exchange.

Like what, dirty panties?

Dick chokes on his hemlock then coughs that shit all over the register. Fuck no! If I want soiled underwear there's plenty in a joint like this. Nah, something, uh ...

Tangible? Like proof of life?

Yeah, something like that.

Why not ask her for some DNA?

Fuck yeah! That's a good idea, that is, can you do that?

In this world, Dick, you can do anything you fucking like.

And that is true, up to a certain point. I am preparing for the Brits today, sorting out my shit so to speak, although I'm regularly bothered by my new posse of stripper girlfriends. Their so-called manager, Dwayne, has left, done a bunk with the bread and abandoned these long-legged silicone-enhanced specimens of womanhood right in my crib. Being surrounded by this much hair makes me feel like I'm in a 'Poison' video but, hell, you can't just turn gals like this out on the street, not at this time of the year – although I'm pretty sure they'd survive somehow. I have them in a six-bed dorm, where every night is a sleepover, and I have to get shot of 'em before the Doc returns trim and taut from another expedition into financial recklessness. Maybe I can offload them onto a few Brits? That'd work. And I'm in negotiation with BK next door, him of the failing bar business, trying to manipulate him into installing a few poles; girls with legs like these have got to be worth something.

I have seen everything since I've been here, the whole world and its debauched carryings on have arrived at my bolt hole looking for refuge. Nothing else can take me by surprise; I am au fait with bugs, bastards, bum bandits, braggards and bolshy Germans. We have survived, and are due some R&R on the company tab, moreso if Jo's conviction that the Doc will stiff us come pay-out time happens to be true. That is why I have wee stashes here and there, secreted around the place like a dope fiend's emergency supplies. I have covered every base, and not even Zsa Zsa will throw her monkey wrench in my gruel. That crazy bitch hasn't once asked how I am feeling, not even when I was the colour purple during a hacking-up fit. The tiara of thorns she's awarded me just because I wouldn't get lathered up in the communal love tub ain't hurting me at all.

I can do without it all, thanks, head-screwed bosses and their toy boy lovers, emotionally-crippled work colleagues, deviants, numbnuts and con merchants, not to mention the inane questioning that accompanies so-called seasoned travellers with as much experience of adventure as Bambi. As for that aloofness that travellers haul around, the know-it-all-guide-book-street-savvy-chic that is so the rage on the road, well, I can do without that too. Some of these dickheads treat those guide books like bibles, ticking off all of the guide book sights they've seen – even though the fool who wrote the review hadn't seen them himself. These people do not travel at all, other than in a physical sense. Their minds stay right back on the old home-town street corner, loitering dumbly.

But not the Brits. I've high hopes my country people will arrive like rent-a-crowd and show the rest of these doped-up fools how you ought to behave when abroad – if there's one virtue the Brits are renowned for worldwide, it's their overseas antics. The British will bring me all the trace elements I require to survive the world; stories of the auld country, the patois of association football, binge drinking, good-natured sexual assault and many sing-along toons – ain't it great to be British?

I wait eagerly, like a faithful mutt on a foggy night ...

I advise BK to get plenty of grog in, the Brits go at it hard. He has the cool store out back stacked to the ceiling with warm beer. Forget the nibbles, I tell him, boil up 50-dozen eggs and order in a hundred cartons of ready-salted chips, that's all those freaks need; that, a pool table, dart board and a decent jukebox – get that shit in place, my jovial jelly-bellied friend, and all your ever-tightening monetary problems will vanish.

I know my natives. That's where I grew up, picking locks, fleecing Japanese tourists at Piccadilly, stealing milk off doorsteps and generally being a Fagin-esque juvenile delinquent. But, good Christ, I was a real boy back then, whereas now I'm Pinocchio in drag. Even so, I've still got the gift of the gab; I can converse on all levels with all three sexes. This'll be like stealing black jacks from Mr Lee's corner store.

I'm briefing my better half, not that she needs much briefing seeing she's an unabashed anglophile. She stops my discourse mid-flow, tells me she thinks we ought to camp it up, a bit like Mavis and Rita from The Cabin on *Coronation Street*. And who'll play Mavis? I ask her, already knowing the answer.

Nope, that won't work, you've gotta stand your ground with the British else they'll walk all over you. Look at India.

What about Mrs Slocombe and Miss Brahms from *Are You Being Served?*

Well, that's a better option, I tell her, but only if I'm Miss Brahms.

You'd be better with the pussy jokes, though.

Look, why don't we just be us, okay?

The first thing I see is a Sheffield Wednesday shirt. Then a Leeds United, then a Preston North End, then a Newcastle, then a QPR – Jesus, even the girls are into it big time, wearing their tribal colours tight across surgically enhanced chests. Ay up, luv! the first mug says, and I realize it's on now for young and old, here we go here we go here we go …

They drink BK's watering hole dry by four in the afternoon, and they're still arriving. Congregating like they do when abroad. By six I have a snaking conga line from the bar to the kitchen and back, singing terrace tunes, changing the lyrics of well-known pop ditties and generally playing the fool. They have bought all the phone cards, there is a roughhouse game of five-a-side being played in the dining room, and all the videos that have any British content – *In The Name Of The Father*, *ID*, *Braveheart* – are on continual loop. There's about 500 bucks on the sides of the pool table and I wish to god I was in there playing.

They are at the hole in a continual stream of unconsciousness asking about clubs, cheap beer, hot action, chips, steaks, frozen peas … they are heavenly creatures of habit. Home or abroad they will cling to what they know, install a little British Empire wherever they set up camp.

All that bread BK has invested in the big-screen cable is reaping handsome rewards now. I can hear football commentary loud and clear, jeers, cries of despair, shrieks of joy. I tell some half-bred waster wearing a fucking Man City shirt to go find out who's playing and what the score is. Fuck the America's Cup, that's what I say.

Keep the aspidistra flying, long live Hooky Street!

Just call me Del boy: I knew I'd offload those strippers cheap. Here they are arm in arm with a half dozen ruddy-cheeked specimens from Barnsley. Those gals are in for one hell of a night. Come sun-up they'll have enough dosh to set themselves up someplace new, maybe even Barnsley. The joint is rocking with deals being brokered, two for one, stay three get the fourth free. Fair exchange is daylight robbery – it's just like my old schoolyard when we played conkers and traded football cards for lunch tickets. None of that bitchin' and whinin' you get from your foreign types. This is straightforward under or over-the-counter business – makes no matter so long as the deal gets done. The Doc is being fleeced big time courtesy of me, I am undercharging and being generous with rules about blanket deposits, extra towels and those individually wrapped soap slivers the Doc likes to flog for half a buck a pop. I've put the box up on the counter and it is all but empty. Bog rolls too, and laundry detergent that I'm supposed to bag and sell like cut dope for two fifty a score I'm giving away by the cup. Screw all this petty bollocks, the stupid machinations of financial profit and loss. Let the good times roll.

And you see how we're rewarded? Look here, the pizza guy has just arrived, staggering under a leaning tower of family-size delights, groaning with the strain of it all. They descend upon him like vultures, stuff more hard cash than he should carry around streets like these into his mouth, and as they surge past reception a kid wearing a Birmingham City shirt slaps a Hawaiian on the counter and tells me 'n' Jo that it's for us coz we're top birds. Ain't no Israelis, no Germans, no Yanks who'd do that.

Six beers arrive fifteen minutes later, courtesy of our friends from Oldham in BK's thriving watering hole. This is living, more how I'd thought that running a hostel would be, and right now I'm glad I didn't walk away, Renee.

And ain't it strange how the British can find a common

cause for good when they're offshore – how they can temporarily put aside, even while bedecked in their finest replica merchandize, those puerile parochialisms that dull their minds and blur their vision back home in the Isles? Sure, they'll joke about it, be playful with that Catholic versus Protestant bollocks, that north–south antiquity, that Arsenal Tottenham juvenile mentality. Abroad the British are very fine company, even the Welsh, and god knows those poor bastards don't have too much to crow about. But here, a zillion miles from Westminster, from warm beer on a Saturday night, street brawling, petty vandalism and all things oh so quintessentially British – away from The Disease – the Brits are all right. I even find myself liking them, laughing right along with their tales of the Motherland. Wondering, Why the hell did I ever leave?

You can take the boy outta England but not that St George fervour for fisticuffs outta the boy, ain't that what they say? Here's a guy sporting a Celtic shirt, ripped on warm booze, hanging on the arm of a posh bird from Surrey who under home-guard circumstances would most likely have had this legless Jock arrested for assault. But not here, here she's happy to join in the gang bang, to let Britannia rule, to breed for Queen, country and unity. These crazy British: walking, talking, gobbing, drinking, fucking, fighting – just like me, or at least, like wot I used to be. Two decades away from these influences haven't rendered me indifferent to my birthright obligations. And how do my ilk view me? Are they really sensitive New Age Europeans without a care in the continent when it comes to gender-bending likely lads? Most likely not. Pissed, your average Brit will screw anything with a pulse, no matter how faint. Sober it's a completely different matter. The British hinnies on the other hand don't seem to give a hoot. British women are annealed to their men folk's penchant for deviancy. They fully understand that their men are complete wasters devoid of even the simplest scruples, that given even a glimmer of an opportunity they will be faithfully unfaithful, that is the British way.

Maybe tomorrow I'll be under the microscope, in the hot seat on *Mastermind* where my specialist subject of choice will be Sex Swapping. It'll be interesting, from a sociological point of view; especially given that not twelve months ago me and the Ink Girl were meandering around Cool Britannia by various modes of transportation and, for the love of Christopher Wren, we couldn't assimilate. But here in the great green paradise of open slather on diversity, maybe there'll be peace.

The next day, Freddy has checked in another two planeloads of grunts of the British variety. They are fleeing Oz by the multitude now, none wanting to miss the Last Party on Earth before normality and regularity claims their bodies and minds for the long march to a cemetery in a cold climate. For most if not all of the specimens I've witnessed through my window on the budget world, this is their last shot at the Big Ride until they turn up again sporting two-piece shell suits in 40 years' time. By that stage it'll be clean drinking water, hot-water bottles and denture adhesive that occupies what remains of their coddled brains. This is the last fling of the young, time to cast off all those imposed inhibitions and societal structures that from hereon in will govern their lives. This is why they are in my reception doing the funky chicken while wearing adult diapers. Why they are drinking Guinness for breakfast and slathering each other's faces in red, white and blue zinc cream. Their bus is outside idling, their very own chartered chariot of the adventure-gods.

Nothing but thrills matter today, the more stupid, the more

reckless, the more impervious to danger you can be up on the high wire today, the more you can revel in your daredevil antics tonight. I feel like the ringmaster as I count them, corral them, collate them and cosset them onto their big green throbbing machine.

They pull stupid faces at me through the bus window and shoot me a full moon here and there; nothing has changed since that school outing to Windsor Safari Park. I have no compulsion, no longing, to be on that bus and experience what those fools are going to experience; this is the reality of adventure travel – nothing that glitters is gold.

I hear from the Doc. He is on the satellite phone someplace near that big dish in Australia where they spy on extraterrestrials and dopehead budget travellers. Communication hasn't improved since 1961, either that or there's a thousand galahs on the line, plus one holding it. All I can hear is fuzzy warm static and what sounds like a 4x4 speeding away. He is trying to tell me something about nothing, so I just say yep where I think that yeps ought to fit.

Was that the Rev? the Inkster asks me as she rifles through a sheaf of UK passports that have been left as deposits for various hostel items we'll never see again.

I think they've tossed him and Zsa Zsa into one of those detention camps someplace, I tell her, not that either of us are really bothered. Just so long as the direct debit functions we'll hang on. This is all that it means to us now, the continuation of payment.

The Brother and his wo-man jetted out last night for some atoll where a major publishing house is conducting a children's writing course. Maybe those cannibals will marinate that big lump and stew him up with some seaweed. Dick? Well, Dick's in a real lather about something, most likely to do with his boy's latest failed bid for parole and this bundle of demands for motor registration renewal that has been clogging up our pigeon holes for far too long.

I flip through a few names dodgy enough to warrant MI5 surveillance. Who are all these fucking people? I ask the old bastard angrily, the whole office is getting overrun with this government documentation. How long are we supposed to hold all this shit?

I dunno, Dick says. Until the fuckers come back from wherever they've bin, I suppose. What am I, a fucking public servant?

Oops, Dick's picking up a bit of my bad vibe. Maybe I ought to quit bugging him about such shit given he's deep into a pre-nup agreement with a cyberspace Dr Legal. I've been here five months almost and not once has some fool come to the hole searching for a registration renewal document. I begin feeding them through the Doc's heavy-duty shredder, and find the task cathartic.

Holy shit, what's all this fucking paper everywhere? Jo asks me when she returns to the hole from an expedition to the golden arches to grab our lunch. I'm still quite happily feeding unopened envelopes into the ever-hungry slot. You do know that that's an offence, don't you, tampering with Crown mail?

What are you, some kind of undercover spook?

You can get ten years for that, she tells me smugly.

Bullshit.

Why'd you think the Doc keeps it all, huh? You're supposed to write 'return to sender' and stuff it all into a mail box.

No one told me.

It's here in the manual, look. It is too, so I feed that fucking thing through the shredder as well; it gobbles it voraciously.

You've gone la-la, honey!

Maybe she's right, my grip on the state-sanctioned level of sanity was always tentative, so why bother to cling to the ledge? The phone rings again. I tell Jo that if it's the Doc, tell him I'm knee-deep in house cleaning. He'll like that. Within the hour I am buried in shredded correspondence and all I can hear is the near-perfect humming of a manmade machine that eats paper and spews out vermin-nesting materials. Brother, I love this job ... oops, that wasn't supposed to be shredded, that's mail for Dick from across the ditch, legal looking too. Nor that ... that's the Doc's gym membership renewal form and, Jesus, how'd a demand for unpaid council rates get in with this pile of crap?

Too late now, this machine's a ravenous fucking beast: those Chinese sure know how to design sabotage equipment. Oh look, a demand from Sally Lim on behalf of those kooky Chinese she sent here, must be the People's Court turfed them out into the Square to run the tanks ... Ah well, the Doc don't need this shit in his in-tray when he gets released from that detention centre. I hear Dick around the other side of the counter, calling me. Shit. I stick my head around the office door. What? I ask him.

Where's all the fucken mail gone? You got a letter from my kid's lawyer in there?

Ain't seen nothing from Oz with your name on, Dick, but I'll keep an eye out, okay?

Yeah, thanks, fucking postal service. If I don't countersign that fecken form me kid's fucked, fecken crap it is ...

Trust in god, Dick.

29.

If You're Not Part of the Solution, You're Part of the Problem

And that much is true, especially so in a rat mound like this; I am now officially a part of the problem. Or so I presume. We have been overrun with greenbacks of the counterfeit kind. God knows how, we don't even have any Yanks in-house, and yet my night man Freddy has been hoodwinked good and proper. Must be those four gooners who checked out early yesterday. I knew they were good-for-nothing North London crooks; as soon as I saw that massive discrepancy, I knew Freddy had been diddled. What'y take as payment for these four, I asked him, seeing the big blank space on the register. When I see big blank spaces I get edgy, just like my soon-to-return boss. When Freddy handed me a wad of purple greenbacks I knew something was wrong. Since when has Bill Clinton been on a 50-dollar note?

You fucking idiot, didn't you use the ultra violet lamp the Doc got us?

Fuck no, I thought that thing was for making cheese toasties. No wonder it takes all night to get one brown.

Well, you've screwed up big time, Freddy my son, your arse is in the sling. No way am I gonna take the rap for this.

Can't you just rewrite the register, make it all disappear?

What'y think I am, the great Gonzo?

I'd make it worth your while. Sweet merciful crap, I need this fucking job, shitty as it is, to stay on probation.

I glanced at my watch, the shocking pink Donald Duck one I lifted from unclaimed property yesterday. Donald tells me it's too close to call, but when I press this knob here, Goofy tells me to go for it. I am all for the big risk so I start scribbling like a demented commodities trader covering his tracks. Freddy watches nervously, scared of every shadow. Don't look over my shoulder, I tell him. I have friends in high places in the WPCs' locker room; those girls think I'm kinda neat. Don't you worry, Freddy my man, I'll see ya right.

Dick accosts me as I erase like buggery. My mail arrived? he asks. What's up with the fecken register?

Nothing. You know how it is with these by-the-hour night spooks.

Sure. Any mail?

The mail ain't arrived yet; when it does I'll buzz ya.

Okay. Say, what's all that fecken shredded paper all over the show?

Freddy, I tell him.

The Doc is due any minute. Why I'm sweating I don't know, I really don't give a toss any more. He arrives, all shiny and new, like a stranger. That outback heat and the detention centre diet must have agreed with him. Howdy! he greets me.

Howdy? This is not going to be a good day. Hi, I respond, as I brush a zillion pieces of just-erased circumstantial evidence off the counter.

How's tricks? he asks, as he grabs for the credit card transaction receipt that is just spewing outta the machine.

All under control, boss, I tell him straight-faced. It will take an hour or so for the Doc to implode, for his chirpy mood to disintegrate, for him to realize there is no shit paper, soap or laundry powder in-house, and that despite my most valiant efforts, I cannot make the books balance. Okay, no need to sweat it, play it cool, Teri Lou, you're too close to the finish line to crack now . . .

I go off to supervise something that really doesn't need supervision, leaving the golden one basking in the glow of his over-cooked skin. God knows what that merciless Aussie sun has done to Zsa Zsa, most likely she is a giant, overripe, sun-dried tomato right now.

This is what happens, when I'm summoned on the hotline 50 minutes later.

I go into reception where Dick is sat on his stool like an angry little imp. Jo, manning the register, has had no time to forewarn me of the events about to unfold and so I am not forearmed. The Doc is on me like a ghoul, his mood oscillating dangerously between clucky hen and randy rooster. He has bookwork spread out everywhere, as if we have just been raided by the Feds. Dick is scooping dregs of laundry powder out of the all-but-empty 50-kilo box into small clear plastic pouches. He looks like some inscrutable opium dealer on Freak Street, all he needs is a Fu Manchu moustache and a rat tail.

The depths of my mischievousness bewilder the Doc. Now is the time to pin it all on Freddy – make him my fall guy, as I'm way low on fall person options. But I hang tight, silence is worth 10,000 words of mitigation in such circumstances. I watch Dick while he watches me through his reptilian eyes.

About the mail? the Doc finally asks. Now we're deep into it. The mail, yes, Jo was right. Getting Freddy to haul all those bin bags stuffed full of shredded correspondence wasn't my brightest idea. The mail? I reply, innocently. Now is the time to draw upon my reserves of naughty schoolgirlish charm.

Where'd all the mail go?

I don't know, I think the post office came and hauled it all away . . .

A likely fecken story, I hear Dick say.

What's up his corset? I ask the Doc.

Missing mail, his kid's missed his parole.

Well, he ought to take it up with the post office, huh?

And what about the soap, where's all the soap gone?

Jesus, people need to wash you know. I've had a house full of filthy Brits the past three weeks; no way can I sell soap and do all this other stuff . . .

Other people manage.

Other people ain't been near death, have they? Yeah, I drag out the sympathy card real quick, hoping to play on the Doc's empathy with the ill and infirm.

I know, and about that . . .

That's when the phone rings: the Doc answers it, my phone-answering privileges having been temporarily suspended. It's for me, Lady Zsa Zsa, no less. Hi, I say.

Look, she says gruffly, what's the matter with you now? It is the emphasis on the word 'now' that really bugs me, the insinuation that there is *always* something wrong with me.

TB, I mutter, it's all I can think of.

Well, she replies, we all get sick now and again, but you know what wards off illness, don't you?

I could give her a hundred answers, all of them verifiable by a doctor. But I don't. What? I say in a deadbeat, disinterested way.

Hot tubs, that's what. Never fails, I swear by them.

So, my shot at redemption. All I have to do is relent, grab my bathers, maybe those nice camouflage ones I found last week, size twelve, and stuff a rag down my pants. I can take the ride and then splash around and all my recent sins will be washed away in the bubbling hot water ... but I don't. I just make a funny sound, like a stifled laugh, and she picks up on it real quick. There is an uneasy silence. I glimpse Dick drawing his thumb across his own neck, signalling the Doc that I am all but finished, only ... I'm not.

Well, Zsa Zsa sighs, are you seeing a doctor?

Like, what does she think I've been doing? Self-medicating? Sure, I tell her.

Are you going to be written-off? It's as though she's talking to the insurance broker about water-logged computers. Am I going to be written-off, scrapped, replaced? Is third-party fire and theft coverage needed?

I was going to be written-off, I told her, but instead I carried on working.

Uhm, are you feeling better now?

A bit, I sniffle, a bit.

Okay, hand me back to ...

Shit, yes, I've avoided the black spot yet again. I hand the phone to the Doc, who cleans the mouthpiece with an anti-bacterial wipe. Making a gun gesture with my own fair hand, I cock it at Dick, then at my own head. This is all crazy crap. I wink at Jo and rummage through the paperwork on the Doc's desk while he gets his orders direct from the nag's mouth. He hangs up and turning to me says the most ridiculous thing: Now, I want to brief you on the skiing portfolio. I hear Dick gasp. Jo, too. The ski portfolio? Don't they ski in winter? Isn't winter three months away? Doesn't our contract expire in four weeks? What kind of crazy word has come crackling down that line? Maybe the Doc has misunderstood?

Skiing? I hear myself say.

Yes, skiing, the Doc replies. I've bought this snow-making machine in a bankrupt stock auction and I'm thinking of getting a few mean pistes made up at the manor. What'y think?

Dick topples clean off his perch with a downy thump, like a ripe gooseberry dropping. Me, the Doc and Jo all look at him queerly. Not one of us offers to give him a hand up.

The Doc gives us the rest of the day off.

We are in the Irish bar. Liam pulls two pints and while they settle, we offer him one on us. Ah, tiz most kind of yer, ladies, but Lord knows I never touch a drop, as God is me witness, to be sure I don't now.

I look at Jo. A teetotal Irishman, what next? We sup up and the discussion on this unexpected overnight pass turns, naturally, to what has just occurred. We are both baffled and as you're well aware by now, I am not the kind to be out stumped. By god, I tell her, you know I've done everything a girl could do, bar putting us on the block for immediate dismissal, to convince these numbnuts we've had a gutful. What in the hell is wrong with these people?

Liam tells us, on the QT, that he's off to Capital City come season's end. Too fucking cold and quiet down here.

I mull it over, and ponder why these goddamned Kiwis can't seem to be up-front about anything. It's all ducking and diving, saying one thing and making grandiose promises, then doing abrupt U-turns as if such practices were completely normal. Maybe it's the confrontation they abhor. You get invited to the hot tub, which to them is above the water line and kosher, and when you graciously decline they make your life hell. Why?

Why aggravate what are possibly the best, grooviest, hostel managers you've had in a decade, over something as trivial as communal bathing?

It makes no sense, nor does the upshot. You readily accept the fact you and they will part ways less than amicably, and then, then they start talking to you about winter fixtures when they've not said one baa about contract extensions?

I gulp down the remains of my pint, belch, and Liam smiles in appreciation. We are off to see Miz Ruby, ex-Singapore, to get some rogue hairs ripped and stripped. As I lay there in the soft beautifying light, letting Miz Ruby's nimble fingers do the talking, she tells me she's off to Capital City in a fortnight, she's scored a top job in a big store there, it's too cold and too quiet down here. Jesus, everyone's up and leaving. Soon enough, this town'll be nothing but a ghost town.

We are in an Indian restaurant on Colombo Street. Ali the waiter tells us he is off to Capital City soon, that's where it's all happening. I start laughing about the whole mess; us up at the manor, mob-handed, digging pistes and bobsleigh runs overseen by the Hunter. Screw that crap, these are folk are queer as, not at all what god intended. I blame the isolation. I tell Jo I'm gonna buy us a car, that we're gonna quit, take the high road to Capital City, it's all happening there.

That makes her happy and back in our garret she is soon to the business of ripping down our Marilyn Manson posters and packing up our vintage fash. I can see, as I lie on the sofa sucking hard on a bottle of suds, that we'll need a station wagon. No sedan built could carry this much shit. We are no longer travelling light.

The following Friday I am on the trombone talking to some Kiwi about the station wagon he's got for sale in the local rag. No way am I gonna buy one from some raggy-arsed budget traveller with a stone-age foot.

The Mitsubishi is $800. The guy is gonna bring it down about five for me to look over. The deal is conducted relatively quickly over the phone, to both parties' satisfaction – only, this guy tells me he'll need a lift home, after he's been to the gym. These Kiwis are mad for the gym. Walk down the street after five and glance up to where the music emanates, and you can watch a hundred office girls with nine-to-five sedentary arses doing Pilates, or whatever they call it. I'm not happy about having to run this fucker home in three hours time, but I don't wanna pay for the cab. I'll have to take this goon to Belfast, so I ask Dick where the fuck that is.

Jesus, fucken Belfast? That's kidnap country, that is. All trailer homes, swamps, bee farms and bad breeding. Rather you than me!

That old fucker, he's just yanking my chain, given that he thinks me and him are in for a long relationship. You wanna come, I ask him, ride shotgun?

Fuck, no. The All Blacks are on TV, and besides, I fancy waking up in the morning!

When the car guy does turn up, the vendor is well pissed. Gym, my bollocks, this bastard is just after a free ride home after a night on the tiles spending my money. So, reluctantly, off we go, out through the one-way maze until the city lights fade and the highway turns to dirt. There are no more lights and my passenger is as crazy as a loon, telling me stories about all the 'fresh meat' he sees tramping these highways at night, how easy it'd be to just grab one and . . .

I reach for the mace I have in my flak jacket pocket. If this crazy SOB says just one more word I'm gonna douse him good, roll him out onto the verge and reverse over him. Onward we press. I have no idea where we are as all the signs that still stand have been peppered with buckshot. This has to be some kind of sick Kiwi wind-up, and the gas is getting way low. Where's the next gas station? I ask him. The guy just laughs, ain't no gas out here, but not to worry, he's got a jerry can in the shed at home, it'll only cost me ten bucks and that ought to get me home. Most like it's meths. I ought to turn around right here, save myself. Finally we turn off up some high-hedged drive and ahead I see the dim flicker of oil lamps. Holy fucking crap ... I do not turn off the engine, or open my door. Not with that slobbering beast of a hound pawing at it.

You want that gas? he asks me, a half-cocked smile playing on his lips like warm blood.

Thanks, but no thanks, I tell him, already popping the clutch even though he still has a hold of the passenger door.

Oi, me tools! he yells.

Mercifully, the rear door is unlocked. He begins rummaging around while I watch him in the mirror. There goes the spare and the jack, I'm thinking. The bastard. The door slams shut, he comes back to the passenger door and leans in. This is my last sight on Earth ...

You want that gas?

Nope, thanks, gotta go, see ya! I am doing 80 up the drive, the dog is bounding after me, tongue lolling. I'll never make it back to civilization with so little juice, and especially without knowing where I'm going. Why don't these bastards put up road signs? Left or right here? Hell, no time to lose, look at that fucking needle ...

I drive like a manic moth, always heading toward light, and

as the piece of junk I've recently taken ownership of begins to shudder dangerously, I hit highway. Out I spew, fishtailing. Just a few more kays, darling, I coax my new vehicle – just a few more ks, hell yes. I push it the last two ks to the gas station. I could see it but I couldn't drive to it, every bit of gunk and shit from the sediment in the bottom of this tank has been sucked through the lines and filters. I fill it right up, pray that it'll start, if not it's gonna be a long lonely night.

Where the hell have you been? Jo shouts when I finally re-enter reception. I have no time to tell her the story; I am shagged, I need beer, a hot bath, never ever again to be that far out into the boondocks solo – I grab her hand and we head upstairs. At least we're mobile now.

Your car's exactly the same as mine! Dick exclaims proudly, while we stand outside the next day admiring my new wheels. It is, too, the exact same make, model, and year of first registration. How odd is that? They are like evil sisters, side-by-side in the lot. Great cars these, Dick continues, fingering my bonnet lovingly while he keeps one eye on a scurvy backpacker trying to hump start his love wagon. Best fucken cars made that year. Want me to show you which cables to remove? he offers. These bastards know a hot set of wheels when they see one.

No thanks, I tell him. I am mortified over my poor choice of car – which unintentionally flatters the old bastard and makes me depressed. Dick shrugs, then goes off to continue his daily ritual of spearing up used rubbers, squashed beer cans and other junk dumped by our guests in their haste to hit the road. I watch him, out there in the square courtyard, stabbing at litter, mumbling to himself, prancing around like an Andalusian at a dressage rehearsal. It really is time we moved on . . .

30.

Square Exchanges are Still Daylight Robbery

The truth is that budget travel has ceased to exist. This hovel might well be the last vestige of what was once a real-deal dirty experience.

The Doc and his Madam will offload this place to a scrap merchant one day soon. That silver-tongued Svengali has raked in about as much hard cash as he can from a dump like this, pumped enough untreated effluent uphill. Creature comforts are all the rage with budget travellers these days: hair dryers, hand creams, half bottles of cab sav.

During this very hands-on tenure of ours, we have run the gauntlet of complaints – a few are warranted, sure, but Jesus, the rest are just the bitching of the New World order; those who presumed slumming it would look great on their CV. The people who arrive here might look filthy, but it's only designer filth, they are filthy rich too, shabby chic out on the highways. They are the new wealthy – young, fit, mentally fucked and desperate for a guide book tour of anywhere a guide book says it's cool to tour. Blame Lonely Planet for making the world anything but lonely. You can never be alone with your thoughts, not that these people have thoughts to be alone with . . .

We are writing our resignation, me and young Jo, and yes, she's young, but not so young her mother could file a Missing Person's report. We have made three stabs at it, none of which really serve the intended purpose of a resignation letter, which is to disentangle ourselves from the intricate web of lies and deceptions we have become enmeshed in. Walking out won't suffice here, nor will fleeing in the pitch of night – not when there's a CCTV you yourself have stupidly set up, and your boss owes you several weeks of hard-earned. There is little to be gained from giving word-life to your innermost thoughts either, as I have just told Jo.

Look, you can't take a statement of affairs like this down. All this slander and personal accusation. How'd you think our last two weeks would be if we handed in something like this? Jesus, girl, try to be a bit more discreet, okay?

You mean, we're gonna crawl outta here on our hands and knees, grovelling in thanks for the swell time they've shown us?

If it means we get that fucking cash, yes, that is the name of the game, sweetmeat. Leave with your bread and balls intact. Trust me, I'm old and wise.

You idiot, no way am I gonna spend my last two weeks here biting my tongue.

Then, my dear, you leave me little choice but to pump you full of other folk's prescription drugs and happy pills.

Shit, I hate it when we have to do crap like this.

Indeed, pretty maiden, but she who laughs last, laughs longest, huh?

And what exactly does that mean?

To be perfectly frank, I've no idea. Now, hand me those bennies there . . .

Jo's lost the toss, and so it is her rotten duty to go down first tomorrow and give the Doc our brief and to-the-point letter of intent to get the hell out of here. I ought to do such grubby work myself, of course, given it's my role in this saga; but she is young and her cum-hither smile might dissuade the Doc from protracted protestations. Not that I expect him to protest. These people will always accept defeat sullenly, keep on bailing out even when the bucket itself is beyond the chore. I expect nothing less than stone-cold quiet on the subject; no hotline calls arguing the pros of prolonged tours of duty, no offers of more bread and less hours, just the good old Kiwi wooden wall of silence.

The Doc and his fickle bride in mayhem made us sign some fourteen-page covenant when we first came here. For a simple six-month contract. It is page after page of gibberish, greedily slanted in favour of the boss man. Down here in paradise they call it a worker's agreement; you work and they agree that they will not only taste, but gorge, on the abundant fruits of your labour. They will vanish into the funk whenever they choose and you will work extended hours, including any and every public holiday, for which you, the simpleton who signed such a deed, will be recompensed in pay but not in lieu; and not double pay, I might add. The only double time that exists in New Zealand is the time you and your partner in grime agree to work as two halves of one dumb brute of a being. This way, Kiwi labour law ensures, and enshrines in doublespeak, the legal ownership of two bodies where one obviously won't cut the mustard. I am still leafing through that voluminous contract of employ to this very day, still searching for any get-out clauses I might have overlooked while my brain was robotized and my lawyer serving time for clerical misdemeanours in Tampa.

All it says in respect of terminating is that we, the signa-
tories, are required under both penal law and rum law to give
two full weeks of intent to separate ourselves physically from
our employ or parts thereof. It is technical mumbo jumbo,
obviously thought up by public servants during one of those
taxpayer-funded conferences on trade laws where the room
keys are put in a large candy jar and divvied up after dark by a
shop steward high on red ink.

But, ho hum, we have saved a fair stash of dough, enough
to set ourselves up somewhere swanky, and that, friends, is
all that really counts. I arrive on deck two hours after Jo has
(I hope) delivered up our resignation. The Doc, counting cash,
smiles at me beguilingly as I take the reins from the Jo'ster and
start my day's business. There are fewer problems now that the
crowd has thinned – except, although I believe I have seen it all
and done it all, I have never seen a Peruvian in a poncho until
now. He has pan pipes too, and he enquires if there is a chance
he might sing for his supper, so to speak, to aid him along his
journey of discovery. It suits me, so long as he stands in reception from seven till ten doing his business each night. It would
lighten my load but, alas, the beast master's eyes bore into my
very soul through the two-way glass so I regretfully decline my
little friend's request and give him the daily rate.

The Peruvian doesn't take it badly. Obviously he has been
on the Great Western Highway of capitalism a while and
understands the core principles of our set-up. He rummages in
his leather pants and produces a crumpled-up greenback. I do
my duty, go out back and run it under the scanner, rub it to
make sure the ink is waterproof and finally return to check
the little pilgrim in for one night of threadbare comfort.

It is great to be a First World citizen.

The Doc, as he readies to leave, has still made no

reference, veiled or otherwise, to the letter he has obviously perused. Make sure to tally the ticket receipts, he tells me, as if, after five months of doing so, I would suddenly forget. Tallying receipts is as engrained into my psyche now as shaving my armpits. Of course, I tell him jovially – it is a game we shall play, I presume, for the next fourteen days, barring any dramatic changes of heart on either side.

Saturday morning. I am through one week of termination notice without any hiccups. The Doc has been neither seen nor heard for the past four days – since, in fact, we handed in our resignation. Me and Jo are still at the helm, in tandem, doing all that good hostel managers are supposed to do.

I pick up the Saturday paper, as is my way. Very shortly a hot bacon sandwich will be delivered by Jo. I will eat it as I read. They have a good Saturday paper here, that is one thing in their favour, and I have enjoyed my Saturdays idly flipping through it, seeing other folk's jobs up for auction to the lowest bidder.

Even my old pals at Puppy Love were advertising a few weeks back ... hello ... what the f –

WANTED!
Couple to assist owners in day-to-day management of
100-bed hostel on South Island.
Live-in accommodation supplied. If you want to be a part
of a dynamic set-up, please apply in writing to –
The Owners C/-

I recognize the address, as I'm standing in it! Ye gods, if it's in the paper it must be true. So the Doc hasn't told us he has accepted our resignation but they're advertising for our replacements.

Lady Zsa Zsa exerts a cruel and manipulative hold over our boss, pussy-whipped doesn't even begin to describe that kind of power. Maybe he don't even know that she's advertising? It wouldn't surprise me. Jo arrives with the bacon butty, dripping animal fats, and I show her the paper. She laughs out loud.

Our boss man and his Imelda have, if you've noticed, carefully re-worded their advertisement. No more managers required. Jo and I have proved that fresh meat can perform a multitude of roles simultaneously in the workhouse; why promise the Earth when all you're really interested in offering is a coalface? I pity the poor dumb fools who will be sucked into this black hole quicker than a Tour de France competitor can test positive for steroids.

Well, it really is all over now, I tell my girl, while I demolish the bacon sandwich.

Do you care? she asks.

Really, I don't, this is a far better result than having to do the fandango over contract extensions; at least now we all know where we stand. I just want to lay up somewhere warmer a while. I have a great idea for a novel, one that has been developing over my last few night shifts. I want my health back, sea air, and the chance to lie fallow and vegetate on the taxpayer tab – that is a pastime I excel at. Still, the thought of these cutthroat pirates just sticking an ad in the paper for our replacements makes me feel kind of bilious, as if everything we've done here has been pointless.

A few days later, in my duty as post sorter, I notice cute hand-written envelopes addressed to The Owners. Obviously, there is more than one fool birthed every minute.

It is on my penultimate night shift that I successfully pick the lock to the Doc's secret drawer. And so what? He has encroached on my life enough. There is all the usual shit in there, most of it not secret at all – except for the income statements for all the rubes who toil here, from which I can see just how little the Doc is paying slaves these days. I also spy a few returned letters from the tax department about my reticence in supplying a tax number. I am not stupid. I have played dumb, said I've had mucho problems getting the damned thing, even though I've had it since I arrived. It's only over the name business, but to get paid out, I will have to hand it in this week and confess my true gender.

Here is what I'm after, a whole sheaf of applications for the job I am now not quite doing to the best of my abilities. TRIAL!! That is what the Doc has scrawled across two particular applications; he is quick to smell his quarry. The first is from a travelling American couple called Hank and Dana. Hank is a marine biologist and will, I presume, immediately understand the flow of effluent. He will be handy with a set of rods. Dana, on the other hand, appears to be knee-deep in home economics, and that is business pertinent to a place like this.

But they have stiff competition in the guise of Ilana and Ivan. Knowing as I do the Doc's penchant for ship-jumping Soviets, my roubles are already stacking up on these two wannabees. Ilana is a dab hand with anything domestic and dirty; her passport-booth photo strikes me as the portrait of a washerwoman. She has a stern face, which, if I know my boss's whims and fancies, edges her out of the 'front-of-house' stakes; Dana is more of a looker. And Ivan? Well, Ivan knows boiler-making and tending furnaces.

These are the front runners, insofar as I can see. It's a straight superpower battle, cold war.

My Peruvian amigo arrives around four in the morning, still stuck on Lima time. We discuss the Incas and Machu Picchu a while. When he asks if a thumping rendition of something on the pipes might buoy my mood, I tell him why the hell not, and off he goes, whistling Dixie on his instrument – there is nothing like being serenaded by an Andean hustler in the wee small hours before a big dank hostel crawls back to life. I'm nearing my last stint on patrol and, hell, I'll be kinda loath to hand over this bunch of keys. They've become as much a part of me as the hips they bounce against while I walk the corridors of power . . .

31.

White Girls

Okay, bedhoppers, here we are now, checkout time.

I am in cruise control. Jo and I have packed up our hidey hole. We have raided the linen cupboard and stocked up on life's necessities. We have had the water pump on that piece of crap I bought completely replaced, and I have visited my quack to get the all-important letter of referral.

I cannot move without paperwork these days. The risk of being stranded someplace, no matter how civilized, without a doctor's referral for continuation of hormonal drugs is now a deep-rooted fear. My doctor here has been among the best I have so far encountered on my cross-gender travels. More compassionate than that bow-tied quack in London who insisted I ought to be implanted in the butt. I will miss this doctor, and I think she'll miss me. Shut, Turry, I'll muss you, that's what she said. She put me on the inhaler then slapped my flank once more for old time's sake. I still have the remnants of that chest infection, maybe I always will. Whenever I get flu and my chest goes all 70-year-old guy on me, I'll think fondly of the South Island of New Zealand. Travel affords you many memories, vivid flashbacks that dance across your mind like skittish schoolgirls on their way to a big day out someplace. I can't think of anything else I'll take away from this experience, only experience itself, I guess.

My boss is due back briefly. He trusts us enough, it would appear, to see out our days in a professional manner. He hasn't even changed the safe combination. As word of our imminent departure spreads, a few of the long-term inmates have come to offer condolences and compliments: we are the best managers this joint has ever had, we have done heaps for the business, the guests loved us. The Doc arrives, chipper with the season's bounty. He counts our cash, tallies our books and is gone in a whiff of duty-free cologne. The guy is just a figment – no, a filament, likely to burn out at any moment. No one, no matter their constitution or tolerance levels for sex with geriatrics, can go on living like he does. Look at Casanova.

I am ready to do this last night shift, in fact, I am deliriously happy about doing it. I haven't been delirious for a long time, apart from all those prescription drugs. I am whistling, although I rarely whistle; whistling is a boy thing and they forced me to stop when I did my voice therapy. Still, jaunty Jayne and her metal ruler aren't around tonight so I can whistle like a skylark. Maybe my little Peruvian buddy will hear and come down and accompany me on the pipes? Why not – I think to myself – do a fucking top-notch job on this kitchen and dining room? Leave a clean full stop, I suppose.

I really give that place a going over, the most thorough job I've done in weeks. I'm pretty chuffed with myself, whittling away these otherwise tiresome nocturnal hours doing what I get paid to do. I finish it all ahead of time. All I've left to do is retrace my steps and find those little stashes I hid here 'n' there just in case ... but first, I ought to go do a final check upstairs, jangle those keys one last time.

On this job, especially the night part of it, if you're lucky it'll just be you and your thoughts – and your instincts. Maybe the hairs on the back of your neck will bristle, you'll hear something untoward, or detect an alien smell. Something will be out of kilter.

Like this shithouse door here on landing two. There ain't no guests up here so why's this door locked from the inside? I rattle it once or twice, and listen. Either some fool is dead or dying in there, or more likely it's a vagrant lock-in. The latter seems more viable because there's an odour wafting out from under this door that I recognize ... C'mon, Tommy lad, I say, let's be having you, eh?

I hear the catch unlock, see the shock of bright red hair, then the freckled face. It's appropriate, I think. Tommy knows the rules and he offers neither argument nor apology, wouldn't insult my intelligence by doing so. He shuffles along in front of me as we head back to the stairs that will lead to his usual point of exit. Hold on, I tell him as I jangle my keys. Six months ago it took me an eon to find the right key to the right door but now I can do it by feel alone. I open the linen closet, grab two blankets, re-lock it and hand the blankets to Tommy who just looks at me. I motion him to follow with a nod of my head. I take him to the upstairs TV lounge and tell him to bunk down on the sofa. I'm not to see or hear him again tonight and tomorrow and he has until midday to leave, does he understand?

Sunrise is pink and mallowy, the promise of a good Sunday. The bells will begin soon enough and our time here is all but done, our sentence almost completed. Six months of hard labour, and what is the cost? To me, it's what my shrinks might call regression, sacrificing what I had struggled to be for almost two years before I took this job. A role reversal in reverse! But it doesn't just affect me, does it? No, it has an impact on

Jo. Who, gawd bless her, was a bona fide dyke when I came crashing into her life. I guess she thought we'd always be like that – and she's told me this day and night these past six months. Told me what a shit I am, a coward, a liar, a fraudster. Our spats have been vicious up in that wee hidey hole at times – spats that involved bad 'guy' words and suitcase packing and the whole shebang that the 'straights' act out. She's seen us more like that; more straight, more Adam and Eve, more her having to act a subservient role to me, the man. It's true I've had to assume that aggressive, mouthy, bullying role I learned many moons ago. That is how we've got through this nightmare. But I ain't proud of it.

I ain't proud of jettisoning the identity I waited four decades to assume, and I ain't proud of dragging Jo down to that level of pantomime. Soon I will have to re-assume my role as woman and I don't know how I'll cope with it, how I'll regain my mannerisms, speech pattern, and deference. And what of the long-term damage that's been done to Jo and me?

I sit watching a bum rummage in the bin across the street, my mind chock-full of scenarios. Just how in the hell do you go about convincing the girl you love that the real you is back? I've been too busy to think about it, day to day, too busy surviving. But Jo, she's been finding time to worry about how we'll be, who we'll be, when this whole shit pile finally gets flushed down the pipework of life ... The routines we've endured here, the charade, will be a big gig to get over. Together we may get through. Find me, her, and us, not exactly where we left them, but hopefully, close by.

We follow our normal routine; that is, I go off shift and Jo comes on – well, not quite. I have gotten used to watching for her on the CCTV coming down the rear staircase. She's a tad later this morning but I don't mind. I see her, and then suddenly I don't. That's queer, maybe it was just my imagination, wishful thinking. I do a rewind. Nope, my eyes, bleary as they are, weren't playing naughty little parlour tricks. Something ain't kosher here ... I wait a few minutes, still nothing, so I roll down the cage and lock the door; money first, that's the rule. Off I go, up the back stairs though not too far; the sugar-coated cereal over the stairs tells me all I need to know. Jo is flat on her back, groaning, an empty cereal bowl in one hand, spoon in the other. I help her up and check for obvious breaks. All good. She has missed a step, grappled thin air for balance, lost, then slid arse first down this flight to the dog leg. Lucky it was there, huh? That well-endowed butt of hers has saved her arse. Does it hurt? I ask her.

What you think?

Want me to rub it?

Kiss it better, she orders. What the hell, life is for the living ...

I return to the hole around eleven, find the good ship *Desperate Times* still afloat, thanks to capable captainage rather than seaworthiness. The phone rings. It's my boss.

Not planning to rush off tonight are you? he asks.

No, I say, I'll always take a free bed when there's one going.

Good-o, he tells me cheerfully, I'll see you tomorrow to settle up.

At least he plans *to* settle up.

Overnight we have the daddy of all storms. Terrifyingly loud thunderclaps, whiplash lightning, and what sounds like golf balls raining down. Minus the keys – which makes me feel naked – I go for an early morning stroll around the landings. In the corridor I pass a huge brute dressed in just a full-length faux mink stole. I bid him a good morning. There are three or four rooms with their doors flung open, their ceilings caved-in, water drips into strategically placed buckets and pots. Jesus, what a stinking mess – but not my problem any more.

We finish packing the car, which is full to bursting, and go see the Doc on the bridge, Han Solo. He tells us he hasn't had a second to do our payout; can we wait a couple of hours?

At midday we get a call that everything is ready.

What'y think he means by everything? I ask Jo as we descend the stairs one last time.

Handcuffs, I should think. Will you write me?

Sure, babe, and I'll dig us a tunnel!

The Doc has given us a fat cheque, and tells us that our regular pay went through as usual, all we gotta do is sign this disclaimer. What the . . .? Oh sure, work laws and all that, the Doc smiles, can't have you suing us for underpayment now can we?

Whatever. It's all done. Well, I say, see ya . . . and that's when we hear loud, hacking coughs followed by desperate gulps and attempts at throat-clearing. The Doc is peering around me. Who's that red-headed guy chok – I turn around too. Tommy's face is no longer freckled, it is blue and his eyes are bulging and he has both his hands around his throat. There are a few lugubrious types loitering around reception but none are moving. I step behind Tommy, lock my arms around just under his ribs and push in and up in the same fluid movement. A projectile of some sort exits his mouth at warp speed and lands straight on the Doc's just-done register. The Doc looks at it in disgust. Tommy breathes again.

Where on earth did you learn the Heimlich? Jo asks me.

On some TV med-show I think.

You've just saved a life, sugar.

Before I can answer the Doc has me in some macho hug.

I swear he's sobbing. I do not know if he is sobbing because I'm leaving or because I've just spared him and his hostel a front page headline in the local daily: 'Vagrant Chokes on Stale Bagel in Downtown Hostel!'

He lets me go and grabs up Jo. Gives her the full perform-ance, wipes a tear from his eye. What in the name of Captain Cook is wrong with these people? Did he presume we wouldn't go? Does he really care? Do we really care?

Dick around? I ask, as the Doc grabs up a handful of tissues.

Dick's ill again . . . We both know he's lying but it makes no matter now. Silly old sod, too proud or too stupid to know or care. I shrug and offer my hand in a man-gesture; the Doc pumps it voraciously. Then I have to go through the whole routine again with Tommy – and I so loathe shaking hands. As we make to leave, the Doc stops Jo, takes an envelope from his back pocket and hands it to her. We head straight for the car before anyone else needs first aid, and we hit the road.

What is it? My curiosity has got the better of me. She opens the envelope as I struggle to keep one eye on this ridiculously maddening one-way system. She has 700 greenbacks in her paw and a look of stupendousness on her face. Who'd have thought, huh?

Tomorrow we will cross to Wellington. We have a booking in a mid-range motel for a week, all paid up. This is a way-sweet life, just the open road, well, some open sea too, plenty of readies, a good staunch woman each, a pre-paid bed and the whole world at our disposal. From tomorrow, anything could happen . . . and that, big boy, is the only reason *to* travel.

What's the plan? Jo asks after a few silent miles.

Once we stop tonight, my plan is to shave my goddamned legs and wear a bra again.